Ending Poverty as

Guaranteeing a [

Ending Poverty as We Know It

Guaranteeing a Right to a Job at a Living Wage

WILLIAM P. QUIGLEY

TEMPLE UNIVERSITY PRESS
Philadelphia

Temple University Press, Philadelphia 19122
Copyright © 2003 by Temple University
All rights reserved
Published 2003
Printed in the United States of America

Library of Congress Cataloging-in-Publication Data
Quigley, William P.
   Ending poverty as we know it : Guaranteeing a right to a job at a living wage /
William P. Quigley.
     p. cm.
   Includes bibliographical references and index.
   ISBN 1-59213-032-1 (cloth : alk. paper) — ISBN 1-59213-033-X (pbk. : alk. paper)
   1. Wages—United States.   2. Poverty—United States.   3. Wages—Law and legisla-
tion—United States. I. Title.
HD4975.Q54   2003
331.2'15—dc21   2002043553

2   4   6   8   9   7   5   3

Contents

Acknowledgments

Over the years I have worked side by side with many good people who were poorly paid for delivering newspapers, stocking warehouse shelves, painting signs, repairing highways, building mobile homes, being aides in nursing homes, doing community social services work, and surveying for the census. In my work as a lawyer I have also worked alongside many, many people who were paid quite a bit less than their work was worth. These folks showed me the true value of work and human dignity and the need to make good work pay. They inspired this book.

Thanks to the many people who helped me think and write about guaranteed good jobs at good pay: Ramona Almonte, Steve Bachman, Jackie Berrien, Kim Bobo, Beth Butler, Odessa Carew, Glen Cater, Nancy Collins, Danya Cunningham, Ron Chisom, Jason Deparle, Don Everard, Lillian Flavin, Mike Gallagher, Claire Gisel, Lani Guinier, Penda Hair, Barbara Jackson, Jeraldine Johnson, Jim Klebba, George Lundy, Marnie Mahoney, Barbara Major, John Makdisi, Tony Mazzochi, Jack Nelson, Lois Nelson, Karen O'Keefe, Helen Prejean, Fran Quigley, Wade Rathke, Adolph Reed, Jocelyn Sargent, Lory Schaff, Jerry Siefken, Patrick Stevenson, Susan Sturm, Gerald Torres, Louis Westerfield, Jennifer Willis, Barbara Wilson, Fran Wild, and Maya Wiley. Thanks to Emilie and Bill Griffin, who helped me at a very early stage to believe that a book like this was possible and who helped me shape my initial thoughts. Ongoing thanks to my sisters and brothers in the clinic and at Loyola, who supported me all the way. Special thanks to Peter Wissoker, who truly made this book possible.

To my mom and dad, my sisters and brothers and their families, and Debbie's family, thanks to all of you for never giving up. Most of all I am grateful to Debbie, Patrick, and Joey for supporting me and the writing of this book over all these years. I love you all.

I INTRODUCTION

1   Why a Right to a Job at a Living Wage?

> When it shall be said in any country in the world, my poor are happy;
> neither ignorance nor distress is to be found among them; my jails are
> empty of prisoners, my streets of beggars; the aged are not in want, the
> taxes are not oppressive; . . . when these things can be said, then may that
> country boast of its constitution and its government.
> —Thomas Paine, *The Rights of Man*

THERE ARE approximately thirty million people in the United
States who are working full-time but earning poverty-level wages. In
addition, there are approximately fifteen million people who are either
out of work or working part-time but would like to be working full-
time. Historically, the first response to poverty has been to advise the
poor to work. But if the poor are already working or cannot find a job,
what's the next response? Usually, silence. And because of that silence,
more and more people join the ranks of the poor.

There is, however, a solution. By amending our Constitution to guarantee every person the right to a job at a living wage, we can end poverty
in America. A surprising amount of support exists both for a guaranteed
right to a job and a guaranteed right to be paid a living wage. The need
for such a national commitment is real and growing, and implementing
a constitutional solution to poverty in the United States is possible.

In my twenty-plus years as a lawyer and law professor, I have come to
know hundreds of poor people by representing them in legal matters
and working with them on issues such as public housing, public education, health care, living wages, and welfare reform. As a teacher, I have
discussed poverty and economic justice issues with thousands of others. Since I live in the South, many of the people with whom I discussed
these issues are deeply conservative. As a result of these experiences,
I have learned something about how people, both the poor and those
better off, think and feel about poverty.

Fundamentally, the vast majority of us believe in the American dream—that people who work should be able to support a family and build for the future. We also tend to think that work—the historic path that many Americans have followed to a more affluent life—is the way out of poverty.

While I applaud the sincerity of these beliefs, as a longtime student of poverty issues I know that they simply are not true. However, if we understand poverty as it truly exists in our country, we can end it for every person able to work. To do so, we will have to scrap a number of myths about poverty that stand in the way of positive change.

First, ask yourself two questions:

- Do you think that every person who wants to work should have the opportunity to do so?
- Do you think that every person who works full-time should earn enough to be self-supporting?

For years now I have posed these questions to audiences in places as varied as housing developments, church cafeterias, union halls, and university lecture auditoriums. No matter where I ask them, the responses have always been same:

- Everyone who wants to work should have the opportunity to do so.
- Everyone who works full-time should also be able to support his or her family.

These are things we all believe. But there is a big problem.

Poverty is much more widespread than most people understand. Poverty is not confined to inner-city welfare recipients—it extends to many who work but cannot afford health insurance, to those who work but still have to rely on churches or other charities for food.

Tens of millions are working but still cannot afford health insurance and housing and child care and food and transportation. Many can afford some of those needs, but most cannot afford all of them.

We need a new definition of poverty that reflects reality. People are poor if they cannot take care of themselves and their children without help. That is what real poverty is, and we need to recognize it.

Once we recognize what poverty is and how widespread it is, we need to do something about it. I think most people are willing to do something about poverty, but since they have been told so often that there is nothing that can be done, they turn away. Yet there is something we can do about ending poverty as we know it.

Sharol is a thirty-one-year-old single parent of two who works full-time as a cashier in Allentown, Pennsylvania. Despite working as many as fifty hours a week for wages considerably higher than minimum wage, she could not make ends meet. She had to go to a church social agency to ask for food and clothing for herself and her children. Sharol is not officially poor, yet she cannot provide for herself and her family. Economic hardship and poverty for Sharol is not the result of laziness. Sharol and millions like her are working and still too poor to make ends meet. As Diana Pearce, a faculty member at the University of Washington's School of Social Work, points out: "This is not about people doing a bad job of budgeting or making bad choices. They simply don't have enough to make it."[1]

Sharol is not alone. One in five single mothers who is working still remains below the official poverty line, even after counting all the government benefits she could possibly receive. Without government assistance, one in three remains in poverty. The U.S. Census Bureau reports that at least 75 percent of the poor people in this country, even under the current artificially low federal poverty guidelines, live in families where at least one person worked at some point in the previous year.[2]

A close look at what it *really* costs to raise a family shows a more disturbing picture. Millions of hard-working people with full-time jobs— who are not *officially* poor—are not earning enough to make ends meet.

This is not news to the millions of people who are working and earning less than living wages. Want proof? Visit the web site of the Family Economic Self-Sufficiency Project at <www.sixstrategies.org>. The site includes calculations by several great organizations showing the actual costs for workers to raise a family in many of the states in this nation. Look for your city and state or a neighboring state. See how much it actually costs a working single mom or dad with two kids, or a family with two kids where both parents are working, to make ends meet each month.

In city after city, state after state, you will find out what working families already know. The official government poverty guidelines do not begin to measure how much it actually costs to live. The reality is that poverty and work go hand in hand.

Americans sense that what these statistics tell us is true. Low-wage work does not suffice.

Even using the inadequate official government poverty guidelines, it takes approximately double the minimum wage for a family of four to meet its basic needs. Two examples demonstrate. First, if you look at the Food Stamp Program, you will see that Congress has decided that tens of millions of working people still need help feeding their families. In 2002, the year I wrote this book, a family of four did not phase out of eligibility for assistance under the Food Stamp Program until the worker earned $23,530 a year; that's more than $11 per hour for a single parent.[3] Second, the official 2002 poverty guidelines, for all states except Alaska and Hawaii, still count as poor a family of four that earns $18,100 a year, which is what a full-time worker making $8.70 an hour would earn.[4] As you will see, tens of millions of people work and earn less than $8.70 per hour.

It turns out that work has not been such a good escape route from poverty and dependency. Some workers do escape poverty, but many do not. Although the national economy generates many jobs, their wages and benefits, in good times and in bad, often are not sufficient to lift a family out of poverty.

Americans also know that there are fewer and fewer good jobs than there used to be. While many people have prospered, many are struggling just to make ends meet. Friends and relatives have experienced downsizing of their jobs or termination because the companies they worked for were sold. Everyone has heard horror stories from friends or family about trying to find another job, let alone another good job. This is no secret. Our nation needs more jobs at better pay, but we are unsure how to proceed.

Somewhere along the line we seem to have lowered our expectations for our nation. We have been led to believe that there is no way we can have a guarantee of good jobs paying good wages for our citizens. The "free market," we have been taught, will not allow it.

It is not enough, though, to say that a change would interfere with the free market. First of all, there is no such thing as a free market. Businesses are in Congress and every state legislative session getting laws passed to protect and benefit themselves. It is only when the economic needs of workers or safety issues or the environment come up that opponents of those ideas start talking about the free market. Many who claim that government has no business interfering with the market really mean that they are satisfied with current government arrangements and opportunities that favor business interests. Those who benefit from the current arrangements do not want change. So, the real question is not whether a constitutional amendment guaranteeing work at a living wage would interfere with the market, but whether the action is in the common interest and whether it would work.

We can, if we choose to do so, shape market forces in such a way as to make good jobs at good pay a priority. If we do so, the market will adapt and incorporate the needs of the common good. It has been done before. It can be done again.

Gainful employment for all who want to work is in the best interest of the entire country. Our common interest is served by people supporting themselves rather than being supported by others. Allowing people to work allows these very same workers to contribute to their own well-being, to their family's well-being, to the community's well-being.

Likewise, it is in our common interest that people who work full-time should not have to remain poor. Workers who are compensated enough to support themselves and their families do not need to rely on financial support from government, churches, family members, or others just to survive. The opportunity to work should be the right of every person.

As a nation, we can respond to the needs of tens of millions of our fellow citizens for jobs that pay living wages.

Work and poverty should not be partners. That partnership is not in our common good.

But wait a minute, some say. If we just allow the economy to work on its own, the economy will solve these problems on its own.

Is it realistic to expect the current market economy to look after the common good totally on its own? No. The market has no inherent interest in the common good. The market is interested in making money. That is its job. Period.

Expecting only the unguided market to steadily create good jobs at good wages is like expecting your car to watch your kids. It cannot happen. The common good is irrelevant to the market. Looking after the common good is the job of civil society and democratic government.

The guiding principle of most free-marketeers is that self-interest of individuals is good and that allowing that self-interest the maximum amount of freedom to operate will help the common good. Trust the invisible hand of the economy, they say, and all will get better.

Trust the market on its own? On its own, the market will give us recessions and depressions as well as good times. Recall that prior to current government regulation of the free market, our nation suffered the massive crisis of the Great Depression in the 1930s. The financial and unemployment nightmare of the Great Depression retreated only in the face of a massive public job creation program and World War II.

We need to think about what exactly is meant by those who use the term "free market" to oppose assistance for workers and legislation for the common good. We will discover that most people who advocate for a free market actually mean a business climate that is free of any regulation on commerce for the common good.

At the exact same time as these folks are telling people to trust in the free market, their representatives are furiously lobbying Congress and every single state legislature for rules and regulations to assist businesses and to structure the legal, economic, and work environment in such a way as to advantage them. Their advantages disadvantage others.

Blind trust in the market, or neutrality, or a hands-off attitude, is essentially acceptance of the status quo. This status quo involves poverty as we know it—tens of millions of people unemployed or employed at wages so low they are still unable to be self-sufficient. As Bishop Desmond Tutu said, "If you are neutral in situations of injustice, you have chosen the side of the oppressor. If an elephant has its foot on the tail of a mouse and you say that you are neutral, the mouse will not appreciate your neutrality."[5]

This is not a book that appeals to people contented with the status quo. If you have thought about it and have concluded that the economic system is working fairly and justly for all, providing good jobs at good pay for everyone who is willing to work, this book is not for you.

If, however, you think that since human beings have created the current economic system, which works well for some and not so well for others, and human beings can change it to make it better, then I hope you will read on.

It is in our common interest to fix problems with our current system that unfairly penalize work. It is in fact the responsibility of civil society and democratic government to fix such problems.

This book calls for American citizens and our leadership to transform the current economic and legal rules, which benefit some of us, and to bend them just enough to increase the benefit to the common good.

The ways we have been dealing with poverty up to now are inadequate. Thus, I propose that we eliminate poverty by means of a constitutional amendment that guarantees everyone a right to work for a living wage.

Those who are benefiting the most from our current economic system will certainly cry out in protest. This amendment, they'll say, is unrealistic and violates the natural rules of economics. Some people can be expected to oppose guaranteeing a job for every person who wants to work, arguing that full employment is inflationary and thus bad for America. They would accept millions of people out of work as the price the nation must pay for keeping inflation low. As this book will show, that does not have to be the case. There will also be others who suggest that government has no business interfering with economic life. Yet, as every tax lawyer, business owner, labor official, and legislator already knows, there is no economic activity that is not already immersed in government regulation right now.

Certainly a constitutional amendment guaranteeing work at a living wage will not be a perfect solution. The economy and rules and regulations and social welfare laws are routinely manipulated by the rich and powerful and special interests, but that is not a reason to give up. Though there are economic "predators" who look for opportunities and seize them, that does not relieve the community of seeking structural improvements in our society.

Many thoughtful economists already acknowledge the possibility, and support the idea, of full employment and living wages. And there are many ideas already proposed detailing how we as a nation can make jobs for all and decent wages possible.

While I have been writing this book, the United States has experienced both a booming economy and an economic downturn. Unemployment dropped to new lows and then started back up. The stock market soared, then fell, then rose, then fell again. Unemployment and the stock market will continue to go up and down as the years go forward, but some things will not change.

Despite the unemployment figures or where the stock market is on any given day, millions of our fellow citizens are not able to support themselves and their families even though they are hard at work. At week's end they are still left with insufficient funds to pay their family bills. Millions more are part-time workers but would like to be working full-time. And millions are not working at all, but they would like to be.

Our American political history supports the sort of change I propose. Three times during the twentieth century a guaranteed right to employment was seriously considered in the United States. Providing opportunities for work when the private sector has faltered has been done on all levels of government. Public job creation has an extensive history on the national, state, and local levels. Public incentives for private employment have also been enacted at all levels of government.

Public opinion polls have consistently shown support for government providing good jobs to those who need them. A 2001 poll showed that more than eight in ten Americans support creating temporary government work programs for the unemployed in needed areas such as school and road construction. This cuts across all party affiliations, with 82 percent of Republicans, 90 percent of Democrats, and 83 percent of Independents supporting such a measure. A 2002 poll found nearly nine out of ten voters (86 percent) believe the federal government has a responsibility to do away with poverty. The same poll showed 77 percent of voters favored increasing the minimum wage from $5.15 to $8 an hour. An even higher percentage, 79 percent, favor raising the minimum wage to keep up with inflation.[6]

There is also a hundred-year tradition of significant religious support for both the right to work and the right to earn a living wage. If the public supports the idea, our churches support the idea, and the idea is just and in the common good, there is reason to explore how it can be done.

Our nation has continued to search for ways to improve the constitutional rights of its citizens, particularly in regard to voting rights, freedom, and liberty. But the brightness of rights with regard to personal liberty and political participation dim for those who have no work or are working but still unable to support themselves and their families.

Therefore, it is time to recognize the need for creating the opportunity for all persons to support themselves and address that need with a constitutional amendment.

The amendment I propose is simple: Every person shall have the right to work and to receive a living wage for their work.

The amendment contains two principles: (1) The right to work, and (2) the right of people who work to receive a living wage for their work.

These principles must remain linked together. Without the other, each is considerably weakened. A right to a job without a right to decent pay is as weak as the right to decent pay but no right to a job. Placing this promise into our Constitution would direct us as a nation to create ways to live up to our shared dream—that every person who wants to work can do so and every person who works full-time will earn enough to be self-sufficient.

Amending the Constitution would be hard work, but it could and should be done. The Constitution itself contains the process for amendments. Amending the Constitution is meant to be a hard, time-consuming, and politically demanding task. Could such an amendment be enacted by the needed two-thirds majority in Congress and three-fourths of the state legislatures? Not today. But in the future? It can be done if we are serious about making the American dream come true.

If this amendment was enacted, how would it actually operate? Fortunately, we know some of the answers to some of the questions.

First, the process of implementing this amendment would operate in the same way as other constitutional obligations; that is to say, with considerable care, deference, and judgment. Because the initial steps are the responsibility of the legislative bodies, Congress would be expected to craft appropriate laws consistent with the Constitution. The executive branch would be called upon to carry out the laws. The judiciary would carry out its traditional role of evaluating actions in purpose and practice to ensure they are consistent with the Constitution.

Second, the process engaged in by the judiciary would remain the same as for other constitutional rights. Even though judicial interpretation and enforcement of a constitutional right to work for a living wage would itself be unprecedented, legal scholars point out that enforcing social rights requires the same degree of judicial action as enforcing civil rights.

Third, for Congress, the possible ways of enacting laws in support of this right are literally limitless. To support jobs creation and retention, Congress could introduce new tax incentives and wage subsidies for private employers and employees. Congress could modify existing labor laws in areas such as raising and indexing minimum wages. Wages themselves could be supplemented by tax credits for low-wage workers and expanded for larger families. For those who are not employed in the private sector, a state or local public or WPA-type employment corps could, for example, help clean and teach and police our nation's communities.

The right to work must be a right of opportunity. "Every person shall have the right to work" simply means that there must be an opportunity for work for those who seek it. No one will be forced to work, and the voluntarily unemployed would not benefit from the amendment. This proposed amendment is not the sloganeering right to employment of those working against unions, but a real right to the opportunity to work. As a part of the U.S. Constitution, it would be a legally enforceable right for all citizens.

People who work would be entitled under this amendment to receive a living wage for their work. A living wage means compensation sufficient for workers to meet the needs and demands of everyday life, lived in a manner consistent with human dignity. What precise amount of money this is will vary over time and with national standards and expectations, but it is intended to cover the commonly accepted living expenses for workers and their dependents. Since it is a living wage, and because it is expected that many workers will be supporting families, the lives of those dependent on the worker must also be considered. What living wage certainly does not mean is the statutory minimum wage, which is far below the wages needed for most workers and their dependents to live in dignity. A living wage would also become a legally enforceable right.

The Constitution enshrines the highest goals of this nation, which has always valued working to earn enough to secure a dignified living. A constitutional amendment guaranteeing every person the right to work and to earn a living wage simply yet forcefully elevates accepted American principles to protected rights.

What does this mean in a practical sense? The key to ending poverty is linking the right to a job with the right to a living wage. As you will see, the details of how that will be done can be constructed, debated, changed, and reconstructed in many, many different ways. I am offering one vision of how those rights might be implemented. There are probably many other ways, some no doubt superior to the one I sketch out here. I offer this plan not to end the dialogue but to start it. But, no matter what the details are, the key is keeping the link between the right to a job with the right to a living wage.

Amending the Constitution to guarantee every person the right to a job at a living wage is no small task. But when this amendment is passed, it will be up to Congress to enact laws to make the right to a job at a living wage a reality. While implementing change will not happen overnight, it should certainly not take more than four or five years to phase in the elements that are necessary.

The first step is for Congress to determine what level of income constitutes a living wage. I suggest that we scrap the current federal minimum wage and create a new federal minimum living wage. This minimum living wage has to be high enough for one working person to support herself and her family in dignity. Thus it must not be tied to the existing inadequate federal poverty guidelines, but to what it actually costs to be self-sufficient in the United States. The federal poverty guidelines should be raised by 100 percent to reflect what it really costs a working family to make ends meet. The federal minimum living wage has to be set to that newly revised poverty level, and it should change annually. In 2002 dollars, I suggest that the hourly wage should be at least $8.50 if health insurance is provided and $10.50 an hour if health insurance is not provided. Working people with dependents whose wages fall below the revised poverty thresholds should receive a wage supplement in each and every paycheck, to lift them out of poverty and to ensure that their work provides them and their families with enough to live on.

The second step is to create the system that guarantees every person who wants to work the opportunity to do so. The specifics of that are also up to Congress. What I propose is a mixed system that primarily relies on private employment but creates a permanent flexible safety net of public employment opportunities for people when there are insufficient private jobs available. Private employment can be increased, enhanced, and assisted by tax deductions and credits. Public employment can be created by federal block grants to states or counties that will be free, with federal oversight, to make their own choices of how to provide living-wage jobs for every person who wants one.

If Congress fails to act, or acts in a manner inconsistent with the constitutional right to a job at a living wage, then it will be up to the courts to act. The courts routinely fulfill their traditional role of evaluating constitutional issues, and they will have to do so in this area as well.

What about other practical issues such as cost? Honestly, it will cost billions. But our current broken system is already costing us billions. Later in the book I will share some of the ideas already circulating about how to create enough jobs for everyone as well as ideas about raising wages and some of the estimated costs.

While this new right undoubtedly has financial implications, our nation is already paying a high price for our current system, which tolerates unemployment and poverty-level wages.

Who pays for the living costs of low-wage workers now? If low-wage workers need food and rental assistance and medical treatment, the reality is that the living costs for low-wage workers are already being supplemented by all levels of government as well as family members, friends, and churches.

The same holds true for the unemployed. Who is supporting the unemployed now? In a very real sense, we are: the same families and friends and churches and all levels of government.

But a constitutional amendment could begin to effect positive change. Everyone could then have a chance to work at a job that paid a living wage. I believe the widespread effects of a constitutional amendment would bring new hopefulness and encouragement to our society.

America has always valued and even demanded work. But valuing work and demanding work are not enough. Currently, the only right to employment that exists is the right to look for an employer and, once found, to engage in enormously unequal bargaining with that employer over the availability of benefits and terms of employment. But unless a real opportunity to work exists, commitments to work and opportunity ring hollow. If we truly value work and demand that people work, we must give people the opportunity to do so, or else we are not serious.

Is this kind of change really possible? History shows us that truly significant social progress is possible.

Take Social Security, for example. My students have a hard time believing that when their grandparents were born there was no Social Security for seniors. Pensions for older people are now an accepted part of our way of life. Yet it was not always so.

In 1795, Thomas Paine published a pamphlet, *Agrarian Justice*, that called for the creation of an old-age pension system funded by a tax on inherited wealth. In 1889, social insurance for older people was adopted in Germany at the urging of Chancellor Otto von Bismarck. In 1909, the U.S. Congress introduced the first pension proposal for people over age sixty-five. In 1912, Theodore Roosevelt, while running for president on the Progressive Party platform, campaigned for old-age social insurance. In the early 1930s, Huey Long proposed a pension for every person over age sixty as part of his program of "Share the Wealth." The Social Security Act was signed into law by President Franklin D. Roosevelt on August 14, 1935.[7] Thus, over time, pensions for seniors grew from a radical idea into a realistic proposal and became law.

The same will happen with the right to a job at a living wage. Is it five years off, twenty-five years off, or more? As you read this book you will see that the idea is much further along the path toward a realistic political proposal than many believe.

If the U.S. House of Representatives can repeatedly pass a proposed constitutional amendment to ban flag-burning, isn't an amendment ensuring the right to a job at a living wage possible? Is the trouble of a constitutional amendment worth it? Are we willing to go through an uncertain process of legislative, executive, and judicial implementation to get millions of people out of poverty? I think millions of us will answer yes.

The time for this idea has come. The right to a job at a living wage has remained a popular concept among the general public for decades. We can—and should—call up the spirit of the New Deal, which combined economic self-interest of the nation with the moral demands of full citizenship, to advocate for the right to a job at a living wage.

Local living-wage campaigns are among the most exciting social justice activities taking place across our country. These campaigns, which combine efforts by community organizations, organized labor, and religious and social justice workers, are an important step toward helping us forge national coalitions so that the issues of living wages and the right to a job can become inextricably linked. Local living-wage campaigns deserve the support of everyone concerned about work and poverty. I have invested years of work in this effort, both as a lawyer and as a writer.

A right to a living wage and a right to a job together are much more powerful than either standing alone. While each alone provides valuable and important props for families, together they create a solid foundation for treating work with the respect it deserves and making work pay the wages that can support families.

This book holds up to the light of reality two principles deeply embedded in American thought and shows that we are not living up to our principles in our current approaches. While I propose a process for our nation to strengthen our commitment to end poverty as we know it and to allow every working person to support themselves and their families, I do not attempt to offer an economic treatise or the definitive analysis of specific programs that the country might use to fulfill the promise of the constitutional amendment. Others can do that. Although I have been talking and writing about the idea of this constitutional amendment for years, others have been discussing these ideas as well. In 1791, Thomas Paine proposed another idea that people who needed work be given a job and room and board with no questions asked. In 1893, the respected labor economist John Commons specifically advocated for a government-backed right to employment for every person. More recently, Adolph Reed Jr., Philip Harvey, David Gil, the Labor Party, the National Jobs for All Coalition, Gertrude Schaffner Goldberg, Sheila Collins, and Rep. Jesse L. Jackson Jr. have all been advocating the idea of a right to a job at a decent wage as well.

This idea was most clearly articulated more than sixty years ago, in words that still ring true today:

> Our nation so richly endowed with natural resources and with a capable and industrial population, should be able to devise ways and means of insuring to all our able-bodied working men and women a fair day's pay for a fair day's work.[8]

Those were the words of Franklin Delano Roosevelt in 1937. Despite the progress made since then, we as a nation still have a long way to go.

I think most Americans would like to make this happen.

I now share with you the evidence that we can make this happen.

II REEDUCATING OURSELVES ABOUT WHAT IT MEANS TO BE POOR

2   Myths and Facts about Poverty and Work

> It's not what we don't know that hurts us,
> it's what we know for certain that just ain't so.
> —Mark Twain

THE VERY first time I taught my course Law and Poverty, I asked my students midsemester to anonymously suggest a person they'd like to have as a guest speaker. Some students, no doubt intending to challenge my liberal perspective, asked me to invite David Duke, then a Louisiana state representative, to speak about poverty to my class. Duke had just lost a close election to the U.S. Senate in Louisiana, even though he had received hundreds of thousands of votes. I was surprised by the suggestion and frankly did not know how to respond. Since I was a brand new teacher I went to talk it over with Loyola's dean and my friend, Louis Westerfield. Louis was Loyola's first African-American dean and was personally not too thrilled with the idea of a visit to the law school by Duke, but he reminded me that I was in a university and that we needed to be open to controversial ideas and people. I agreed to invite Duke to speak to my class, and he promptly accepted.

Duke was very articulate. As an experienced and able speaker, he spoke at some length about poverty. He spoke about the problems of the welfare underclass, the need for tough love, the need to put welfare recipients to work, the need for drug testing of all welfare recipients, and other issues that had not yet achieved the national acceptance that they would later achieve.

David Duke was great at answering questions, even the challenging ones, with quick and easy responses. He had spoken all over the world hundreds of times and was very comfortable with the give and take of questions about poverty.

Except one.

A student asked, "We've heard what you'll do about the poor who aren't working—you'd put them to work—but what do you propose to do about those who are working but are still poor? Hundreds of thousands of workers in our state aren't on public assistance, but they're so poor that their kids still qualify for subsidized school lunch. What are we to do about those people who are poor?"

For the only time in the nearly one-hour session, Duke was at a loss for words. He stopped, a slight bit flustered, and then uncharacteristically fumbling for a response, he told of his allegiance to the cause of the working poor. Then, he switched gears and launched into a criticism of those who cheated in order to qualify for free or reduced-cost school lunch.

Like Duke, few of us think of people who work when we think about the poor. Yet most of the people in poverty live in homes where someone is working. Few of us consider that for many Americans, work and poverty go hand in hand.

In fact, when I speak to groups I often start by asking people to close their eyes to summon a picture of poverty in the United States. They report common visions.

A homeless person begging for money.

A dark-skinned welfare mother with kids living in inner-city public housing.

A lonely widow in an empty apartment.

Of course, there are poor people like this in America, but these visions are seriously inadequate when it comes to describing the poor in a comprehensive way. Further, if these are the visions of poverty, then the proposed solutions to the poverty they exemplify are also likely to be, and indeed have been, inadequate.

Most of what the general public believes about poverty and work is inaccurate. Common understanding of poverty is built on myths instead of facts. Unfortunately, statements that are not actually true can still be thought of as accurate if they are repeated often enough. Let's take a brief look at some of the most common myths and facts about poverty and work.

Myth #1   Most poor people do not work.

The fact is that most poor people live in families where someone is already working. In 1998, seven out of every ten of the able-bodied employable poor people worked at least part-time. One of every four worked full-time, year-round.[1]

Myth #2   There are plenty of jobs out there for those who want to work. Just look at the want ads!

A university study in Washington, D.C., checked the accuracy of this often-heard assertion. Researchers looked at the number of job openings in the *Washington Post* and found there were more than 3,000 jobs advertised. At the same time, there were 36,400 people reported unemployed and another 28,000 adults receiving some sort of public assistance payments. Close examination revealed that most of the jobs advertised required educational or prior employment experience that the poor just did not have. The study concluded that only 354 of the advertised jobs were obtainable by the low-skilled poor, and those were usually filled immediately by job seekers.[2]

The reality of the job market is more like the situation at the city-sponsored job fair in New York City, held at the height of the booming economy in late 1999, where forty companies agreed to accept résumés. Approximately five thousand people showed up, and some waited more than three hours in line to put in a résumé. The line included everyone from welfare mothers to recent college graduates. Many said they had been job hunting for months. As one employment expert said, "There is a huge pool of people with entry-level skills and not enough jobs for them."[3]

Myth #3   Unemployment is at a very low level and few people actually need jobs.

Unemployment is often twice as high as people think, even using official government information. For example, in May 2002, the U.S. Department of Labor (DOL) reported that the unemployment rate was 5.8 percent and 8.4 million people were unemployed. That in itself is a real reason to be concerned—more than 8 million people out of work. But the real number of people in May 2002 who needed work, numbers also reported by the DOL, was actually more than 17 million.

Here is how it works. Every month the DOL releases information on the unemployment rate and the number of people who were unemployed. But this number does not count millions of other people who need work. In the same May 2002 report, in data rarely picked up by the media, the DOL reported an additional 3.8 million persons who were working part-time but wanted to be working full-time, and another 5.4 million people were unemployed and wanted jobs but were classified as no longer actively looking for them. Some were classified as "discouraged" workers, people who wanted to work and were available to work but could not find work and have given up looking for work. Others were unable to seek work because of disability or home responsibilities. Thus, the number of people who are either out of work or not working full-time and who would like to be is around 17.6 million, well more than double the total usually reported by the media. And instead of an unemployment rate of 5.8 percent in May 2002, our nation was really facing an unemployment and underemployment rate of more than 12 percent.[4]

> **Myth #4**   If people would just work, even at minimum wage, they would not be poor.

The fact is that full-time minimum-wage work has not been enough to lift most families over the poverty line in years. With the minimum wage at $5.15 per hour, the full-time minimum-wage worker earns $10,712 per year. That has not been above the poverty level for a family of three since 1990, or for a family of four since 1984. Even when the minimum wage is inevitably raised, full-time minimum-wage work will not likely lift a family out of poverty. For a single parent with two children, the official poverty guideline for the year 2002 was a yearly income of $15,020. For a parent with three children, the yearly income was $18,100. A parent with two children working full-time would have needed to make at least $7.22 per hour, and a parent with three children would have needed to earn $8.70 per hour, to at least earn enough to be over the 2002 official poverty threshold.[5]

> **Myth #5**   Minimum wage is not important because hardly anyone except teenagers earns minimum wage.

Not true. If the minimum wage had been raised in 2001 by $1 an hour, more than 10 million workers, or 8.7 percent of the entire workforce in the United States, would have seen a direct increase in wages and another 9.7 million workers, who earned up to $7.15 an hour, would have also likely seen an increase. Despite the prevailing wisdom that only teenagers and part-time employees work for minimum wages, 68.2

percent of the workers affected would have been over twenty years old and close to half, 45.3 percent of the workers, would be full-timers. The majority of the affected workers would have been women, 60.6 percent, and African American and Hispanic workers would disproportionately benefit.[6]

Myth #6   Minimum-wage and other low-wage jobs are important to the community because they give unskilled people training opportunities and experience at wages employers can afford, which in turn allows the workers to improve their skills in order to move into better-paying jobs.

The fact is that more than one out of every four workers in the United States earns low wages—too little an hour to lift a family of four over the official government poverty line. That translates into more than thirty million people in this country who work and earn less than $8.19 an hour. These are not entry-level workers who are moving on up the economic ladder. Sixty-three percent of these folks are over twenty-six years old. One in four has attended college. Certainly there are some who are temporarily in these jobs on their way to higher-skilled, better-paying jobs, but most are not. Low-wage work is a permanent fact of life for millions of workers.[7]

Myth #7   There are really not that many poor people out there.

There were between thirty million and forty million people living below the unrealistically low official poverty line during the last ten years. This means that there are more officially poor people in the United States than all the people who live in El Salvador, Haiti, Honduras, Ireland, New Zealand, and Nicaragua combined.[8] Put another way, the official total American poor represent more than the total combined populations of the states of Alabama, Arkansas, Iowa, Kansas, Kentucky, Maine, Minnesota, Mississippi, Nebraska, North Dakota, Oregon, South Dakota, and Tennessee.[9]

If you add in the numbers of people below 125 percent of the official poverty level, a modest increase that some researchers suggest is a more realistic poverty line, there are between forty-five million and fifty million people living in poverty.[10] That is more than the total combined populations of all the states mentioned above plus the total populations of the states of Delaware, Hawaii, Montana, New Hampshire, New Mexico, Rhode Island, Vermont, West Virginia, and Wyoming—a total of twenty-two states.[11]

Myth #8   Apart from the poor, most people in the United States are doing pretty well.

The fact is that more than one in every four workers in the United States, more than thirty million people, earns poverty-level wages. These people are all adults, and not counted in this number are the millions of children in their families. The Economic Policy Institute calculates "poverty-level wages" as those that would still leave a full-time year-round worker earning less than the official poverty threshold for a family of four. The institute's 1999 calculation found that full-time year-round workers earned poverty-level wages if they made less than $8.19 an hour. In 1999, 26.8 percent of all workers—more than thirty million workers—earned less than that.[12] The effects of these low wages are serious. The U.S. Conference of Mayors identified low-paying jobs as the number one cause of hunger in urban America.[13]

Myth #9   Most poor people are African American or Hispanic.

The fact is that there have always been many more poor white people than poor African-American or Hispanic people. Poverty afflicts a much higher percentage of Hispanic and African Americans than whites, but in actual numbers there are more white poor people.

For example, the 2001 *Statistical Abstract of the United States*, published by the U.S. Census Bureau, reported on the details of poor people in 1999. Of the thirty-two million people below the official poverty line in 1999, approximately twenty-two million were white, eight million were black, and seven million were Hispanic. Thus, approximately 10 percent of whites were poor compared with 24 percent of blacks and 23 percent of Hispanics.[14]

You cannot realistically discuss poverty without discussing race and the effects of racism. Unfortunately, the media do a disservice in this area when they repeat and reinforce unconscious racial stereotypes by portraying poverty as primarily a problem for minority Americans. For example, a Yale University study showed that television and print news was much more likely to portray black people as poor than other racial groups.[15]

There are some clear racial patterns in poverty. The rate of joblessness in many urban minority poor areas in the 1990s was as high as 66
percent.[16] Median incomes of white families are much higher than those
of black, Hispanic, or Native Americans.[17] When looking at savings and
retirement, the situation is worse; white families have as much as twenty
times the accumulated wealth of black families.[18]

While among all children one of every five or six lives in a poor family,[19] one of every three African-American and Hispanic children are
poor.[20] The infant mortality rate for black babies in the 1990s was more
than two times the rate for white babies.[21]

As with children, the poverty rate for those over age sixty-five is also
much higher among minorities. Nationwide one in nine or ten persons
over age sixty-five is poor, but one in every four African Americans and
one in every five Hispanics over age sixty-five is poor.[22]

> **Myth #10** Most of the poor are nonworking, middle-aged, pan-
> handling bums.

Even though "can-you-spare-some-change" men may be more visible than others who are poor, they are really a very, very small part of
poverty.

Gender and age are important predictors of poverty, but not for mid-
dle-aged men. In fact, women are more likely than men to be victims
of poverty. Approximately one-third of all female single-parent households live under the poverty line, and these mothers and children ac-
counted for around fourteen million people in poverty in the mid-
1990s.[23] The poverty rate for women in the labor force is higher than
men.[24] The *Wall Street Journal* reported in 1995 that women in the United
States earned 75.9 cents for every dollar earned by men; by 1999 that
figure had risen by 1 cent.[25] Women earn substantially less than men,
even when comparing women and men with similar educational back-
grounds.[26] Child support is of limited help; researchers for the DOL
estimate that only just over one-third of all the children of absent fathers
receive child support.[27]

Of all people, children bear the highest burden of poverty. One of
every five or six children lives in a poor family.[28]

Of those over age sixty-five, one in about every nine or ten are poor.[29]
Those over age sixty-five represent the one group where the antipoverty
efforts of the twentieth century (primarily Social Security, Medicare, and

Medicaid) have really worked. In 1959, 35.2 percent of those over age sixty-five were poor; by 1970 this declined to 25 percent; and by 1998 poverty among those over age sixty-five was down to 11 percent.[30]

Myth #11 Poverty is really just an inner-city problem.

The fact is that wherever there are people, there are poor people. Percentagewise, there is not much difference in the presence of poor people in the country, the suburbs, or the cities. Nationwide in 1998, poor people made up just over 12 percent of all persons in metropolitan areas with populations over fifty thousand, 18 percent of persons living in central cities, and 14 percent of all persons living outside metropolitan areas.[31]

Myth #12 The United States provides more help to poor people than any other country in the world.

The United States ranked twentieth of ninety-six nations in percentage of government expenditures on social security and welfare, behind, among others, the United Kingdom, Italy, Canada, Finland, Norway, the Netherlands, Denmark, Switzerland, and Sweden. Of the ten developed nations in the international Luxembourg Income Study, the United States is the only one without a child allowance. Compared to ten other industrialized nations, the United States has the highest percentage of its population with incomes less than half of the median income level. And, it ranks first in the percentage of poor families with children and second only to the United Kingdom in the percentage of elderly people who are poor.[32]

In a study of fifteen prosperous nations, children in the United States had the highest percentage of poverty, the second lowest standard of living, and the highest gap between rich and poor than any of the nations.[33]

The World Bank reports that the United States ranks behind all other developed nations in how much of its economy it devotes to international development aid to poor countries, one-tenth of 1 percent of our gross national product. Other countries are pretty stingy too, most giving substantially less than 1 percent—Britain 0.23 percent, Germany 0.26 percent, Japan 0.35 percent, France 0.39 percent, the Netherlands 0.79 percent—but the United States is at the bottom.[34]

One of the realities about poverty and work is that poor people rarely have input in the laws that affect them. If laws about prescription drugs are being considered, there are many people involved—the drug makers, the research community, pharmaceutical retail outlets such as drug stores, and health insurance providers. The same is true for most other areas of law; there are built-in lobbies of people who will help push and pull and shape the laws regulating their area. That is not usually true about laws affecting poor people.

Poor people are fairly powerless in the political arena not only because they have insufficient funds to contribute to candidates, but also because voter participation is closely correlated with income. The poorer the person, the less likely he or she is to vote. In a 1996 study of registration and voting behavior between naturalized and native-born Americans, the U.S. Census Bureau found a correlation between income and voter participation:

- 41 percent of those with incomes of less than $9,999 voted
- 49 percent of those with incomes between $10,000 and $14,999 voted
- 53 percent of those with incomes between $15,000 and $24,999 voted
- 56 percent of those with incomes between $25,000 and $34,999 voted
- 62 percent of those with incomes between $35,000 and $49,999 voted
- 69 percent of those with incomes between $50,000 and $74,999 voted
- 76 percent of those with incomes over $75,000 voted[35]

Thus, most of the laws about working and nonworking poor people are formulated by nonpoor people, debated by nonpoor people, and mostly enacted due to lobbying that is not conducted by poor people.

Often these laws are formulated based on the common myths that are described above and are not really in the interest of poor people, but are part of some other political or religious or cultural agenda.

Any realistic discussion of poverty in the United States must look to the facts about who lives in poverty. While numbers and statistics are not everyone's favorite topic of discussion and are as subject to spin and manipulation as any other facts, they are important. The official poverty numbers, as reported by the Census Bureau, change every year. For the latest statistics, check the poverty link at the bureau's web site at <www.census.gov>. While the precise numbers change each year, there are some general trends which do not change and are reflected in the figures given above.

The facts are important. If our common idea of poverty is flawed, then our proposed solutions are also likely to be, and frequently have been, flawed.

In a very real way our commitment as a nation regarding how we address the problem of poverty comes out of our history. That history, going back to the English poor laws, is a very big part of the unconscious background that has shaped our current poverty-fighting policies. Let's take a brief look at what we can learn from our history of dealing with poverty and poor people.

3 Our History Shapes Our Thinking

"UNLESS YOU start saving your money, you're going to end up in the poorhouse!" Ever heard someone say that? Where does that saying come from?

My students generally do not know that the United States was dotted with government and private poorhouses in the early part of the twentieth century.[1]

Poorhouses were real, and the fear of landing in the poorhouse was also real. That is where that warning comes from. The fear of ending up in the poorhouse has been handed down orally from generation to generation, even after the poorhouses disappeared. Yet poorhouses continue to shape our consciousness about poverty and behavior.

There are plenty of other examples of how our shared history and culture unconsciously shapes our outlook on poverty. To properly analyze poverty and work, we have to consider that we have some preconceived notions already imprinted on our thought process.

In the mid-1990s, some politicians declared that they had a new idea—it was time to "get tough" on poor people, time to "force poor people to work." It was time for welfare reform.

It may come as a surprise that their efforts were nothing new, that, in fact, our laws have been trying to "get tough" on the poor for more than 650 years.

In 1349 England enacted the first law to get tough on poor people. What the English did to their poor people is important because the United States inherited many of our basic legal principles of how we deal with poverty and poor people from the English. Our American colonies essentially adopted the English laws about poor people, and those colonial poor laws became the basis for many of our state laws.[2]

In the mid-1300s, the English government was becoming concerned that there were too many poor people wandering around. Too many poor people who appeared to be able to work were choosing to beg. Therefore, England made it illegal to give alms to beggars who were able to work by enacting its first law to classify who among the poor was worthy of help and who was not.

This is what the law of 1349 said:

> Because that many valiant beggars, as long as they may live of begging, do refuse to labour, giving themselves to idleness and vice, and sometimes to theft and other abominations; none, upon the said pain of imprisonment shall, under the colour of pity or alms, give any thing to such, which may labour, or presume to favour them towards their desires, so that thereby they may be compelled to labour for their necessary living.[3]

Translation? There are too many homeless beggars roaming around who could work if we were only tougher on them. These folks are lazy and probably petty criminals. They will only work if we force them. So, we are now making it illegal to feed them or give them any more help, and that way they will be forced to work. The law was sent to each of the bishops, who were asked to order people in their communities to obey it.[4]

Sound familiar? It should. It is familiar. This old English law, enacted more than 650 years ago, and some of the ones that the English enacted later, sound quite a bit like the "welfare reforms" enacted by the Congress in the 1990s.

Nearly two hundred years later, in the 1530s, England continued to be concerned about the number of poor people, beggars, and vagrants. English law was changed to allow only "the aged poor and the impotent" (so severely disabled that they were unable to work) to beg for alms or charity. Even then, the aged poor and the disabled were not allowed to beg unless they were given official written permission, and they were limited to certain locations. Everyone else under age sixty who was poor but who could work was prohibited from begging and was forced to work, even children. Those of whatever state or condition who violated the law were whipped. Repeat offenders were subject to having their ears cut off.[5]

Poor children? The local justice of the peace was given the responsibility of taking poor children, ages five to fourteen, away from their families if the children were found begging and place them as apprentices.[6]

This was England's welfare reform of the 1500s. The English thought that helping the poor only encouraged dependence and actually increased the number of poor people. On grounds quite similar to those raised by contemporary opponents of public assistance to the poor, some even criticized religious monasteries for feeding the poor:

> It is obvious . . . the monastic institutions . . . had the effect of increasing tenfold the evil which they were designed to cure.[7]

Translation? Helping poor people only hurts poor people. What the poor need is not the tender help of generosity, but tough love.

These English poor laws of 1349 to 1601 share several common themes with U.S. welfare "reforms" of the mid-1990s.[8]

First, poor people can work and are choosing not to, so they must be forced to work. Second, helping poor people actually hurts poor people, so it is time to get tougher on them for their own sake. And third, poor parents are likely bad parents, and we should take their kids away from them.[9]

Is it a coincidence that these laws, hundreds of years apart, are so similar? No. These old English laws became the primary basis for the laws enacted in the American colonies when colonial legislatures decided how to handle the problems of poverty on the continent. These laws, and the assumptions they contain, became part of the unconscious backdrop of how we view poverty. And they are such good scenery that we often do not consciously understand how they set the tone for the current actions that take place.

These old English laws are like the poorhouses. They are not actually here anymore, but they continue to influence our thinking.

Many other important forces shaped colonial and early American thought about poverty, including Puritanism, Calvinism, and our national sense of the frontier culture. All of these influences were, like the English poor laws, pretty intolerant and skeptical of poor people.[10]

The "reforms" in welfare at the end of the twentieth century resulted from decades of concerted conservative attacks on the principle that government can or should assist poor and working people.[11] These campaigns increasingly relied on stigmatizing, shaming, and stereotyping poor people as immoral, undermotivated, urban, nonworking, overpopulating, living in and creating a culture of poverty, and dark-skinned. Think tanks and institutions tapped into the historical roots of antagonism against poor people and the age-old proposition that helping poor and working people only ended up harming them. Poor people were analyzed and categorized by those who had no accountability to poor and working people.

In these campaigns, life was simple. Government was bad. Business was good. Rich people were righteous and productive. Poor people were immoral failures. The market was free and self-regulating. Public laws to regulate for the common good were unrealistic and counterproductive. The smaller and less intrusive the government, the better off we all are.

The relentless efforts of conservatives to undercut public assistance to the poor were matched by similar efforts to undercut government regulation in other areas of the economy that were characterized as "antibusiness." Systematic dismantling and decreased funding of government agencies was not just good for business interests, but was in the common good.

Laws were changed accordingly. Not surprisingly, the changes reflected some old themes.

Anyone who has ever heard a talk radio discussion of welfare will be familiar with what the 1834 English Poor Law Commission called "less eligibility." In the English welfare "reform" of the 1830s, "less eligibility" meant that in order for the poor relief system to work, the living standards of the best-situated nonworking poor person must be worse than the worst-situated working person. Translation: the best welfare can never be better than the worst job, or else why would anyone take the bad jobs?

As the twentieth century closed, nonworking poor people were the most visible group to lose welfare. But less publicized cutbacks occurred in many other areas as huge holes were systematically cut in the government safety net.

Working people lost just as much. The real value of the minimum wage dramatically declined. The influence of organized workers in unions declined. The gap between the rich and the rest increased.

In thinking about a public response, we must be constantly aware of these historical themes that are often deeply embedded in our unconscious views and stereotypes about poverty. These old themes and laws are like the poorhouses our parents warned us about. The poorhouses are not here anymore, but they continue to influence our thinking.

The challenge for those who want to engage in serious discussion about these issues is to first acknowledge our ingrained presumptions and then examine them to see what is actually true and what is not.

Part of that discussion has to include an examination of the official definition of poverty.

4   Current Official Definition of Poverty

What is the official definition of poverty? How does the government decide who is poor? The news media report that the numbers about poverty went up or down or how many people are poor, and yet few of us know the official definition of poverty being used.

Before discussing the official definition of poverty and its problems, I want to illustrate some of the problems with deciding who is poor by sharing two exercises that I conduct with my students.

The first exercise shows the difficulty of trying to define what poverty is because our definition of poverty carries with it our thinking of why people are poor.

I ask the students to imagine that they are driving a car. As they approach an intersection, they see me as one of "those people" holding up a hand-lettered sign. How, I ask, do they think the general public would react to me when they see the sign?

The first sign I hold up says HUNGRY, PLEASE HELP.

Reactions are mostly negative. There are many comments about alcoholism, manipulation, and laziness. There are also a few positive remarks, many fewer than the negative ones, about the lack of jobs for the unskilled, layoffs, and worry about hunger.

Everyone admits that a person holding up a sign and begging at an intersection is likely to be poor, but they question why they are poor and why they need to ask for help.

As the discussion goes on, I list the positive and negative reactions on the blackboard. Then I hold up a sign that says WILL WORK FOR FOOD and ask for reactions.

Reactions remain mostly negative. There are acknowledgments that a sign-holder who expresses his or her willingness to work generates marginally more sympathy. But most don't think that the person holding up the sign would be telling the truth.

Even if the person was believable, the students think he or she would likely be a source of danger. Pick that person up, drive him or her to the place of work, and then supervise the person? Not likely. I continue to list the positive and negative reactions.

Then, I hold up another sign: DISABLED NEED HELP.

Reaction begins to be more positive. If people are actually disabled and cannot work, the students think, then they should be helped. There is still skepticism—if people are really disabled the government probably helps them, so why should I?

Then I show more signs.

PLEASE HELP ME FEED MY CHILDREN.

DISABLED VIETNAM VET NEED HELP.

Reactions to these signs are, begrudgingly, turning more and more positive as students list the attractiveness of the need presented by the person. Almost reluctantly, they begin to look to structural societal reasons for the poverty of the person holding the sign. Some have actually seen people begging with their children there with them. Helping children is valued, and students would probably help even though they are very critical of the mother. Veterans have helped us, so we should help them. But aren't vets cared for pretty well already?

I show another sign: WORKING FULL-TIME, NEED EMERGENCY HELP.

This gives the room pause. There is again disbelief that the person is actually working. But if they could be sure that the person is working, they would help. There is discussion of low-wage work and the unmet needs of the working poor.

I hold up the final sign: JUSTICE REQUIRES YOU TO SHARE YOUR WEALTH.

There is a second of silence while the students read the sign, then the room bursts into laughter.

At the end of the exercise there are two lists on the board. The longer is the negative one. It lists laziness, deception, drugs, alcohol, crime, lack of self-control, and lying. The positive list, which is shorter, includes unemployment, need to share, innocence of children, contributions of veterans, and low wages.

In reality, the way we define poverty depends in part on the way we view the poor and the way we view why people are poor. That is, we have different reactions to the poor people we think are "worthy" of help and those we think are not.

Also, the way we view poverty and its causes will shape our decisions about whether we will help poor people and what help they need.

If we think poverty is caused by laziness, drugs, alcohol, lack of self-control, and lying, then we are likely to have a different response than if we think people are poor because of unemployment, low wages, and the need to raise children.

In my experience, our ways of addressing poverty are much more likely to have originated from thoughts prompted by negative preconceptions about poverty than positive preconceptions.

The second exercise is about money. Obviously, people in poverty do not have enough money, but how much is that?

As one of my first assignments, I ask my students to write out a monthly budget for a family of three—one adult and two kids. No luxuries, I tell them; just meet basic needs. Questions immediately start to fly.

How does one define basic needs?

What's a luxury?

How old are the kids?

Does the adult work?

Where do they live?

I decline to answer the questions, directing them to make those decisions themselves. But, after a few minutes, I begin to compare answers from different parts of the room.

How much did you budget for housing?

For utilities?

For food?

For transportation?

For health care?

For education?

For recreation?

For laundry?

For child care?

For newspapers, magazines, television, books?

There are disagreements, of course, premised on what each one thinks the basics and the luxuries are.

Is air conditioning in New Orleans a basic or a luxury?

What does affordable basic housing cost?

Is public transportation available?

Are there relatives (for child care) nearby?

Since the students come from all over the country, they educate each other about differences in the cost of housing and utilities and transportation between places such as urban New Orleans (where I teach), urban and suburban New York, and rural Montana and New Mexico.

At the end it is clear that the students' budgeted amounts vary widely, often ranging from a high-end monthly budget that is twice that of the lowest estimate.

This exercise illustrates the threshold problem for any serious discussion of ending poverty, forcing us once again to ask the question, just what is poverty?

Most people today don't have a precise working definition of poverty. As Supreme Court Justice Potter Stewart said about obscenity, people know it when they see it.[1]

We have an official definition of poverty. It has some serious problems and will likely be changed to reflect that many more people in this country, especially working people, are poor than the official numbers indicate. How did the government come up with the current definition?

Our current official national definition of poverty originated in work done in the early 1960s. But our national struggle to define who is poor and who should be assisted by the government did not start in the 1960s. It started right after the Revolutionary War of 1776.

In 1792 our government created our first social welfare legislation when it decided to give life pensions to disabled and impoverished veterans of the Revolutionary War.[2] The government could not afford to give pensions to every veteran of the war, so it limited them to those who were disabled by war wounds and were in need.[3]

Right away there were problems determining who was actually disabled and who was poor and worthy of public assistance and who was not.

So, in 1793, Congress decided that it was necessary to reform the newly created system because it was found "by experience inadequate to prevent the admission of improper claims to invalid pensions, and not to contain a sufficient facility for the allowance of such as may be well founded."[4] In other words, Congress, for the first of many subsequent times, determined that some of those who should be receiving government help were not receiving it, and some of those who should not be receiving help were getting it. In response the government tightened up the process of determining who was disabled by requiring additional medical certification of disability.[5] Over the next century and a half, the federal government continued to make adjustments and amendments to the laws giving pensions to soldiers, then their widows and children, and in these laws continually adjusted the meaning of poverty and disability.[6]

Since then there have been numerous social welfare programs for the poor enacted by the federal government and the states, but there wasn't a national definition of who was poor until the early 1960s.[7]

The current official poverty line was calculated by Social Security Administration staff economist Mollie Orshansky in the mid-1960s.[8] It is actually very simple. Orshansky used an economy food budget calculated in the 1950s for minimum dietary needs as the basis for the definition. Orshansky took that minimum food budget and then multiplied it by 3, on the assumption that food expenditures represented about a third of the family budget.[9]

Setting the official poverty line has always been as much politics as science. President Lyndon B. Johnson resisted setting the initial poverty threshold too high because he wanted to show good numbers in his War on Poverty.[10]

This measure was soon adopted by other federal agencies as the official poverty threshold, and the Census Bureau started publishing annual statistics on poverty in 1967.[11]

The result was the first rough estimate of who was poor and who was not. If a family had income higher than that line, they were not officially poor. If their income was lower than the line, they were counted among the official poor. With minor modifications, these figures have been annually recalculated by the Census Bureau in light of the Consumer Price Index and continue to be the way we officially define poverty.

The current official calculation of poverty, then, compares the pre-tax cash income of a person or family to see if it is above or below the annually recalculated poverty threshold.

The poverty guidelines are recalculated early each year and released by the federal government. They are available at several government web sites.[12]

For 2002, the official definition of poverty in the government guidelines were:

Family Size	Income
1	$ 8,860
2	$11,940
3	$15,020
4	$18,100
5	$21,180

For each additional person, add $3,080.[13]

The official poverty line determines who has income low enough to be classified as poor, but makes no effort to answer the question about why each person is poor.

Most people know that the official poverty line is unrealistic. In a poll conducted in 2000, 69 percent of respondents thought it would take a family of four at least $35,000 to make ends meet.[14] In 2001, when the official poverty line for a family of four was $17,029, three out of five Americans said that a family of four with an income of $20,000 a year was poor. Two out of five said a four-person family with an income of $25,000 a year was still poor.[15] In other opinion polls, Americans seem to agree that the line is too low and would draw the poverty line well over $20,000. They insisted it takes that much, if not more, to "get along in their community," to "live decently," or to avoid hardship.[16] In another 2001 poll, more than 40 percent thought a family of four with an income of $25,000, well above the $17,029 poverty line in 2001, was still poor.[17] A 2002 poll of voters found that half believed a family of four needed an income of at least $45,000 to make ends meet.[18]

There have been many studies showing that the Americans who were polled were right—these official lines are far, far too low.

In 1996, when the official poverty line was set at $16,183 for a family of four, the Economic Policy Institute calculated what it would cost that family to live in Baltimore. The researchers found what most families of four already know, that it actually took $34,732.28 to meet basic needs. As a consequence, many basic needs such as health care, quality child care, and decent housing were not fully met.[19]

In 1999, the Indiana Economic Development Council produced "basic needs" budgets for families in Indiana. The council concluded, for example, that a single parent, working full-time, with one or two children needed $20,700 to stay out of poverty—not counting child care costs.[20]

In 2001, when the official poverty line for a family of four was $17,650, the Women's Educational and Industrial Union in Boston calculated a "self-sufficiency" standard to measure the real cost of living, including securing adequate housing, child care, food, transportation, taxes, and medical care. The union determined that it took $43,000—a full-time wage of more than $20 an hour—for a family of four to make it in Boston, more than twice the 2001 official poverty level.[21]

The old official poverty line is inadequate for the reality of American life. We need a new measurement.

Surviving poverty is also not the same as achieving the American dream. Not so long ago Americans were asked, "How much income per year would you say you (and your family) need to fulfill all of your dreams?" In 1987, the median response was $50,000; in 1996, $90,000.[22]

Another thing. Poverty is relative. American poor people are rich beyond the wildest dreams of the poor in impoverished countries, where one billion people survive on about a dollar a day. Similarly, the American rich are always complaining about not having enough money for their vast and varied enterprises. Just as there is no agreement on exactly what poverty is, there is no agreement on what constitutes riches.

The relative nature of poverty has to be kept in mind, but we are not usually content to conclude that our citizens who don't have access to what we call the basics are better off than the poor in other parts of the world. Our citizens live side by side and are constantly inundated by a culture that equates dignity with income, possessions, and the ability to be self-supporting. While we can decry that economic pressure, we cannot ignore it.

What are the changes coming in the official poverty line? That is not yet settled. It looks as if the line will be raised to reflect that more people are poor than are currently counted.

According to Professor Rebecca Blank, there is no scientific consensus on how to set a new poverty line. "What there is here are a set of judgment calls, now being made, about what is needed to lift people to a socially acceptable standard of living."[23]

The most persuasive critics say that the current official definition of poverty is too low and thus substantially undercounts the real number of poor people, particularly the working poor.[24]

They first point out that the current system counts pretax income as income and disregards the federal, state, and local taxes that the poor—particularly the working poor—pay. If after-tax income was used as income, many more working poor people would fall below the current line, thus expanding the number of people in poverty.

Second, these critics point out that family expenditures on food no longer constitute one-third of a family's expenses. Rather, food accounts for only about a fifth of family spending. They thus conclude that multiplying the cost of food by 5 rather than 3 would be more accurate. This would raise the poverty line and expand the numbers of people below it. In fact, some experts say that food only constitutes one-sixth of the average family budget, thus the poverty line would be six times the thrifty food plan instead of three and end up much, much higher.[25]

Third, the critics point out that when the poverty line was first set in the 1960s, it was half of the median income for a family of four (a standard widely used to define poverty in Europe today) but has drifted downward to only about 40 percent of median family income, again thus understating the number of people in poverty. That means that the poverty line, which used to measure the poor, now measures only the very poor.[26]

They also point out that the current method effectively assumes the same standard of living as the late 1950s, despite the obvious widespread changes. If adjustments were made to realistically correct these deficiencies, the critics suggest, the poverty line would be raised by 50 percent, thus including millions more people, mainly many more of the working poor, within the official definition of poverty.

John E. Schwarz, writing in *Atlantic Monthly*, offered a version of this analysis of the inadequacy of the official poverty level:

> Many of the expenses necessary for minimally decent living in most areas of the country today were not part of the lives of many Americans in the early 1950s. Even though food prices have risen since 1955 at practically the same rate as general inflation, food today accounts for barely a sixth of the average family budget, rather than a third. [If the current poverty line was adjusted to reflect the actual cost of food as one-sixth rather than one-third of the family budget], the poverty line in 1994 would have been about $26,000, not $15,100.[27]

Schwarz also notes that if you just start with $4,576 (the inflation-adjusted equivalent of the 1955 thrifty food budget) and add HUD's suggested cost for a low-cost rental unit of $512 a month (which includes utilities and local phone service), Social Security and federal and state income taxes totaling $3,270, household expenses of $3,900, $2,000 for all medical care and medicines, some money for an old car and/or public transportation ($3,700), you come up with about $25,000 a year, with no provision for entertainment, child care, emergencies, or savings.[28]

Further supporting the argument of those who say the official poverty line is too low is the fact that several government social welfare programs set a considerably higher level for determining poverty.

For example, the National School Lunch Program provides federal funds for meals served by schools to children who come from low-income families. The program provides free meals to those from families with incomes below 130 percent of federal guidelines and reduced-cost meals to children from families with incomes between 130 percent and 185 percent of the official poverty guidelines.[29] In the decade of the 1990s, between 10 million and 13 million children received free lunch and another 1.5 million to 2.4 million received reduced-cost lunch.[30]

Likewise, the Legal Services Corporation offers free legal assistance to people whose incomes are less than 125 to 150 percent of federal poverty guidelines.[31] The Earned Income Tax Credit was available to low-income working taxpayers up to a phase-out income of $30,580 in 1999, nearly twice the poverty line for some families.[32]

A different school of critics think the current official definition of poverty actually overestimates the number of people in poverty. Their criticisms are primarily based on the manner in which the current method evaluates income of people and calculates inflation. The Census Bureau counts all pretax income, including income from cash welfare programs such as social security, disability income, and welfare but does not count as income other noncash governmental benefits such as food stamps, medical care, social services, education, job training, and housing benefits. Because the Census Bureau does not calculate assets, people with large savings or significant resources such as houses who may have temporary low incomes in any given year are counted, erroneously, as poor. These critics also urge that inflation should not be calculated by using the Consumer Price Index, which includes increases or decreases in the cost of buying a house, but on an alternative scale that incorporates adjustments in the cost of renting a house. They recommend an alternative index for inflation and another definition of income—one that includes state and federal tax benefits, employer-provided benefits, food stamps, housing, school lunches, and a fungible value for some government-provided health care. With something like that, they conclude, the number of people in poverty would decrease substantially from current levels, lifting millions of people over the poverty line. While there is merit to the notion of counting food stamps as income, it would be very difficult to calculate many of the other benefits as income. Additionally, the argument about where to set the poverty line is not really important to the very, very poor who are on government assistance, for they will be counted among the poor in any definition. It is how to count those who are working but still poor that is the main source of contention.

A committee of the National Research Council (NRC) has proposed some reforms in the current calculation of the official poverty line that would incorporate some of the criticisms voiced by each school of critics.[33] These include adjustments for actual costs of food, clothing, shelter, and other needs as well as adjustments for geographical differences in the cost of living and the counting of noncash government benefits such as food stamps. The overall effect of their proposed changes would be to increase the number of people defined as poor and include many more of the working poor.[34]

Experts in the Department of Labor and the Census Bureau experimentally applied the proposed newer standards and concluded that the NRC proposals would identify millions more Americans as being in poverty, and in the newer calculations "the poor are more likely to be white, to be married, and to have a member of the family in the work force."[35]

Personally, I agree that most of the reforms suggested by the NRC are helpful. However, my experience is that even with the council's suggestions for reform, the official poverty levels are way, way too low. The NRC suggestions will make the current formula reflect more accurately the official definition of poverty as it was conceived in the early 1960s. But instead of reforming the old official poverty levels, it is time to re-think and recreate an entirely new definition of poverty, one more in accord with contemporary American reality and aspirations.

5   A New Definition of Poverty

> By necessaries I understand not only the commodities which are indispensably necessary for the support of life, but whatever the custom of the country renders it indecent for creditable people, even of the lowest order, to be without. —Adam Smith, *Wealth of Nations*

ANY NEW definition of poverty in America must be a reflection of our national commitment to justice, fairness, and the dignity of each and every human being.

As Adam Smith noted in the *Wealth of Nations* in 1776, a country's definition of what the necessities of life are is also a test of our national sense of decency.[1] No doubt there are a few in our nation who think that the avoidance of starvation is enough, and their definition of decency and poverty reflect that.

I, on the other hand, believe that a majority of Americans takes seriously our national commitment, that all of us are created equal and entitled to certain inalienable rights such as life, liberty, and the pursuit of happiness.

I also believe that a majority of Americans is committed to justice, fairness, and the inherent dignity of each and every human being.

Finally, I believe that the majority of America supports the idea that each person should be entitled to the opportunity to be self-supporting and self-sufficient. This means that everyone is entitled to the chance for self-determination.

The lack of these rights in a country, as Adam Smith said, "renders it indecent for creditable people, even those of the lowest order, to be without."

That is poverty.

I believe that most Americans want a nation where everyone has a real opportunity to live lives of human dignity. Therefore, we need to craft a new definition of poverty that incorporates this shared understanding, so that all people have the right and the opportunity to provide for themselves and their families. We need to focus not only on economic deprivation, but also on what justice demands. What we want for ourselves and our families is what we want for others: not a free ride, not a handout, but the right to work ourselves out of poverty, with a realistic chance to be self-sufficient.

A new definition of poverty is called for if we as a nation are going to address poverty. A real understanding of poverty requires that, apart from whatever formula the government uses at the time, we as a nation recognize that all humans have a basic dignity and a set of rights that should enable them to survive. As Patricia Ruggles said, "in the final analysis setting the poverty level requires a judgment about social norms, and such a judgment cannot be made on statistical grounds alone."[2] Poverty is not just numbers, it is the lack of opportunity.

A real understanding of poverty demands that, apart from any official formulaic calculation, the definition includes people who do not have the ability to provide for the basic needs of themselves and their families.

Poverty is something everyone can recognize. The official government poverty line is inadequate and outdated. Our official determination of poverty needs to be revised to be more in line with contemporary understandings and contemporary reality.

More than anything else, we need to recognize that poverty is, at its heart, the inability of people to provide for themselves and their families. As we grow to understand that the lack of self-sufficiency is the true test of poverty, we will also understand that ending poverty means not only providing income support and services to people, but providing everyone with the opportunity to support themselves and their families by giving them the right to a job that pays a living wage.

People who are working and yet are still too poor to adequately provide for their families present America with its greatest challenge. If work doesn't really provide a way out of poverty, how can we expect people in the neediest groups to choose or accept work? If we cannot make work pay, how can we expect to motivate realistic change?

The standard of living for the majority of Americans has moved up while the standard for what we call poor has declined. That is out of step with what most people think of as poverty—the inability to provide the basics for one's family. The current official formulation is woefully inadequate because it does not reflect our national aspirations or commitments.

I do not here propose a specific formula for a new definition of poverty. Poverty is not just numbers. While numbers will be involved, they must be numbers that reflect the basic realities of what it takes for people to support not only themselves but also their families. While specifics are important and will be as controversial as are all important ideas, there is opportunity enough to set the specifics after a new common national understanding of what it means to be poor emerges.

There are, however, several basic elements that must be incorporated into any new understanding of poverty.

First, our understanding must be built on a foundation of justice and fairness.

Second, we must as a nation be willing to take our national aspirations and commitments seriously.

Third, we must look at a general understanding of what is necessary in order for each of us to lead lives based on those principles.

Fourth, we must exhibit a willingness to be resourceful and accept change in determining how these rights are to be implemented.

Finally, and most important, we must recognize that if we truly believe that all humans are entitled to human dignity, then each must be given a realistic opportunity to be self-supporting in order to become self-sufficient.

A right to self-determination and a right to the means to self-sufficiency are consistent with our own national goals, with our declared international goals, and with our religious beliefs based on natural law.

We can begin from the national goals that we all hold in common, ones that shaped us from the beginning. Where better to start than with our own Declaration of Independence, enacted by Congress on July 4, 1776:

> We hold these truths to be self-evident; that all men are created equal; that they are endowed by their Creator with certain inalienable rights; that among these are life, liberty, and the pursuit of happiness.[3]

Internationally, there is a similar document that points to our common goals. It is the 1948 Universal Declaration of Human Rights, adopted by the General Assembly of the United Nations. Like the Declaration of Independence, it does not carry the force of law but carries a moral and political force that can help us understand what the basic expectations are for each person.

Article 1 declares that

all human beings are born free and equal in dignity and rights.[4]

If we truly believe that all of us are born free and equal in dignity and rights, then we must recognize there are consequences to that belief.

Article 22 begins the statement of economic, social, and cultural rights:

Everyone, as a member of society . . . is entitled to realization, through national effort and international co-operation and in accordance with the organization and resources of each State, of the economic, social and cultural rights indispensable for his dignity and the free development of his personality.[5]

Article 23 specifically includes both a right to work, and a right to

just and favourable remuneration ensuring for himself and his family an existence worthy of human dignity, and supplemented, if necessary, by other means of social protection.[6]

Religious beliefs also support these common goals. In 1963, Pope John XXIII, in his encyclical "Peace on Earth," confirmed that natural law promises each person the means for proper development, including a right to work and earn a living wage, and that

every man has the right to life, to bodily integrity, and to the means which are necessary and suitable for the proper development of life. These means are primarily food, clothing, shelter, rest, medical care, and finally the necessary social services. . . .

When we turn to the economic sphere, it is clear that human beings have the natural right to free initiative in the economic field and the right to work. . . .

Furthermore—and this must be specially emphasized—there is the worker's right to a wage determined according to the criteria of justice. This means, therefore, one sufficient, in proportion to the available resources, to give the worker and his family a standard of living in keeping with human dignity.[7]

I think a majority of Americans understand that people need, and deserve, shelter and protection from extreme cold and heat.

I think a majority of Americans understand that people need, and deserve, adequate nutrition and access to adequate medical care.

I think that a majority of Americans understand that people need, and deserve, healthy, safe child care and opportunities to achieve their full educational potential.

I think a majority of people understand that people who want to work should be given the opportunity to do so.

And I think a majority of people think that if people work full-time they should be able to provide the basics for themselves and their families. Anything short of that is poverty.

A working person should be able to be independent, to raise a family, and to be self-sufficient. If a working person is not self-sufficient, he or she is really still poor.

Our current federal poverty guidelines are not at all accurately tied to independence or self-sufficiency, so they should be raised by at least 100 percent, phased in over a number of years, to a level that reflects reality.

Setting a poverty line should be about selecting an economic level beneath which people should not have to live. It is a human dignity issue. Setting a poverty line is not just a measuring stick to see how many people are poor, but a way for society to determine its value of itself and its people. No one should live below the poverty line unless there is a scarcity of resources sufficient to go around to provide for basic needs. Such a scarcity does not exist in the United States.

Try to calculate a family budget for the current official poverty thresholds and you will quickly see that they are unrealistically low. My students try to do that every year. Doesn't work. No way can you cover even the basics of food, shelter, utilities, clothing, medical care, and child care at the levels that government has set for poverty.

For example, the 2002 U.S. Department of Health and Human Services (HHS) poverty guidelines were set at $15,020 for a three-person family. Can a mom and two kids make it on that? Pay for an apartment, utilities, food, clothes, health care, child care, transportation to and from work and school? No way. And what about paying for the rest of the things that most in our country take for granted? Can this family buy a newspaper or some books, have a phone, access the internet, visit relatives, afford after-school and summer activities, go to the park, have a savings account? Not a chance.

A 2002 national poll confirmed what most working families already knew. Half of the voters surveyed believed that a family of four needs an income of at least $45,000 a year to make ends meet. That is 150 percent higher than the current federal poverty level. Another quarter said at least $35,000, about 100 percent higher.[8]

Our current definition of poverty does not meet the basics and does not even attempt to include many parts of life that are important.

Many have tried to calculate actual budgets that families could live on and have come up with budgets that are in excess of 100 percent higher than the federal poverty thresholds.[9]

A much more realistic way to set the poverty level is to try to determine how much money it takes for a person or family to become self-sufficient. Self-determination is the truest test of whether a person is poor or not.

Fortunately, these types of calculations have already been done. Two efforts in particular have done the best job of figuring out how much it actually costs working families to live.

The first group that estimates the actual costs of self-sufficiency for working families is the Family Economic Self-Sufficiency Project. This project is a joint effort of the Corporation for Enterprise Development, the Ford Foundation, the Ms. Foundation for Women, the National Economic Development and Law Center, Wider Opportunities for Women, and Professor Diana Pearce of the University of Washington School of Social Work.

The self-sufficiency standard figures out how much it actually costs working families to make it each month in today's economy. People who work at low-wage jobs already know that they cannot make ends meet. The self-sufficiency standards explain why. These standards are much truer indicators of poverty than the official government guidelines.

A number of state nonprofit organizations have actually measured how much income a working parent needs to meet basic needs in their state. These calculations, conducted with the assistance of Professor Pearce, take into account the actual costs of food, housing, utilities, transportation, child care, and even taxes in many different regions of the country for many different types of working families. The standard assumes that employer-provided health care is provided and employees pay part of the costs. The calculations differ by geographic region and by whether or not there are children and whether or not those children are of school age (a very big issue, as all working parents know). The self-sufficiency standard accounts for state and local sales taxes as well as payroll taxes and figures in any credits available under the

Earned Income Tax Credit or the Child Care Tax Credit. The standard does not include any other private or public subsidies, such as food from a church food bank, food stamps, Medicaid, public housing, or housing shared with parents or others. It also does not include any money for dining out, church contributions, or retirement savings.

I encourage each reader to look at the self-sufficiency budget for your individual state. These budgets are a good reality check when discussing poverty, work, and living wages. You can find these self-sufficiency budgets on the web site of Wider Opportunities for Women at <www.sixstrategies.org.states.cfm>. These budgets are mostly based on local and federal government information about costs.[10]

It is interesting to compare the actual self-sufficiency budgets calculated for the states with the 2002 federal poverty guidelines for a family of three with an annual income of just over $15,000.

For Arizona, the 2002 self-sufficiency budget—what it actually cost to live month to month on a no-frills budget—for a working mom and two children in Phoenix was about $40,000, 160 percent higher than the current poverty levels. In Yuma, it took $31,500, a 100 percent increase. In Tucson, it was about 125 percent higher, slightly more than $34,000.[11]

The 2000 California study of self-sufficiency had similar findings. For a working parent and two kids in 2000, it took $27,893 to be self-sufficient in Trinity County, $34,661 in Sacramento, and $40,870 in Los Angeles. Compared with the 2000 poverty guidelines, these figures are 97 percent, 144 percent, and 188 percent higher, respectively.[12]

In Louisville, Kentucky, it took more than $36,000 for a working parent and two kids to be self-sufficient in 2001, 146 percent higher than the 2001 federal poverty guidelines. In Bowling Green, a working parent with two children needed just over $29,000, 98 percent higher.[13]

In New York in 2000, a working parent and two children needed $28,968 in Plattsburgh, 104 percent higher than 2000 poverty guidelines. The same family needed $32,472 in Buffalo, 129 percent higher than the 2000 guidelines, and $44,592 in Brooklyn, 215 percent higher.[14]

The Texas self-sufficiency study was conducted in 1996, and even then it took $28,920 in Abilene for a working parent and two children to make it. This is 122 percent higher than the 1996 federal poverty guidelines. It took $32,040 in Waco, $35,532 in Dallas, and $40,248 in Houston. These are higher than the 1996 federal poverty guidelines by 146 percent, 173 percent, and 210 percent, respectively.[15]

Look at the web site <www.sixstrategies.org> for more detailed information about self-sufficiency studies of cities and states all across the country.

Another respected research organization has arrived at similar conclusions about the inadequacy of the federal poverty line. The Economic Policy Institute published a study in 2001 called "Hardships in America: The Real Story of Working Families." The institute examined the costs involved in creating family budgets that provided a safe, decent standard of living for working families and estimated actual budgets for working families in four hundred communities across the nation. These budgets included the costs of quality child care, preventative health care, and safe and affordable housing. The conclusion? Basic family budgets were actually *twice* as high as the federal poverty line. This study is available on the web site of the Economic Policy Institute at <www.epinet.org>. The study presents the family budget estimates for six types of working families in hundreds of cities across the nation, in every one of the fifty states. Look at these for your community. They are realistic.[16]

Given the information from the national polls of the American people, the surveys of actual costs for working parents conducted in the states for the Family Economic Self-Sufficiency Project by Professor Pearce, and the research of the Economic Policy Institute, it is clear that we need to raise the federal poverty threshold by a minimum of a full 100 percent, phased in over a period of years. This would set a more realistic, yet still quite modest, level for food, clothing, shelter, child care, medical care, and the other basics that are part of the life we expect. Health care should be provided, and geographical adjustments should be made.

This would mean, for example, that the 2002 official poverty line for a family of three, which was $15,020, would rise by 100 percent to a much more realistic $30,040.

There will be much criticism about raising the poverty guidelines from the current official levels to a self-sufficiency level. Some will say that it is politically unrealistic to readjust the federal guidelines.

But the process of adapting to reality has already started.

For example, in 1999 the Connecticut legislature started the process of setting self-sufficiency standards for the state to assist working people. The legislature now uses the standards to identify working people who are underemployed and those who are working but still earning insufficient wages.[17]

This has started on the national level as well. In the U.S. Congress, Rep. Lynn Woolsey (D-Cal.) introduced the "Self-Sufficiency Act" (HR 3667) (107th Cong., second session, introduced January 29, 2002) to create self-sufficiency standards for each state and assess welfare reform by those standards.

Raising the poverty guidelines will count many, many more people as poor in our country than current figures estimate. But it is time to face the fact that many, many more people are poor than current poverty guidelines indicate.

The reality is that it takes a whole lot more money to survive on than the federal poverty guidelines suggest. The official guidelines are outdated. They are unrealistic. They need to be changed to reflect the real costs of living. Millions of working people already know they are not making ends meet—they are working but are not self-sufficient. This will not come as a big shock to them. Critics can complain, but this is the real world. It is time that government estimates conformed to the reality of the lives lived by the people.

I caution the reader that even raising the level by 100 percent would not be the end of the poverty threshold discussion, because over time our societal expectations for living would change. But it would be a good immediate start. Changes in our understanding of what it takes to be self-sufficient should trigger changes in our setting of the poverty level. This is an issue that Congress would be required to decide upon, and Congress could change it for geographical areas (as the National Research Council suggests is possible) and as times change.

III Poverty and Lack of Work

6   The Extent of Unemployment
        and Underemployment

Our nation has a peculiar work ethic. It insists that people work for a living, which is a valid expectation, but it does not insist that the private and public sectors provide enough jobs at livable wages for everyone who wants to work. —Jesse L. Jackson Jr., *A More Perfect Union*

THERE ARE people who sincerely believe that there is a decent job in our country for every person who wants one. They are very, very mistaken.

Millions of people in this country are not working at all, and millions more are working part-time when they would like to be working full-time. This lack of decent work occurs in good times and in bad. Whether the economy is up or down, there are millions of people who are un-employed, many apparently permanently. While millions of the poor do work, other millions of the poor do not work. Of these, the largest group is children. Others are too sick or too limited to work. Some have given up trying to find work. Others work but not full-time. The reality of unemployment and underemployment is that lack of work in good times and in bad continues to be a problem in our country, especially for minority and lower-skilled workers.

Start by considering that the unemployment figures usually reported by the media estimate only about half the number of people who actu-ally need jobs, as noted in Myth #3 (see Chapter 2).[1] What is usually termed as the "official" unemployment rate is, as one writer put it, a "gravely misleading statistic."[2] If you count the people who are work-ing part-time but would like to work full-time as well as those who have stopped looking for work, a more realistic picture of the lack of jobs emerges—a picture usually twice the size reported by the general media.[3]

For example, in May 2002, the U.S. Department of Labor (DOL) reported that the unemployment rate was 5.8 percent and that 8.4 million people were unemployed. That in itself is a real reason to be concerned—more than 8 million people out of work. But the real number of people in May 2002 who needed work, also reported by the DOL but not usually picked up by the media, was actually more than 17 million.

The official number of unemployed does not count millions of other people who need work. At the same time as the DOL reported in May 2002 that 8.4 million were out of work, the department also reported that there were an additional 3.8 million persons who were working part-time but wanted to be working full-time, and another 5.4 million people who were unemployed and wanted jobs but were classified as no longer actively looking for work. Some were classified as "discouraged" workers, people who wanted to work and were available to work but could not find work and have given up looking. Others were unable to seek work because of disability or home responsibilities. Thus, instead of the 8.4 million figure reported, the actual number of people who are either out of work or not working full-time and who would like to be is around 17.6 million, well more than double the total usually reported. Instead of an unemployment rate of 5.8 percent in May 2002, our nation was really facing an unemployment and underemployment rate of more than 12 percent.[4]

Unemployment is a constant and predictable part of our current economic system. As Robert Solow, the 1987 winner of the Nobel Prize in Economics, said, "There is absolutely no reason to believe our economy holds a substantial number of unfilled vacancies for unqualified workers."[5]

Further, no matter what the national unemployment rate is, unemployment among minority workers is usually double that of white workers.[6] For example, unemployment among black adults has been above 10 percent since the 1970s, about twice the rate of white unemployment.[7]

Nationwide, new jobs have indeed been created, but much of this growth in employment has occurred "in the suburbs, exurbs, and non-metropolitan areas far removed from growing concentrations of poorly educated urban minorities,"[8] which is another way of saying that the poor could not get to the jobs. Many poor people do not own cars. Of course, they could use public transit, but public transportation often does not extend far into the suburbs. This is not likely to improve, since the federal government has cut back mass transit funds by $57 billion since 1980.[9]

During recent decades, cities that lost the largest numbers of blue-collar jobs and other lower-skill jobs simultaneously added large numbers of poorly educated minorities to their working-age population.[10]

What we have in the inner cities is unemployment at rates 50 percent higher than during the Great Depression of the 1930s. Urban unemployment rates are as high as 40 to 60 percent for young black males aged eighteen to twenty-four.[11] In the 1990s, in several neighborhoods in Chicago, the unemployment rate for adults over age sixteen was 66 percent![12] This is a rate half again higher than the overall rate of unemployment during the Depression, which peaked at 24.9 percent in 1933.[13]

Glenn C. Loury, an economics professor and director of the Institute on Race and Social Division at Boston University, stated that "unemployment among black men ages 20 to 24 in April 1999 was 17.6%. The rate for white men of the same age was 6.2%." But Loury went beyond statistics:

> In good times and bad, unemployment among young black men is two to three times as great as it is among whites. . . . The unfortunate reality is that race-based barriers to job access are a seemingly permanent feature of the economy. . . . By all means, let's celebrate the fruits of our economic success. And let's keep it going as long as we can. But we would do well to remember that even a fast-rising tide won't lift the sunken boats. The only way to keep them afloat is to do the hard work of rebuilding them.[14]

Both race and gender are sources of staggering inequities in jobs and wages. Indeed, low-wage work and the lack of work are both deeply embedded in our social problem addressing race and gender. The bottom rungs of the economic ladder of work belong exclusively to no one race or gender, but race and gender are certainly overrepresented. The push for the right to a job at a living wage should help the nation as a whole, but it will help those at the bottom of the economic ladder most of all. The campaign for passage of a constitutional amendment can be an opportunity for social justice action that should create organizational opportunities that will demand linkages between workers and all social justice advocates.

Race in America is like the miner's canary, according to Lani Guinier and Gerald Torres. What does that mean? Miners carried canaries down into their deep enclosed work sites. Because canaries have respiratory systems more sensitive than ours, canaries would suffer the ill effects from poisonous gas in the air and die long before humans. Thus, when the canaries were in trouble, it was a sign that the mine workers were in danger, even if they did not know it. So too with race. When the racially marginalized are in trouble, it is not just their problem—it means that big troubles loom for the rest of us as well.[15]

Examples of the racialized impact of unemployment and low wages abound. Employment among young, less educated African-American men lags significantly behind other young less educated white and Hispanic males, with only 52 percent of these young men employed today compared to 62 percent twenty years ago.[16]

Gender and low-wage work also go hand in hand.

Nearly all women work at income-producing jobs. The DOL estimates that ninety-nine out of every one hundred women in the United States will work for pay at some point in their lives. Yet full-time working women still earn only about seventy-seven cents for every dollar earned by men.[17]

Over a lifetime of work, this translates into several hundred thousand dollars less income than the average working man. The Working Women's Department of the AFL-CIO estimates that college-educated women lose $990,000 over their lifetimes due to wage discrepancies. In addition, fewer than 40 percent of female employees have employer-provided pensions, compared to 60 percent of male employees.[18]

Black women, notes Professor Jacqueline Jones, continue to labor under the double disadvantage of race and gender, consistently earning less than men of all races and other women who are white.[19]

Professor Gwendolyn Mink has pointed out that

> the failure to pay women a just wage saps a mother's ability to secure an income that will sustain her family and purchase surrogates for her care when she is working outside the home. These injuries are especially daunting for mothers of color, for inequality in the labor market is not only gendered, it simultaneously is raced. African American women who are employed full time earn only 64 cents to every dollar earned by white men and only 84 cents to every dollar earned by white women. The wage

gap for Latinas is even larger: they earn 55 cents to the white man's dollar and 72 cents to the white woman's.[20]

As a result, many of the struggles for worker justice are often in fact struggles for justice for women and people of color.[21]

Serious problems of unemployment remain for less-skilled workers of all races. As Rebecca M. Blank, another economist who studies poverty, says, "For the working poor, unemployment is as high and job availability is as limited as it has always been . . . around 15 percent of those who seek work remain unemployed."[22]

The result of this problem? In 1998, there were 1.9 low-skill job seekers for every available job, according to a survey of 125 cities performed for the U.S. Conference of Mayors.[23]

But how can there be real unemployment when there are so many jobs advertised in the newspapers? Two considerations should be kept in mind when looking at the conventional wisdom that "there are plenty of jobs out there, just look at the want ads." Though there may always be jobs advertised, how many people are looking for those jobs? Comparisons of the number of unemployed in an area and the number of want ads usually shows that the unemployed outnumber the want ads by several multiples. Also, how many jobs in the want ads want people with a high school education or less and pay a wage sufficient to raise a family?

As noted earlier, a study in Washington, D.C., explored precisely this issue. It looked at the number of openings in the local paper and found 3,000 jobs advertised. At the same time, there were 36,400 people reported unemployed and another 28,000 adults receiving welfare payments. Happily, there were more than enough people in Washington, D.C., to fill the jobs. Sadly, most of the jobs required more education or prior employment experience than those seeking jobs had. The study concluded that the poor actually had a chance to get only 354 of the 3,000 advertised jobs.[24]

A better example of the reality of the job market was the city-sponsored job fair held in New York City at the height of the boom economy in late 1999, where forty companies agreed to accept résumés. Approximately five thousand people showed up, some waiting more than three hours in line to put in a résumé. The line included everyone from welfare mothers to recent college graduates. Many said they had been job hunting for months. As one employment specialist said, "There is a huge pool of people with entry-level skills and not enough jobs for them."[25]

Unemployment has been a consistent problem in our country for more than a century. In fact, in only seven of the past one hundred years has the United States achieved an annual unemployment rate of less than 2 percent.[26] Despite our history, some people continue to cling to the notion that there is plenty of work if only the people without jobs would get out and hustle to find work. This is so prevalent that one of America's premier historians of social welfare, Michael Katz, says, "The availability of work for every able-bodied person who really wants a job is one of the enduring myths of American history."[27]

The fact is, as economist Lester Thurow noted, that

> lack of jobs has been endemic in peacetime during the past fifty years of American history. . . . We need to face the fact that our economy and our institutions will not provide jobs for everyone who wants to work. They have never done so, and as currently structured, they never will. When it comes to unemployment, we are consistently the industrial economy with the worst record.[28]

Why do we have such an employment problem?

As Solow notes, there are two extremes on the unemployment question. The first extreme is total optimism; that is to say, there is no lack of jobs, there is only lack of motivation. The other extreme is that jobs are like chairs in the child's game of musical chairs. There is always a smaller number of chairs than there are children to sit in them; therefore, there will always be unemployment. Solow concludes that both extremes are unrealistic. There is some elasticity in the labor market, but there are never enough jobs for the unskilled. Additionally, in the future there will be fewer jobs for the unskilled, thus pitting the unskilled against the low-skilled in a competition for low-paying jobs. Thus, sadly, the primary burden of ending welfare for the unemployed unskilled will be placed on the low-skilled working poor. They will be faced with competition for their jobs from increased pools of workers who must work for whatever they can earn.[29]

Some theorists think that millions of unemployed are good for the nation. Why? Because unemployment keeps inflationary pressures down. In fact, current economic policy of the Federal Reserve nearly dictates that some percentage of the workforce must be unemployed in order to fight inflation.[30] Some economists call it "natural unemployment" when several percent of the workforce is out of work, a term condemned as a "vicious euphemism" by other economists.[31]

Others suggest that the economy is responding to globalization and to growth in information technology, a transition resulting in an increasing number of workers who will be competing for a decreasing number of jobs.[32]

Consider the following examples of what is occurring in the workforce:

- In the 1990s, the steel industry made about the same amount of steel as it did in 1980, but with less than half the workforce.[33]
- Persistent unemployment is so bad that one county in California has taken to giving out flyers to local unemployed people advising them that the county would pay them $1,600 to move out of state.[34]
- Over a period of ten years, the assets of Chase Manhattan have grown by 38 percent, from $87.7 billion to $121.2 billion, while its workforce shrank by 28 percent, from 44,450 employees to 33,500.[35]
- After the Korean War, 35 percent of the workforce was in manufacturing; after the Vietnam War, 28 percent was in manufacturing. Today, 17 percent is in manufacturing.[36]
- General Motors employed 500,000 people at its peak in the 1970s. Today, it can make the same number of cars with 315,000 workers.[37]
- During the boom year of 1998, companies announced the elimination of 600,000 jobs.[38]

Underemployment is similar to unemployment: underreported and little understood.[39]

Underemployment challenges millions, even tens of millions, of workers. The most conservative definition of the problem would count only government reports of four million people who are working part-time but who would like to be working full-time. A more realistic picture of the underemployed would count not only the four million people who are working part-time but want to work full-time, but also those tens of millions of people who are working full-time but are not earning enough to make ends meet. Underemployment also describes people who are working for wages that are less than they earned before. Using any realistic definition, tens of millions of people are underemployed.

Historically, at least prior to World War II, irregular employment or underemployment was the norm for most workers. As Professor Jacqueline Jones has pointed out, whether it resulted from agricultural seasons, natural disasters, economic downturns, or the lulls and spurts of the construction industry, underemployment was chronic among workers of all regions of the country.[40]

Official government figures are the best place to start to reveal the extent of underemployment, even though they seriously underestimate the number of underemployed people just as they do for the unemployed. These numbers are inadequate because they only count the number of people who are working part-time but would like to work full-time and because they do not count those who are working full-time but are not earning enough to be self-sufficient. As already discussed, the DOL releases monthly figures on employment and unemployment. Part of those figures, which are publicly released but are rarely ever reported, give a hint about the numbers of underemployed people. The DOL report for May 2002 found 8.4 million people unemployed, or 5.8 percent of the population. Further, in the same report you can find that there were another 3.8 million people officially classified as working part-time because that is all they could find or because that is all business conditions allowed.[41]

Part-time work is now a permanent part of our economy. Economists Barry Bluestone and Bennett Harrison indicate that as many as one in six workers now reports working part-time, one-quarter of whom are doing so involuntarily. Another 6 percent of workers work at two or more jobs.[42]

Remember also that the U.S. Census Bureau reports that at least 75 percent of the poor people in this country, even under the current low federal poverty guidelines, live in families where at least one person worked at some point in the previous year.[43]

Full-time workers and their families know that the paychecks of many full-time workers leave them underemployed, if the term "underemployed" is used realistically. One state, Connecticut, uses the definition for underemployment that counts all people, even full-time employees, who do not earn enough to support themselves. Connecticut General Statute 31–111(10) defines the underemployed worker as a person whose education and skill limit her or his capacity to earn 100 percent of the self-sufficiency standard. There are many tens of millions of people across the nation who meet this definition; they are working but not earning enough to be self-sufficient.[44]

When good jobs are eliminated, often low-wage jobs take their place. For example, between 1979 and 1996, forty-three million jobs were lost in the United States, but according to the DOL, in the same period of time more than forty-three million jobs were created. Yet, while there has been a net increase in the number of jobs, only 35 percent of laid-off full-time workers end up in equal- or better-paying jobs.[45]

Complicating the unemployment and underemployment problem are the numbers of people who have left welfare. As a nation, we used to think that it was in our collective interest to offer poor mothers the option of home-raising their children; thus, beginning with the New Deal in the 1930s, the nation provided Aid to Families with Dependent Children (AFDC). In the 1990s, Congress decided that poor mothers staying home and raising their children was no longer in the national interest, and AFDC was replaced by Temporary Assistance for Needy Families (TANF). One of the most notable characteristics of TANF is that it severely restricts the time that a poor and unemployed mother can spend at home with her children. There is a five-year national cap; some states have limits as low as two years.[46]

Apart from whether it makes sense to separate poor kids from their mothers, there is the issue of jobs—jobs for the mothers who were on welfare, and jobs for the people who were working at lower-skilled jobs who are now facing an influx of new lower-skilled and unskilled workers competing for those jobs.

Will pushing mothers off welfare lead to good jobs at good pay? Not likely. What most mothers who have found work have discovered is that welfare, nonworking poverty has been replaced with working poverty.

Professor Solow has reviewed several welfare-to-work programs and found little short- or long-term success, leading him to conclude, "The burden of proof is on anyone who thinks that welfare recipients forced into the labor market will be very successful in the search for jobs."[47] A December 1997 study estimated that the odds against a welfare recipient finding a job that paid a living wage in the midwestern states of Illinois, Indiana, Michigan, Minnesota, Ohio, and Wisconsin were ninety-seven to one, against.[48] Other research conducted in 2001 found that while the transition from welfare to work has improved self-esteem among some, many have indeed effectively traded nonworking poverty for working poverty.[49]

Many may debate the wisdom of depriving poor children of their mothers in their earliest years, but if the nation demands that these mothers work, is there no reason not to also advocate their right to a job at a living wage?[50]

Our serious problems of unemployment and underemployment have been a part of our history for the last one hundred years. The extent of the problem is about double what the media report, touching the lives of ten million adults. The lack of a job is twice the problem in the black community as in the white, and in all communities lack of work impacts lower-skilled workers much more dramatically. Until now, we as a nation have accepted this situation. At what cost?

7 The Cost of Unemployment and Underemployment

WHAT IS THE cost to us as a nation of unemployment and underemployment?

First, there is a personal cost to the unemployed. Consider the remarks of Shelley Haynes, age thirty-nine, who worked for fifteen years for a business before it closed two offices and laid off workers, including her. Ms. Haynes, interviewed while unemployed and enrolled in a training program, compared the shock of being laid off to the force of a death in the family: "It's like a woman who got married and had kids and her husband passes away, and she has to go out into the working world."[1]

Recall, however, that some people are willing to accept the unemployment of millions of people for what they perceive is a greater economic good. Current economic policy of the Federal Reserve accepts that some percentage of the workforce must be unemployed in order to fight inflation.[2] But these "percentages of unemployment" translate into millions of real breathing people with children and spouses and brothers and sisters, all people who are without work. Yet, several million people out of work is called "natural unemployment" by some economists.[3]

Wouldn't it cost a lot to help these people find and keep jobs?

Yes, it would.

But what does the current economic system that accepts millions out of work cost us now?

It comes down to what they said in the old oil filter commercial, "You pay me now, or you pay me later."

There is a direct cost that we are asking the unemployed to pay for the maintenance of our current economic system. Is it right to ask the least well-off to pay the cost of keeping the economic engine running for the rest of us who are better off?

Additionally, there is the cost paid by those of us who are employed.

Do we really think that the unemployed and underemployed are not eating? Are their children not eating? Are they going without any medical care? Do they not need heat in the winter? Are all of these people on the street? They live somewhere; they are cared for by someone.

We as a society are now paying the price for our current system that accepts millions in poverty. We pay through our public assistance programs, our voluntary and church-based assistance, the support we give to family members, and the illegal economy that grows up in the absence of a legal one. We also pay a big price in the lack of work that these folks could be contributing to our society.

Experts tell us that unemployment takes a toll on society in a variety of ways. First, society must subsidize those out of work with income assistance. Second, society forfeits the additional goods and services that would be provided by those out of work. Third, society then pays for unemployment because of the suffering, insecurity, family strife, and crime that are caused by lack of work. Finally, unemployment makes people question the health of the economic system.[4]

The Congressional Budget Office estimated that a 1 percent rise in unemployment over a five-year period costs the U.S. Treasury more than $400 billion.[5]

Our nation is likely now paying substantial crime-prevention costs for high unemployment among those ages sixteen to twenty-four years old. One recent study found that the decline in unemployment during the mid-1990s may have explained 30 percent of the fall in crime rates. The unemployment rate for those ages sixteen to twenty-four was 26 percent in 1999, compared to 4.2 percent overall. It is unrealistic to think that our communities are not already paying a significant price for this situation.[6]

And then there is the negative impact on society: unemployment has a widespread negative effect far in excess of the damage done to the individual who is out of work. There are the costs of programs for the unemployed, the loss of the goods and services that could have been produced by the nonworking, and the social costs of individual and family suffering.[7]

For those who are not willing to continue to have the unemployed and our communities pay the costs of unemployment, there is a way we can proceed.

To those who think they can tolerate millions of unemployed in the name of fighting inflation, an ugly question remains. If involuntary unemployment is bad for the family, bad for the neighborhood, bad for the city, and bad for the state, how can it possibly be good for the nation?

It cannot. For as religious leaders attending the U.S. Catholic Conference in 1986 said, "The dignity of the human person, realized in community with others, is the criterion against which all aspects of economic life must be measured."[8]

By the criteria of family, neighborhood, city, and state, involuntary unemployment and underemployment is a serious problem we must address. Not to do so says we value economic life over that of the human dignity of people. We are better than that.

IV Work and Poverty

8   The Working Poor

> The working poor remain America's glaring contradiction. The concur-
> rence of work and poverty is contrary to the American ethos that a will-
> ingness to work leads to material advancement, and it negates the preva-
> lent view that the cause of poverty among adults capable of work is
> deviant behavior, particularly a lack of commitment to work.
> —Levitan, Gallo, and Shapiro, *Working but Poor*

THE USUAL first response to poverty has been to advise the poor
to work. But if the poor are already working, what's the next response?
The next response is usually silence.

One of every four workers in the United States, around thirty million workers, earns less than "poverty-level wages" or the hourly wage
necessary to sustain a family of four even at the official poverty threshold.[1] This percentage of workers earning "poverty-level wages" has remained at around 25 percent since the 1970s.[2]

If you add the thirty million people who are making poverty-level
wages to the fifteen million to seventeen million unemployed and underemployed, you can begin to see how the lack of work at a living wage
impacts our country.[3]

The relationship between work and poverty forms the core of our
national problem of poverty.[4] And millions of people who work are directly impacted. There are at least four important reasons to care about
the working poor. First, more than half of the working poor live in families with children. Second, the nine million or so working poor counted
by the government show only a fraction of the real working poor if a
more realistic definition of poverty is used. Third, there is a significant
likelihood that someone you know is already in or going to spend some
time in this category, including one out of every three people between
the ages of twenty-three and thirty-seven. And fourth, the working poor
are the fastest growing segment of our population.[5]

As the *Wall Street Journal* reported in the mid-1990s, even before cut-backs in the welfare program that put many more poor people to work, more than half of the poor lived in households where someone was already working.[6]

Most of the poor in the United States live in working families. Millions of poor people work. The working poor are everywhere, yet many of us don't see them.

Most of the working poor labor in the same buildings as us and frequently visit our neighborhoods, even our homes. They clean and maintain our offices, they pick up our trash, they serve us our meals, they serve and clean up our stores and restaurants and hotels and malls, they ring up our purchases and restock our shelves, they cut our grass, they guard us, they answer our phone calls, they make our copies and run our errands, they care for our children and our parents and elderly relatives. They are everywhere. Some have cars; many take the bus.

Want a good idea of the lowest-paid working poor in your community? Look at the people gathered at the downtown bus stop in the dark in the morning and in the dark in the evening. Or watch as the restaurants and fast food places and shopping centers close for the night.

The end of welfare has put many people to work, but many still remain poor. The director of the Atlanta Community Food Bank reflects on the end of welfare in that city: "There's been a 50 percent drop in welfare recipients, but we've seen a 30 percent increase in need at the food bank."[7]

Journalist and author Barbara Ehrenreich has done a remarkable job of capturing what the lives of the working poor are like. Ehrenreich entered the low-wage workforce to find out what former welfare mothers would experience as welfare reform kicked in. In *Nickel and Dimed in America: On (Not) Getting By in America,* Ehrenreich describes how she got a job at a restaurant that paid her $2.43 an hour plus tips.[8] (Believe it or not, paying a waitress this way is perfectly legal.)[9]

Ehrenreich spent a lot of time working with the poor, waiting tables and sharing breaks. What did she learn about how the working poor live?

You might imagine, from a comfortable distance, that people who live, year in and year out, on $6 to $10 an hour have discovered some survival stratagems unknown to the middle class. But no. It's not hard to get my co-workers to talk about their living situations, because housing, in almost every case, is the principal source of disruption in their lives.[10]

These were the living situations of some of her co-workers:

- Gail is sharing a room in a downtown flophouse for which she and her roommate pay $250 a week. But the roommate, a male friend, has begun hitting on her, making her crazy. Still, she couldn't handle the rent without him.
- Claude is a Haitian cook who wants to get out of the two-room apartment he shares with his girlfriend and two other people who aren't relatives. Other Haitian men on the wait staff seem to have equally crowded living arrangements.
- Annette is a twenty-six-year-old woman, six months pregnant, who lives with her mother, a postal worker. Her boyfriend has abandoned her.
- Marianne and her boyfriend live in a one-bedroom trailer for which they pay $170 a week.
- Tina and her husband are staying at the nearby Days Inn, where they pay $60 nightly. But they can walk to work (and they don't have a car).
- Joan lives in a van, parks it behind a shopping center every night, and showers in Tina's room.[11]

Ehrenreich concludes by recognizing how much those of us who are not poor owe to those who make our lives possible:

> The "working poor," as they are approvingly termed, are in fact the major philanthropists of our society. They neglect their own children so that the children of others will be cared for; they live in substandard housing so that other homes will be shiny and perfect; they endure privation so that inflation will be low and stock prices high.[12]

The U.S. Department of Labor (DOL) estimated that 6.8 million people were both regularly working and still poor in 1999, 4 percent of all full-time workers and 10.5 percent of all part-time workers.[13] Of these workers, 5.4 million were working full-time and were still poor.[14] The DOL also reported that if all the people who worked at any time in the year who still remained below the poverty level are included, the number would add up to 9.6 million people.[15] Among families with at least one person working, 3.8 million families, or 6.2 percent of all working families, had incomes below the poverty level in 1999.[16]

Most of the poor who can work do so. Consider that in 1998, there were more than eleven million poor people between the ages of twenty-five and fifty-four. One in four of these people were unable to work because of illness or disability, or were currently enrolled in school. Of the rest, seven out of every ten of the able-bodied poor worked at least part-time. One of every four worked full-time, year-round.[17]

This same profile of the working poor found that like poverty in general, race and gender were important predictors of who was poor. While the majority of the working poor are white, the rate of white workers who were both working and poor was significantly lower than for black and Hispanic workers. And working women were more likely to be working and poor than working men.[18] As columnist Molly Ivins said:

> In the mid-1960s, women were paid 69 cents for every dollar a man made. After 30 years of struggle and hard work, we now make 74 cents for every dollar a man makes. . . . At the rate of 5 cents every 30 years, we can expect to achieve equal pay sometime in the 22nd century.[19]

Most of the working poor can afford housing or utilities or food or child care or health care, but few can afford all.

Consider the following profiles, taken from recent news articles, of working people and the problems they face trying to make ends meet.

Housing costs are a big problem. In fact, the federal government reported in 2000 that no full-time minimum-wage worker could afford the average market rent anywhere in the United States.[20]

• Laurie Berrios is a divorced mom with four kids. She earned $8 an hour as a nurse's aide outside of Chicago. In order to try to make ends meet she would pull double shifts at the end of each month. Health problems caused financial problems because she has no health insurance. She lost her apartment and she and her kids moved into her sister's one-bedroom apartment, where they slept on couches and chairs. When this became too much for her sister, Laurie and her kids moved into her 1988 Cutlass Sierra. When the police found out and threatened to take her kids away, Laurie moved into a homeless shelter. She continues to work at her job.[21]
• Kenneth Lindo, forty-four, works on Wall Street as a messenger. In 1999, Kenneth earned $5.50 an hour. He has been working at or near minimum wage since he was eighteen. At night Kenneth sleeps in the

30th Street Men's Shelter in Manhattan because he cannot afford the city's rent.[22]

• Ricardo Ramirez works more than forty hours a week in San Jose, California, for minimum wage plus tips. He pays $180 a month to rent space on the floor in a corner of an apartment already occupied by a family of four. The family he is living with lets him store his things in a closet.[23]

Some people cannot afford their utilities.

• Pat Williams, forty-six, lives in Shreveport, Louisiana, and works as an aide caring for aged and disabled people at a nursing home. In April 2001 she was earning $5.55 an hour. In order to make ends meet, after she gets home from work at the nursing home she goes to her second job cleaning offices. In 2000, Ms. Williams earned $10,067; she lives in public housing and gets free medical care for her high blood pressure. Despite working two jobs, she cannot make ends meet. She owes almost $150 to the electric company, $55 to the phone company, $23 on a student loan, and $40 for a burglar alarm. Today, when she came home from work, there was a red ticket on her door—her gas was cut off because she was $477 overdue.[24]

Others cannot afford safe child care.

• Veronica Mason, thirty-six, a former welfare mother, lives in Indianapolis and works the 11 P.M. to 7 A.M. shift at White Castle earning $6.60 an hour. She cannot afford a car and walks to work. She leaves her three daughters, ages eight, six, and five, sleeping on a neighbor's couch. Veronica worries about her children because the neighbor she leaves them with has boyfriend problems and is drinking a lot. She tried to get government assistance to help with child care, but there are seven thousand families on the waiting list for help in Indianapolis. Sometimes when Veronica is called into work during the day, the children ride the bus on their own, cook their own meals, and sometimes have to stay home by themselves.[25]

Some workers cannot always afford to purchase food.

• Ann McGinness, forty, left welfare to work as a bookkeeper at a car dealership. Her $290 a week in take-home pay makes her ineligible for food stamps, but after paying rent, car payments, insurance, and utilities, there is often not enough left for food. As a result, Ann relies on a food pantry at a local church to get her through the month. "I'm tired of always having to say, 'Please help me.' "[26]

• Pamela, forty-five, makes $7 an hour doing janitorial work in Waterloo, Iowa, where she lives with her two children from her twenty-one-year marriage. Pamela does the best she can to stretch her budget, but no matter what she ends up visiting the Cedar Valley Food Bank in Waterloo once or twice a month. The Waterloo food bank serves more than thirty-five thousand underemployed individuals and families each year.[27]

Many have to work extra jobs.

• William Cotto works full-time as a security guard at $7 per hour, yet has to work twenty hours a week extra as a janitor to support his wife and four children. He has no health insurance and had to pay more than $2,000 in dentist bills for removing a molar. "I barely have any money in my pocket," he says. "If I buy clothes for one kid one week, then I have to wait for the next week to buy clothes for one of my other kids."[28]

• Gloria Pye is fifty-seven years old. She earns $7.19 an hour as a home care attendant for a patient with Alzheimer's. Because of high prescription bills, she fell behind on her rent and now has to work fifty-five hours a week to make extra payments on her apartment.[29]

Some are getting by only with help from family and friends:

• Linda K. Williams is forty-three and takes home about $15,700 annually. It is not enough to pay the expenses for her apartment, utilities, groceries, clothing, bus fare to work and back, and to support her teenage son. How does she make it? A boyfriend helps, but the biggest help is from her four sisters, who regularly appear at her home with food, detergent, and household supplies.[30]

• Julie Pinner is thirty-five and works as a receptionist and clerk, earns $15,500 a year, and has two children. Since she cannot really afford to live where it is safe, she is going to move into a house that her father, a retired auto worker, owns. Her father helps her make it. "He picks me up in the morning and drives me to work. If we don't have anything to eat, he'll help. Maybe once a month he pays for the shopping, and my aunt gives me a few dollars."[31]

We advise the poor to get a job and lift themselves out of poverty. While millions have done that, they still remain poor. As Professor Rebecca M. Blank has noted, "employment has become progressively less effective at reducing poverty."[32] In 1998, the U.S. Conference of Mayors identified low-paying jobs as the number one cause of hunger in urban America.[33]

As most know, full-time minimum-wage work hasn't been enough to lift most families over the poverty line in years. Nor has pay close to minimum wage. In 1999, when the minimum wage was $5.15 per hour, it took an hourly wage of $8.19 to lift a family of four over even the too-low official poverty line, a wage that 25 percent of all workers did not earn.[34]

Any way you count them, there are millions of people who work and yet remain poor.

Exactly how many working poor people are there? Estimates in the 1990s ranged from six million to double that number, depending on the year.[35] Using a more realistic definition of poverty—one that raises the poverty line—will find millions more workers who should be recognized as poor.[36]

A quick way to figure a conservative estimate of how many children live in families of the working poor is to look at the National School Lunch Program (NSLP).

The NSLP provides federal funds for meals served by schools to children who come from low-income families. Children of families with incomes below 130 percent of federal guidelines get free meals; children from families with incomes between 130 percent and 185 percent of the poverty guidelines get reduced-cost meals.[37]

If you look carefully at how many kids are in this program, you can see the extent of poverty in working families. Even if you assume that many people will not ask for free or reduced lunch because of pride or embarrassment, the numbers are still large.

For example, in 1999 an average of more than 13 million children received free lunch and another 2.4 million received reduced-cost lunch each school day.[38] If you deduct the numbers of kids whose families were on public assistance, you can figure out a conservative estimate for the numbers of children who lived in working, but still poor, families. During that year there were slightly more than 5 million kids on welfare.[39] There were also about 850,000 school-aged children with disabilities on the Supplemental Security Income program in 1999.[40]

That leaves more than nine million kids who lived in families poor enough to receive free or reduced-cost school lunch but whose parents were not receiving public assistance in 1999. That is nine million kids in working poor families in addition to the five million to six million kids who live in other poor families.

There are many forces that aggravate the financial health of the working poor, but at the center are three: low wages, part-time work, and periods of unemployment.[41]

Though found in many occupations, a disproportionate number of working poor are present in service work, low-skill blue-collar work, and sales.[42] Poverty among workers has also increased because more families are headed by single parents, limiting the potential for two-wage families. In 1998, 24 percent of families were headed by a single parent, compared with 14 percent twenty-five years before. Three in five married mothers with children under age six were in the workforce—twice as large a share as in 1970.[43] And, as we will see in later chapters, minimum wage used to provide a whole lot more for workers than it has in the last decade.[44]

The DOL consistently reports that there are millions of people working part-time who would like to be working full-time.[45] And the number of people actually out of work at any given time is close to twice what the DOL reports.[46] The lack of full-time work and full-time wages is a prime reason for poverty among those who work.[47]

We continue to see companies growing without creating jobs. It used to be the expectation that in good economic times, as a company grew, it added workers. That's no longer the case. We've already noted that in the 1990s the steel industry made about the same amount of steel as it did in 1980, but with less than half the workforce.[48] General Motors employed 500,000 people at its peak in the 1970s; now it can make the same number of cars with 315,000 workers.[49] Such job loss is not confined to the manufacturing industry.[50]

There is another important angle. Much of the job growth in the growing economy of the 1990s did nothing to help raise the wages of the working poor. For example, a December 1998 nationwide study estimated that 74 percent of the jobs with the most growth paid less than a livable wage and 46 percent paid less than half a livable wage.[51] In 1998, experts found that in Illinois 76 percent of the fastest growing jobs paid less than a living wage for a family of four; in Missouri the percentage was even higher.[52]

In 1998 in Los Angeles, where a full-time working parent with two kids was eligible for welfare if he or she earned less than $8 per hour, Alfredo Galindo cleaned floors at the UCLA Medical Center and supported four children on his salary of $6.73 an hour. He was not alone. One in four adults who worked full-time in Los Angeles County, eight hundred thousand people, earned less than $8 per hour. In 1998, the county estimated that it took $7.82 per hour with health benefits to create a living wage for a parent to support two kids, or $9.47 per hour without health benefits.[53]

Across America, the working poor are penalized for low skills and lack of education.[54] Or is it more accurate to say that employers have been successful in keeping the supply of labor high and wages low because of decreased unionization, weakened social welfare support systems, global relocation for cheaper labor, increased replacement of workers by technology, and increased reliance on part-time no-benefits work? Overall, inflation-adjusted wages have fallen among less-skilled male workers. As a consequence, young men with a high school degree can expect to earn less than their fathers earned twenty years earlier because real wages have declined in both manufacturing and service jobs.[55] Throughout the last twenty years, wages have fallen among men, younger workers, and the 75 percent of the workforce without a four-year college degree.[56] As Peter T. Colborne noted in 1995,

> for all but professionals, executives, new college graduates, and the most skilled blue-collar workers, many problems that workers faced only in bad times have become fixtures in all times: some wages are still falling, people must be ready to work 12-hour shifts and 6 day weeks, and no job is for keeps.[57]

It is impossible to discuss why there is so much work that does not pay living wages without also discussing the decline in the role of organized labor. Labor's role in pushing for the right to employment at living wages is absolutely vital. Yet many people are unaware of both the history and current efforts of trade unionism in pushing for workers' rights, living wages, and decent jobs for all workers. The labor movement has a long and rich history of fighting for the rights of low-wage workers. Over the past century no group has invested more in organizing, legislating, and advocating for plentiful jobs and decent wages. Today, unions are active in nearly every local living-wage coalition, working side by side with community organizations and churches. It is a fundamental truth of organizing that people struggling together for justice are stronger than people struggling alone. The forces that have kept wages low certainly work together. The labor movement is the place where people struggle together for justice for workers.

Yet, in my own work with the Interfaith Committee for Worker Justice, usually comprised of religious and social justice people working to support low-wage workers, I have found that many otherwise progressive people are not all that knowledgeable or supportive of the union movement. While there is often deep solidarity in regard to the plight of low-wage workers, there is often too little solidarity with the efforts of organized labor to address the issues that create low-wage workers.

My experience is not unique. Consider Nelson Lichtenstein, who found that even within the coalition working on a living-wage campaign at the University of Virginia, "ideas about trade unionism, worker's rights and class were alien concepts, not only to many low wage workers, but to some of our key activists."[58]

The lack of information about the positive power and potential of organized labor in the social justice and antipoverty community and the lack of coalition work between labor and other social justice groups is a serious omission. That is not to deny that labor unions have created some of their own problems. There are race and gender problems, misleading campaigns, financial irregularities, and inadequate democracy within the union movement. Despite these problems, which in my experience burden all collective actions for justice, a strong labor movement is a necessity for good jobs and good wages. Labor, churches, community, and civil rights groups all are less than perfect on justice issues. But while their problems must be addressed, no one who is committed to justice should use these problems as an excuse for inaction or lack of coalition-building.[59]

Unions seem to have stopped the decline in overall membership through more aggressive organizing tactics, addressing internal race and gender problems, increasing national solidarity with local labor fights, and movement toward more democratic governance. As unions regain their voice, more will have to be done on all these fronts.[60]

Organized labor is also confronted with increasing individualism in our society. This is a pervasive and usually unconscious classical American tendency—I call it "internalized individualism," others call it "internalized classism"—to think that each person's position in society is a result of her or his own positive achievements or negative behaviors. In this thinking, a person's economic position can and should be changed by individuals alone, thus precluding a real critique of the economic systems that create and maintain injustice and also, and, just as important, precluding collective organized action.[61]

As a result of these factors, and despite recent gains, the labor union movement is less powerful than it has been in quite some time. Union membership is down by nearly two-thirds since 1953, and today unions in the United States represent a lower proportion of all workers than any other industrialized nation in the world. In 1953, 32.5 percent of all workers—35 percent of private workers and 12 percent of public workers—were union members. In 2001, 13.5 percent of wage and salary workers were union members, according to the DOL's Bureau of Labor Statistics. In 2001, approximately 16.3 million wage and salary workers were union members.[62]

This is important because union workers earn better wages than nonunion counterparts. In 2001, full-time wage and salary union members had median weekly earnings of $718, compared with a median of $575 for wage and salary workers who were not represented by unions. Nearly four in ten government workers were union members in 2001, compared with less than one in ten private wage and salary workers. Protective service workers, a group that includes police officers and firefighters, had the highest unionization rate among all occupations, at 38 percent.[63]

Union membership has been identified as a central factor in understanding why public service working women get better wages and benefits than private sector working women.[64]

Why does the decline in the power of unions hurt other low-wage workers? Simply because individual workers alone lack the financial, organizational, legal, and political bargaining power to offset the constant gains being made by individual and organized businesses. Unions offered a political counterweight to the significant clout of business lobbies in the law-making arena. Union workers earned better wages than nonunion counterparts for a reason: they exerted the collective power of workers.

In addition to learning about organized labor and coalition-building, we need to improve our social consciousness about the importance of unions and change the weakness of current labor laws in order to help the labor movement efforts to regroup.

No one will openly advocate firing people on the basis of their race or age or pregnancy or religion or gender—society would not approve. It is clearly good policy not to penalize these workers. Yet there are many lawyers in every town who will proudly help companies develop strategies to isolate and terminate low-wage employees who are seeking to bring a union to their workplace, and society openly tolerates such action. Why does our society not view this type of discrimination as just as outrageous? Why is it more acceptable to fire a person who seeks to get employees together to bargain collectively for better wages and better treatment with their bosses than to fire a person who becomes pregnant? Is not social justice advanced by extending social protection to workers who seek to improve their wages and workplace? We need to help our social consciousness catch up in this area. All workers deserve to be treated with justice, especially if they are trying to improve conditions for each other.

Our labor laws are also quite weak in their protection of workers who are seeking to organize. They need to be changed. When working as part of a religious support campaign for workers at Avondale shipyard in New Orleans, I found out that the laws for organizing workers really do not work. Workers who are fired because of their race or gender can go to the Equal Employment Opportunity Commission (EEOC) and if they are not satisfied can then sue for reinstatement, back pay, and damages. While anyone who has tried to go through these laws knows they are certainly not very responsive to remedying discrimination, they are much, much stronger and quicker and provide more relief than the laws protecting workers who seek to organize. Our labor laws need to be dramatically improved to give workers a real chance to be protected when they seek to organize.

Academic research confirms the challenges for the working and poor.

Bluestone and Harrison found that declines in public investment, particularly in education, combined with greater job insecurity, the decline of the influence of organized labor, reduced government regulation of work, and the decline in the real value of the minimum wage all cause structural unemployment and underemployment problems.[65]

William Julius Wilson identified the decrease in the number of quality jobs in inner-city neighborhoods as a result of many factors: decline in mass production, lower unionization rates, increased internationalization of the U.S. economy, increasing movement of jobs to the suburbs, government policy that reduced social services, and an overall decline in employment and wages for low-skilled workers in general and men, especially black men, in particular.[66]

Jacqueline Jones points out that low-wage work and poverty result from many causes. Some are the more recent results of movement of industry to low-wage countries. Other causes are more longstanding. Some regions of the country have always had higher percentages of poor and low-wage workers: Appalachia, the South, and Native American reservations in the Southwest, places with "roots deep in the nation's history of slavery, commercial development and territorial conquest." Other regions of poverty and low wages resulted from migrations by southerners to northern cities and by growing immigrant communities.[67]

In addition to increasing job uncertainty, structural employment problems, and the declining role of organized labor, the country is faced with widening gaps between those at the top, middle, and bottom of the income scale. These gaps have grown significantly and are now wider than any time in the postwar era.[68]

Readers should be familiar with the Walgreen's example of the wage contrast between the working poor and highly paid CEOs. In the same year that the wages for a cashier at Walgreen's were about $12,000 a year, the CEO made $2.6 million. It would have taken the cashier 217 years of full-time work to make what the CEO made in one year. It took the CEO thirteen hours to make what the cashier made in one year.[69]

While corporate CEOs will always make more than workers, the unfairness of the growing disparity between executive compensation and the earnings of the working poor remains a troubling sign that there is much work to do. For example, *Business Week* reported that in 1996 the typical factory worker wage rose 3 percent while the average raise for top executives was 54 percent.[70]

As the Economic Policy Institute has pointed out, this gap has grown dramatically over the years. In 1965, the average CEO made 20 times what the average worker earned. In 1978, the average CEO made 28 times what the average worker earned. In 1989, the average CEO made 56 times what the average worker earned. And in 1999, the average CEO made 107 times what the average worker earned. It took the average CEO half a week to earn what an average worker earned in fifty-two weeks.[71] In 1997, the pay earned by the 49 million lowest-earning workers equaled what the top 1 percent of workers earned; in 1999, it took 100 million of the lowest-earning workers to equal the top 1 percent.[72]

But if some people are doing wonderfully well, doesn't that mean that good times are coming for everyone else? This "a rising tide lifts all boats" school of economics is the essential part of the platform of people who defend extraordinarily high incomes for some.

Professor Blank tells an insightful story about her surprise that the popular slogan was not accurate:

> I was working as a senior staff economist for the Council of Economic Advisors in the fall of 1989. One of our responsibilities was to produce short memos for the White House when major economic statistics were released summarizing the implications of these data. In October, the Census Bureau released its annual report on income and poverty for 1988, which happened to be a year of very strong economic growth and rising average personal incomes. Oddly, however, the poverty rate fell by an insignificant amount that year. I wrote up my summary and brought it to my boss for approval. He read it through, handed it back to me and said, "Add a paragraph explaining why poverty didn't fall last year." I dutifully went back to my desk, sat down at my computer, stared at it a while, and realized I had no explanation to offer.[73]

Professor Blank had run into the same problem later described by Professor Loury: "We would do well to remember that even a fast-rising tide won't lift the sunken boats. The only way to keep them afloat is to do the hard work of rebuilding them."[74]

There is a disconnect between the overall economic health of the country and improvements in the lives of the working poor. Most of the working poor are left out of the boats in the good times and put out of the boats in the bad. The rising tide certainly has lifted many boats, but it does not lift all.

9   Low-Wage Work

The American ethos sets up the expectation that human dignity and the ability to earn a decent living are intimately connected. It is not surprising, as a result, that the dearth of jobs that provide a decent living (not simply the absolute lack of jobs) would be deeply demoralizing in the eyes of workers. —John E. Schwarz, *Illusions of Opportunity*

MILLIONS OF workers, one of every four in the United States, earn "poverty-level wages" or less than it would take to lift a family of four over the official poverty line. The minimum wage is certainly not a living wage, and yet millions of people earn wages within a dollar or two of minimum wage.

MINIMUM WAGE IS HALF A LIVING WAGE

One of the key problems with low-wage work is the minimum wage, which impacts, directly and indirectly, more than twenty million workers.

Consider the following facts about the effect of a one-dollar increase in the minimum wage as of 2001:

- Nearly 10.3 million workers (8.7 percent of the workforce) would receive an increase in their hourly wage if the minimum wage was raised by one dollar an hour.
- Another 9.7 million people (8.2 percent of the workforce) earning up to two dollars over the minimum wage would likely also get an increase
- Almost 1 million single mothers (967,000) with children under age eighteen would benefit from a one-dollar minimum wage increase.
- More than 2 million married men and women with children would benefit from a one-dollar increase in the minimum wage.
- Full-time workers would benefit. Close to half (48 percent) of workers who would benefit from an increase in the minimum wage work full-time, and another third (31 percent) work between twenty and thirty-four hours a week.

• Adults would benefit. Seventy-one percent of those workers who would get a raise if the minimum wage was increased by one dollar are age twenty or older.
• Women are the largest group of people who would benefit from a one-dollar increase in the minimum wage. Almost 60 percent of the people who would get a raise would be women.[1]

The minimum wage is several dollars an hour short of a living wage and even several dollars short of matching its own value of thirty years ago.[2]

At the time of the writing of this book, the federal minimum wage was $5.15, an hourly wage put into effect September 1, 1997.[3]

According to a 2001 report of the Congressional Research Service, the highest value of the minimum wage was reached in 1968. Had the minimum wage been adjusted to allow it to retain its 1968 value, in 2001 it would be approximately $7.72 per hour.[4]

While today's minimum wage is 30 percent lower in real value than the minimum wage in 1968, the economy has become 50 percent more productive in the same time period.[5]

The *Wall Street Journal* reported in 2001 that the minimum wage fell below 45 percent of the average wage in only four of the years between 1950 and 1982. Since Ronald Reagan became president, the minimum wage has never again reached 45 percent of the average wage and in 2001 stood at 36 percent of the average.[6]

The legislative problems with the federal minimum wage are that it was too low to begin with, it is not indexed for inflation, it can only be raised by an act of Congress, and it does not cover everyone.[7] Because the minimum wage, unlike Social Security, has never been indexed for inflation, the federal minimum wage diminishes in value as soon as it is enacted.[8] Additionally, more than 13 million workers are still exempt from minimum-wage protection under the Fair Labor Standards Act, with an estimated 2.4 million of these actually earning less than the minimum wage.[9]

In my experience speaking about work and poverty to dozens of audiences, no one thinks that a person can support herself or himself, much less a family, on wages that pay at or near the federal minimum wage. They are right. A 2002 poll of voters found that half believed a family of four needed an income of at least $45,000 to make ends meet.[10]

The Department of Housing and Urban Development (HUD), which calculates "fair market rents" for every region of the country, says people should not spend more than 30 percent of their income on rent. Using that standard, no full-time minimum-wage worker can afford an average rent in any county in the United States.[11]

For a single parent with two children, the official poverty guideline for the year 2002 was a yearly income of $15,020.[12] For a parent with three kids, the yearly income was $18,100. Working full-time, a parent with two kids would need to make at least $7.22 per hour and a parent with three children would need to earn $8.70 per hour in order to at least be lifted over the 2002 official poverty threshold.

If a more realistic poverty threshold was used, the poverty line for a family of four in 2001 would have been doubled and the insufficiency of the wages would be even more stark.

Low-Wage Work Is Also Not a Living Wage

In 1999, more than thirty million workers, more than one out of every four people working, earned less than $8.19 per hour, the hourly wage that it would take to lift a family of four over the poverty line.[13] As the reader knows, $7 to $8 an hour, while a great improvement over minimum wage, is still not enough for a worker to raise a family. Such workers still need government assistance to be able to survive, and government program eligibility guidelines reflect that.

People who earn wages insufficient to raise a family of four over the poverty line are often defined as low-wage workers. Approximately 40 percent of women workers (about sixteen million women) are low-wage earners.[14]

The health of millions of low-wage families is at risk because of insufficient earnings. People earning poverty-level wages cannot purchase health insurance. Full-time workers with three kids can earn more than $10 an hour and still be impoverished enough to remain eligible for food stamps.[15]

The U.S. Conference of Mayors identified these low-paying jobs as the number one cause of hunger in urban America.[16]

Our government recognizes that low wages are not enough to live on. Workers with two children are eligible for a few dollars in credits from the Earned Income Tax Credit even if they make over $14 an hour.[17]

And it is not just government that recognizes that substantial wages are necessary for survival. In the fall of 2000, the National Low Income Housing Coalition discovered after a national survey of fair market rentals that the average person who worked forty hours a week would need to earn $12.47 an hour to rent a two-bedroom apartment.[18]

In 1999, the Chicago-based Women Employed Institute reported that a mother with one baby in suburban Chicago would have to earn $12.78 an hour to afford rent, child care, food, transportation, health insurance, and taxes. Yet most low-income jobs in the area pay less than $8 an hour.[19] The Massachusetts-based Women's Educational and Industrial Union calculated a "self-sufficiency" standard to measure the real cost of living, including adequate housing, child care, food, transportation, taxes, and medical care. It took $32,280 in 1997 for a single adult and a preschool child to make it in Boston in 1997, a full-time wage of more than $15 an hour.[20]

Yet, a lot of the job growth in the 1990s was in low-wage jobs—restaurant work, security guard, day care work, home attendants for the elderly—that pay less than $25,000 a year.[21]

Low-wage work sustains poverty and continues the cycle for millions of workers and their families. Nonworking people in poverty have, as a result of welfare reform, traded in one form of poverty for another. While it is likely better for self-esteem to work and be poor rather than not work and be poor, many of these people are not actually making ends meet.[22]

Like all motivation, efforts to move people from dependent poverty to self-sufficiency can be done by providing both carrots and sticks.

The sticks we are all familiar with.

Our society criticizes and categorizes the poor, seeking to shame them into action. Our society stigmatizes the poor by labeling them as "underclass" or "project dwellers" or "poor white trash" and showers them with contempt and pity. We pass laws for workfare and tough love and removing dependency by compelling poor people to work. We incarcerate overly aggressive beggars, and we outlaw panhandling. We're good with the sticks. But where are the carrots?

If we as a society are serious about helping people move from poverty to self-sufficiency, then we need to look at how we are rewarding work.

More than a century ago, England established a public policy to create economic distance between workers and those who were dependent on charity. They called their concept "less eligibility."[23] The principle of less eligibility stood for the proposition that aid for the nonworking poor should never be given generously enough that it neared the living standards of the lowest-paid worker. The government felt that overly generous charity to nonworkers made workers consider not working. This concept is familiar to all who listen to political rhetoric in the United States. It has been at the core of welfare policy for some time. Politicians and aspiring politicians know they can get automatic approval for the promise to take the able-bodied off welfare and put them to work because those who are working deserve our respect. Elected officials have recognized that for some time there was little national sympathy for the nonworking poor, and thus assistance to them could be kept low or reduced.

This school of thought resulted in the welfare "reform" of the 1990s. Welfare reform has moved many millions from the welfare rolls, but many studies show it has not been nearly as successful in moving people out of poverty.[24]

Holding the nonworking poor down has been one easy political way to create some economic distance between the nonworking poor and poor workers, but a strong public policy that rewards work would be much, much better.

V A Constitutional Right to a Job at a Living Wage

10   A Constitutional Amendment

Some men look at constitutions with sanctimonious reverence, and deem them like the ark of the covenant, too sacred to be touched. They ascribe to the men of the preceding age a wisdom more than human, and suppose that what they did to be beyond amendment. . . . I am certainly not an advocate for frequent and untried changes in laws and constitutions. . . . But I know also, that laws and institutions must go hand in hand with the progress of the human mind. . . . We might as well require a man to still wear the coat which fitted him when a boy, as civilized society to remain ever under the regimen of their barbarous ancestors.
—Thomas Jefferson, Letter to Samuel Kercheval, 1816

AMERICA VALUES work. We value self-sufficiency. Because of that, it is now time to make the right to a job at a living wage part of our national promise to one another. It is time again to amend our Constitution.

As a country our highest civic values are incorporated into our Constitution. These are promises we make to each other. Many of our most cherished constitutional promises to each other are promises that came about as amendments to our original Constitution: freedom of speech, outlawing slavery, the right of women to vote.

These rights were not always part of our constitutional promise to each other. Freedom of speech was added as the First Amendment to our Constitution in 1791, fifteen years after our country was formed. The Thirteenth Amendment, guaranteeing people the right not to be enslaved, was added in 1865. The right of women to vote was guaranteed by the Nineteenth Amendment in 1920.

While I have been discussing and writing about the idea of a constitutional amendment for quite some time, others have also been pushing for a universal right to employment at fair wages.[1] While not all have suggested amending the Constitution to incorporate a right to a job at a living wage, all have advocated for a right to work and to earn wages sufficient to support a family. Adolph Reed Jr. and the Labor Party have been arguing for a constitutional amendment for years.[2] David Gil and Philip Harvey have each written in support of universal employment at decent wages.[3] Rep. Jesse L. Jackson Jr. picked up on the good work done by the National Jobs for All Coalition and authors Gertrude Schaffner Goldberg and Sheila Collins and has continued the push.[4] The appeal of the idea is such that it seems to have arisen in several places independently—further indication of the potential for future widespread support.

By amending our Constitution to include the right to a job at a living wage, we are making a solemn promise to one another—a promise that those among us who want to work will always have the opportunity to do so and that those who work full-time will earn enough to be self-supporting. As a nation, polls consistently show that we already support these principles. Incorporating them into our Constitution will keep them high on our list of national priorities.

As constitutional rights, the right to a job at a living wage will be a national promise that our legislative, executive, and judicial branches will help us work toward. Our Constitution does not automatically make any right happen, but it does lay the foundation for how our laws should be working. For example, although our Constitution promises all of us equal protection under law, few would consider that we as a nation have achieved that. Yet, because the promise is in our Constitution, we are pledged to continue to try to make it possible.

In my first class of every semester, I stretch my hands out wide and tell my students that one hand represents the law and the other justice. The distance between them represents the gap between what the law is and what justice is. Our job, I remind them, is not to pretend that law and justice are the same, but to narrow the gap. That is what our Constitution tries to do—point us in the right direction to help us narrow the gap.

Our Constitution is the foundation document that guides us as we govern our nation. It embodies our fundamental promises to one another and sets out the procedures by which we resolve our disputes. There is a well-founded reluctance to amend the U.S. Constitution. Only twenty-seven amendments have been enacted in more than two hundred years. Some suggest that it is in this unchanging nature that the Constitution draws its strength. It should only be amended for matters of enduring principle. The right to a job that pays a living wage is the kind of principle that should be integrated into our Constitution because it guarantees our citizens a right to have the opportunity to be self-supporting and self-sufficient. This right is consistent with our national heritage and our national hopes.

Our Constitution provides the framework for our national guarantees to each other. A constitutional amendment is the clearest and most direct way to ensure that all people have a right to work and earn a living wage. It provides an enforceable guarantee that job opportunities and living wages will be among the guiding principles of our nation, as well they ought to be.

The wisdom of this amendment is up to the people to decide. If the American people think a constitutionally protected right to a job at a living wage is not a core right for each of us, then it will not be enacted. But if the people decide that changing times demand changes in our Constitution, they will find support from some of the very people who helped fashion the current Constitution.

Is the Constitution a sacred document never to be modified? Of course not. As Thomas Paine cautioned, we should not boast of our Constitution if there are still those who remain outside of its protections:

> When it shall be said in any country in the world, my poor are happy; neither ignorance nor distress is to be found among them; my jails are empty of prisoners, my streets of beggars; the aged are not in want, the taxes are not oppressive; . . . when these things can be said, then may that country boast its constitution and its government.[5]

While it should not be lightly amended, even its framers recognized that alterations in the Constitution were inevitable.

Alexander Hamilton noted that one of the fundamental principles of republican government was "the right of the people to alter or abolish the established constitution whenever they find it inconsistent with their happiness."[6]

Justice John Marshall, in an 1821 opinion of the Supreme Court, declared: "The people made the constitution, and the people can unmake it. It is the creature of their will, and lives only by their will."[7]

Once the Constitution is amended to include a right to a job at a living wage, all three branches of government will have this right as one of their guiding priorities. Adopting this amendment will not guarantee instant universal opportunity and instant eradication of all want among workers, because none of our other constitutional provisions were or are yet perfectly realized. What adopting this amendment will do is make the right to a job at a living wage part of the agenda for the executive, legislative, and judicial branches in all spheres of the implementation of their duties. Just as no branch of our national government should take action to correct any kind of problem by suspending the protections of the First Amendment, so too will the protection of the people's right to be self-supporting be one of the givens in all subsequent governmental action.

Adding the guarantee of a right to a job at a living wage to the Constitution will not instantly make that promise a reality. It will still take a sustained commitment on the part of all branches of government and the American people to provide these opportunities to all.

Our nation has experienced problems backing up and enforcing constitutional amendments. We continuously have problems with our Constitution as times change and the mood of the country changes with the times. After the terrorist attacks of September 11, 2001, many seemed very willing to trade away constitutional protection of speech and privacy for the hope of increased security and safety. Even though our Constitution promises equal protection of the law, we know that racial profiling and discrimination still occur.

Amending the Constitution will provide a solid foundation upon which to build the home of a new American promise. But the foundation is not the home. Once the foundation is created, plenty of work remains in Congress and in the executive branch to build and maintain the structures that will implement the right to a job at a living wage. And even once built, the legislative and administrative structures that carry out the right to a job at a living wage will have to be maintained.

There are powerful countervailing forces that will challenge the right to a job at a living wage. Once this right is enacted as an amendment to the Constitution, these forces can be expected to use their powers in every branch of government to work against change. And even once legislative and executive branches do create and fund enabling legislation, the forces of opposition will not rest and will try to minimize, undermine, stigmatize, limit, and destroy the right to a job at a living wage.

So, as momentous a process as amending the Constitution is, the fight for opportunity and economic justice will continue long after the right to a job at a living wage becomes law.

Some will oppose this constitutional amendment because they do not value the principles it embodies enough to make them a continuing priority in the governance of our nation. That opposition is expected.

Others will suggest that we put the highest value on universal opportunity to be self-supporting by guaranteeing a job at a living wage to all, but they will disagree with the method of amending the Constitution. That opposition, too, is expected. But these people will be responsible for offering an alternative method of placing a right to work at a living wage as a continuing priority in the governance of our nation.

The preamble to the U.S. Constitution explicitly discusses the need to "promote the general Welfare" as one of the reasons for establishing the Constitution:

> We the People of the United States, in Order to form a more perfect Union, establish Justice, insure domestic Tranquility, provide for the common defense, promote the general Welfare, and secure the Blessings of Liberty for ourselves and our Posterity, do ordain and establish this Constitution for the United States of America.

The Constitution itself provides the procedure for making amendments. Article V points out that either Congress or the state legislatures can initiate the process:

> The Congress, whenever two thirds of both Houses shall deem it necessary, shall propose Amendments to this Constitution, or, on the Application of the Legislatures of two thirds of the several States, shall call a Convention for proposing Amendments, which, in either Case, shall be valid to all Intents and Purposes, as part of this Constitution, when ratified by the Legislatures of three fourths of the several States, or by Conventions in three fourths thereof, as one or the other Mode of Ratification may be proposed by the Congress.[8]

Amending the Constitution is an arduous, time-consuming, and politically challenging task. Senator Dale Bumpers pointed out in 1998 that more constitutional amendments were offered in the prior 32 years, a total of 5,449, than in the first 173 years of the country; none have been approved by the Senate since 1975.[9] Recent efforts to amend the Constitution include campaigns to prohibit flag burning, to enact the equal rights amendment, and, in the 1960s, to overturn the one-man, one-vote decisions of the Supreme Court.[10]

It is not the purpose of this book to map out the details of a realistic organizing strategy for how the passage of this amendment should be effected.[11] Questions about the process of amending the Constitution under Article V are already the subject of many extensive inquiries.[12] The point is that our Constitution provides a method showing how an amendment is to be enacted. If enough agree with the idea of this amendment, strategies will certainly emerge.

Critics of amending the Constitution indicate a great unwillingness to impose what they call social policy. They point to the Eighteenth Amendment, which introduced Prohibition only to be repealed fourteen years later by the Twenty-first Amendment, as an example of why social amendments are unworkable.[13] Others go so far as to suggest that it is precisely the current legal system of largely unfettered economic opportunity that is *the basis* for liberty and justice.[14] They note that in the West, constitutional and human rights have historically focused on civil and political rights and not on economic or social rights.[15]

Yet, as others point out, the history of the Anglo-American legal system includes episodes in which the law has successfully confronted economic power in the name of justice. Slavery, after all, was an important economic system. It was confronted and changed. We know that it can be done.[16]

Looking to litigation to create a right to a job at a living wage without a constitutional amendment guaranteeing it, despite the skill and creativity of those who may try, does not appear to be a realistic alternative. While it might be argued that the Constitution already contains support for the right to work for a living wage, no courts have yet said so.

Some have looked, so far unsuccessfully, to the Supreme Court to establish a constitutional right to a job under the liberty interests of the due process clause.[17] Others have looked, so far also unsuccessfully, for a constitutional right to subsistence or minimum income.[18] And still others have looked, with the same lack of success, for social rights such as the right to a job under the heading of fundamental values.[19] Some suggest that the courts might offer remedies to tie American economic justice issues into the United Nations Charter.[20]

Many have tried looking to Congress alone to reverse trends in unemployment and low-wage employment by proposing admirable and important statutory strategies.[21]

While all of these approaches have merit, they are all, to some extent, already in place and making insufficient progress in combating the lack of work at decent wages because of a lack of commitment by the enabling bodies to go forward in a serious enough manner to succeed.[22] By making the opportunity to work at living wages a key part of our constitutional framework, these efforts will always be a part of the nation's agenda, and there will a reason to hope that they will get the national commitment they deserve.

Thus, if the right to work and to earn a living wage is to be placed squarely in the center of our national priorities, amending the Constitution is the best way to proceed. There is no comparable option for giving weight to the right to an opportunity to work for a living wage. Amending the Constitution is in order.

11   Support for a Right to a Job

It is in affording to the poor the means of labor, instead of a support independent of labor, that your Committee think a judicious change can be
made in the system of State Charity.
—Report on the Poor Laws of Massachusetts, 1831

THE IDEA that everyone should have the right to a job to support themselves has been supported by Americans for decades. Providing opportunities to work has been a preferred governmental response to poverty for hundreds of years. Even prior to the twentieth
century, state and local governments in this country created public job
programs for those who needed work. Three times during the twentieth century a guaranteed right to employment was seriously considered
by the Congress of the United States. While none of these prior efforts
culminated in an enforceable right to work, each moved the country
closer to that goal and provided insight for those considering a constitutional amendment. There has also been considerable religious and
popular support for the idea that those who want to work should have
the opportunity and that those who work should be able to earn a living wage.

POPULAR SUPPORT

Popular opinion has continuously supported a right for every person
to work, even if government has to provide a job so that every person
who wants to work can do so.

In 1935, *Fortune* magazine surveyed the American people and asked
the following question: "Do you believe that the government should see
to it that every man who wants to work has a job?" The vast majority
of respondents—76.8 percent—answered yes. *Fortune* concluded that
"public opinion overwhelmingly favors assumption by the government

100

of a function that was never seriously contemplated prior to the New Deal. . . . [T]he country has definitely accepted the theory of state responsibility for an opportunity to earn a living."[1]

Surveys between 1956 and 1976 showed continued public support (56 percent to 70 percent) for the proposition that "the government in Washington ought to see to it that everybody who wants to work can find a job."[2] Two Gallup Polls, one in June 1968 and another in January 1969, show an overwhelming lack of support for a guaranteed poverty-threshold income for those not working, while at the same time showing overwhelming support for a guarantee of work at a living wage.[3]

A *New York Times*/CBS poll in November 1987 found 71 percent supported the proposition that "the government in Washington should see to it that everyone who wants a job has a job."[4] A comprehensive review of public attitudes published in 1989 found more public support for employment for the poor than for income-maintenance programs.[5]

A 1992 poll found that 71 percent of the people responding favored replacing welfare with guaranteed public jobs.[6] The Gallup Poll reported that in 1994 between 54 percent and 60 percent of the people surveyed favored providing a government-paid job to welfare recipients when there are not enough private sector jobs available.[7]

A 2001 poll showed that more than eight in ten Americans support creating temporary government work programs for the unemployed in needed areas such as school and road construction. This support cuts across all party affiliations—82 percent of Republicans, 90 percent of Democrats, and 83 percent of Independents.[8]

Clearly, the American people support the idea of government making sure that every person who wants to work has the opportunity to do so.

Government and Political Support

Government has been in the business of giving people the opportunity to work for more than four hundred years.

In 1536, England authorized local governments to provide employment for the able-bodied poor, who, noted Parliament, "may be daily kept in continual labor, whereby every one of them may get their own sustenance and living with their own hands."[9]

The Elizabethan Poor Law of 1601, legislation that was very influential on subsequent English and American social welfare law, authorized a number of work-generating activities for local governments to engage in to address unemployment and poverty.[10]

In colonial America, those who were unemployed were regularly put to work by local authorities. This public work was not always provided as only an "opportunity" but also, unfortunately, sometimes as a method of coercion. But because it was provided, it did offer a means of support for those who were capable of working but could not find work.

For example, as early as 1636, the Massachusetts Bay Colony authorized local magistrates to put unemployed persons to work.[11] Many other colonies did the same.[12] The idea that work was the primary solution to poverty was widespread.

The idea that government should provide work to people who needed it was being seriously discussed as early as 1791, when Thomas Paine published *The Rights of Man.* Paine proposed that government set up institutions where anyone seeking work could find it, "so that every person who shall come may find something which he or she can do." Room and board would be provided to these workers, no questions asked. When the workers left, Paine argued, they should be allowed to take with them a portion of the value of the work they performed. Paine saw poverty as a structural economic problem that needed to be addressed by not merely the charity of the well-intentioned and the poor laws, but by fundamental changes in the economic system such as guaranteed employment, subsidized education, pensions, and family allowances.[13]

In the earliest years of the United States, state laws frequently required the unemployed poor to work for their support in private and public settings. Those who could work were put to work.[14]

Publicly funded work projects have been used as a means of relief for the unemployed since the 1800s.[15] In the nineteenth century, authorities in cities such as Baltimore, New York, Newark, and Philadelphia provided public jobs at a set minimum wage in response to widespread unemployment.[16] These local public works efforts continued into the twentieth century. For example, in 1914–1915 more than fifty cities used public works such as laying water mains, improving roads and parks, and repairing public buildings for the relief of unemployment.[17]

The idea of a right to work has long been discussed. In 1893, the respected labor economist, Professor John R. Commons, advocated a government-enforced right to work:

> The rights to life and liberty are practically denied to labourers in our day, by virtue of the denial of the right to employment. There is, therefore, pressing upon us, the claim for recognition of this new and higher right, belonging to man as a man, by virtue of the very dignity of the manhood that is in him. . . . The right to work, for every man that is willing, is the next great human right to be defined and enforced by law.[18]

Three times in the twentieth century the United States considered passing laws giving work to every person who wanted it.[19] The first time, during the New Deal, President Roosevelt led the fight for decent work at decent wages by exhortation and legislation. After World War II, a comprehensive legislative guarantee of employment was considered by Congress. Thirty years later, in the mid-1970s, Congress again wrestled with a way to ensure that everyone had the opportunity to work. Each effort, while ultimately unsuccessful, underscored the continuing concern for and importance of a right to work.

NEW DEAL

The seeds of modern hopes for a right to a job that pays a living wage were first planted in the New Deal. The federal government made great effort to safeguard and create jobs for all Americans at a time when the need was great and the opposition fierce. These actions went forward on two fronts in the New Deal: the creation of public programs providing jobs for the unemployed and a continuing push for the creation of a right to a job for all Americans.

Little of the significance of the New Deal can be understood without some knowledge of the Great Depression. In the spring of 1929, there were 2.8 million unemployed men and women; by January 1930, there were more than 4 million out of work; in September 1930, 5 million were unemployed; 8 million had no jobs by spring 1931; and unemployment continued to steadily increase until the peak of 13 to 15 million out of work in the spring of 1933.[20]

What did people want? They wanted a job. Consider what the head of the New York City relief effort said about those who sought help: "At least 75 percent of the people who came to us wanted just one thing, and that was work; the last thing they wanted was a charity dole of any kind."[21]

President Franklin Delano Roosevelt responded to the widespread unemployment in two ways: by creating specific programs that provided millions of public jobs, and by pushing for the federal government to commit to providing work to all who needed it.

While the most well known of the public employment programs of the New Deal is the Works Progress Administration (WPA), it was not FDR's first effort. The WPA actually arose out of two employment programs enacted in 1933, the Civil Works Administration (CWA) and the Federal Emergency Relief Act (FERA).[22] FERA was signed into law in May 1933 and was a part of the largest public relief program in the world. CWA was created by executive order of FDR in November 1933 to provide decent jobs at good wages to the four million unemployed and underemployed.[23] FERA, CWA, and other programs helped more than twenty million people a year, with expenditures of more than $4 billion.[24] CWA, more than any other New Deal effort, came closest to providing the unemployed "real jobs for real wages."[25]

In 1934, FDR shifted the government focus away from relief almost exclusively to public employment. While forces opposed to social welfare are fond of quoting the oft-repeated line from FDR's 1935 State of the Union Address that "the Federal Government must and shall quit this business of relief," they rarely go on to read the rest of the speech in which he stressed that the federal government must provide jobs to all the unemployed:

> I am not willing that the vitality of our people be further sapped by the giving of cash, of market baskets, of a few hours of weekly work cutting grass, raking leaves or picking up papers in the public parks. We must preserve not only the bodies of the unemployed from destitution but also their self-respect, their self-reliance, and courage and determination. . . . There are however an additional three and one-half million employable people who are on relief. . . . The Federal government is the only governmental agency with sufficient power and credit to meet this situation. We have assumed this task and we shall not shrink from it in the future. It is a duty dictated by every intelligent consideration of national policy to ask you to make it possible for the United States to give employment to all of these three and one-half million employable people now on relief, pending their absorption in a rising tide of private employment.[26]

The Works Progress Administration (WPA) was set up in 1935. Within a year it was an enormous success, employing more than three million people. Over the next several years, it provided jobs to millions of the unemployed, primarily those who were already on relief.[27] WPA workers did much to build and improve the nation's streets, public parks, schools, bridges, hospitals, and playgrounds.

Critics assailed the WPA as "make-work," a criticism with some validity early on because of logistical problems with the start-up of such a large, unprecedented program. Other criticisms of the WPA included: objections to the cost of the program, which was higher than just providing people relief assistance; objections to WPA work cutting into private business and construction opportunities; and objections from those conservative critics who saw uncorrectable flaws in any system of public employment.[28]

While the WPA actually lasted until World War II, Congress cut its budget nearly in half in 1937 and yet again in 1939 (when Congress ordered all WPA employees who worked for the program more than eighteen months to be terminated).[29]

In addition to the creation and administration of programs employing the unemployed, FDR and those who worked with the New Deal significantly expanded the political discussion over whether people should have a right to a job and a right to earn decent wages and how such rights ought to be considered.

For example, FDR created the cabinet-level Committee on Economic Security (CES) in 1934 to develop a comprehensive workable social security program.[30] CES quickly outlined a two-pronged social welfare policy to combat the economic misfortunes prevailing at the time: an income-transfer approach for the needy who could not work, and an employment assurance approach for those who could. Income assistance for the needy was formulated into programs such as the Social Security program and Aid to Families. The economic assurance part of the equation was to provide work opportunities to make people self-supporting. Unfortunately, only one of the legs was made operable, the income assistance programs.[31] In January 1935, the CES not only proposed what later became the Social Security Act, but also issued a report discussing the need for "employment assurance":

> Since most people must live by work, the first objective in a program of economic security must be maximum employment. As the major contribution of the Federal Government in providing a safeguard against unemployment, we suggest employment assurance—the stimulation of private employment and the provision of public employment for those

able-bodied workers whom industry cannot employ at a given time. Public-work programs are most necessary in times of severe depression, but may be needed in normal times, as well, to help meet the problems of stranded communities and overmanned and declining industries. To avoid the evils of hastily planned emergency work, public employment should be planned in advance and coordinated with the construction and developmental policies of the Government and with the State and local public works projects.

We regard work as preferable to other forms of relief where possible. While we favor unemployment compensation in cash, we believe it should be provided for limited periods . . . without government subsidies. Public funds should be devoted to providing work rather than . . . relief.[32]

Despite the novelty of the idea that the government become the employer of last resort, a 1935 poll by *Fortune* magazine found overwhelming support for the principle that "government should see to it that any man who wants to work has a job."[33] A 1939 Roper Poll found majority levels of support among the unemployed, blue-collar workers, and lower-paid white-collar workers. Even among high-income white-collar workers, 46 percent agreed that the government should guarantee jobs to everyone.[34]

FDR continued to keep the idea of a government-guaranteed opportunity to work for fair wages before the public. In 1937, in an address to the Congress, he said:

The time has arrived for us to take further action to extend the frontiers of social progress. . . . Our Nation so richly endowed with natural resources and with a capable and industrial population should be able to devise ways and means of insuring to all our able-bodied working men and women a fair day's pay for a fair day's work.[35]

As war approached, FDR and his advisers recognized that the unemployment of the mid-1930s, which was declining as a result of the war production effort, might well be repeated after the war. So, in November 1940, FDR instructed the National Resources Planning Board (NRPB) to formulate detailed plans for economic and social policies for the postwar period.[36]

The NRPB stressed the importance of a strong national commitment to full employment:

The development and adoption of techniques for bringing about and maintaining reasonably full employment of men and machines is not only a major problem, but is today the Nation's most pressing economic problem, relegating all other economic problems to a secondary position so long as it remains unsolved.[37]

In its report "Security, Work and Relief Policies," the NPRB proposed a "New Bill of Rights," which included:

1. The right to work, usefully and creatively through the productive years.
2. The right to fair pay, adequate to command the necessities and amenities of life in exchange for work, ideas, thrift, and other socially valuable service.[38]

In the body of the report the NRPB called for the assurance of economic security as a right of every American citizen. For those in need of steady work that the private economy could not provide, the federal government should provide a job.[39] This federal strategy for full employment was spelled out in detail:

> To guarantee the right to a job, activities in the provisions of physical facilities and services should be supplemented by:
> (1) Formal acceptance by the Federal Government of responsibility for insuring jobs at decent pay to all those able to work regardless of whether or not they can pass a means test.
> (2) The preparation of plans and programs, in addition to those recommended . . . for all kinds of socially useful work other than construction, arranged according to the variety of abilities and locations of persons seeking employment.
> (3) Expansion of the functions of the [U.S.] Employment Service, strengthening its personnel to the end that it may operate as the key mechanism in referring unemployed workers to jobs, whether public or private.
> (4) Establishment of a permanent "Works Administration" under an appropriate Federal agency to administer the provision of jobs of socially desirable work for the otherwise unemployed.[40]

While no specific legislative action was taken on this report, its suggestions and the discussion it provoked helped pave the way for the postwar Full Employment Bill.[41]

Meanwhile, FDR continued to proclaim the need to guarantee economic opportunity and security for all people. In his State of the Union Address delivered on January 6, 1941, FDR proclaimed:

There is nothing mysterious about the foundations of a healthy and strong democracy. The basic things expected by our people of their political and economic systems are simple. They are:

- Equality of opportunity for youth and for others.
- Jobs for those who can work.
- Security for those who need it.
- The ending of special privilege for the few.
- The preservation of civil liberties for all.
- The enjoyment of the fruits of scientific progress in a wider and constantly rising standard of living. [42]

Later in the same address, he pointed out the four freedoms he hoped would come about in the United States and worldwide: freedom of speech and expression, freedom of worship, freedom from want, and freedom from fear. [43]

In his 1944 State of the Union address, FDR provided the fullest explanation of the reasons for and substance of the economic bill of rights he advocated for so forcefully:

> It is our duty now to begin to lay the plans and determine the strategy for the winning of a lasting peace and the establishment of an American standard of living higher than ever before known. We cannot be content, no matter how high that general standard of living may be, if some fraction of our people—whether it be one-third or one-fifth or one-tenth—is ill-fed, ill-clothed, ill-housed, and insecure.
>
> This Republic had its beginning, and grew to its present strength, under the protection of certain inalienable political rights—among them the right of free speech, free press, free worship, trial by jury, freedom from unreasonable searches and seizures. They were our rights to life and liberty.
>
> As our Nation has grown in size and stature, however—as our industrial economy expanded—these political rights proved inadequate to assure us equality in the pursuit of happiness.
>
> We have come to a clear realization of the fact that true individual freedom cannot exist without economic security and independence. "Necessitous men are not freemen." People who are hungry and out of a job are the stuff of which dictatorships are made. [44]

To establish economic security for Americans, FDR proposed a "second Bill of Rights" under which a new basis of security and prosperity could be established for all—regardless of station, race, or creed. This second Bill of Rights included:

The right to a useful and remunerative job in the industries or shops or farms or mines of the nation;
The right to earn enough to provide adequate food and clothing and recreation.[45]

The New Deal still provides a high watermark for those who look to transform the economic and political system enough to make it more responsive to the needs of the workers and the poor. Through the efforts of President Roosevelt and Congress, America advanced. The federal government became employer of last resort, and millions of people and their families survived massive unemployment.

Although these New Deal public employment projects themselves did not become permanent, they helped millions of people in challenging times. Never since have the New Deal efforts to provide the unemployed with public jobs been matched. But the idea that the national government has responsibility for fighting unemployment and, if necessary, becoming employer of last resort, which had not been seriously considered prior to the New Deal, was now a permanent part of the American political discussion.

During this time, economic independence secured by the right to a decent job at decent pay became more than just a slogan; it became part of the American dream. There was now also hope that the right to a job could become a part of a second Bill of Rights.

EMPLOYMENT ACT OF 1946

The next major push came when Congress passed the Employment Act of 1946, which was originally intended to guarantee full employment. As introduced, the bill contained a proclamation that all Americans had the right to a useful and remunerative job. As passed, it contained less than the right to a job but still stands as an important milestone in the social economic history of the United States.

The bill arose out of continuing worries about unemployment. The vast unemployment problem of the Great Depression in the 1930s was finally solved only by the onset of World War II and prompted serious questions in the 1940s about why unemployment was not as solvable in peacetime as it seemed to be in wartime.[46]

Full employment was now the promise of both the Democratic and Republican parties.[47] The Democrats in their 1944 National Convention adopted a platform that guaranteed full employment.[48] Republican presidential nominee Thomas Dewey was even more explicit than the Democrats:

> If at any time there are not sufficient jobs in private enterprise to go around, the government can and must create job opportunities, because there must be jobs for all in this country of ours. . . . [I]f there is one thing we are all agreed upon, it is that in the coming peacetime years we in this country must have jobs and opportunity for all. That is everybody's business. Therefore it is the business of government.[49]

In late 1944 a coalition of people in and outside of government began drafting a Full Employment Bill. The original draft of the bill opened with a call for a specific right to full employment:

> The Congress hereby declares that all Americans able to work and willing to work have the right to a useful and remunerative job in the industries, or shops, or offices, or farms, or mines of the nation.[50]

The Full Employment Act, as introduced in 1945, contained Section 2(b) of the bill, which stated:

> All Americans able to work and seeking work have the right to useful, remunerative, regular, and full-time employment, and it is the policy of the United States to assure the existence at all times of sufficient employment opportunities to enable all Americans who have finished their schooling and do not have full-time housekeeping responsibilities freely to exercise this right.[51]

The bill's sponsor, Senator James E. Murray of Montana, speaking on the Senate floor, said about the bill:

> Our American system owes no man a living, but it does owe every man an opportunity to make a living. That is the proper interpretation of the "right to work."[52]

The bill called for the president to propose an annual National Production and Employment Budget that would estimate the number of jobs needed during the coming year and also propose a plan to bring the economy up to full employment levels.[53] While the bill did not guarantee a job to everyone who wanted one, its goal, according to Senator Murray, was to assure that there were enough jobs for everyone.[54] Support for the Murray bill came from groups such as the American Federation of Labor (AFL), the Congress of Industrial Organizations (CIO), the American Veterans Committee, the Young Women's Christian Association, the National Council of Jewish Women, the National Catholic Welfare Conference, the National Association for the Advancement of Colored People (NAACP), the National Lawyers Guild, the Union for Democratic Action, and the National Farmers Union.[55]

There was considerable opposition to the bill. A coalition of conservative Democrats and Republicans who feared increasing power in the executive branch warned "of a vast state bureaucracy that would compel everyone to work and determine what jobs they could have."[56] Employers feared that a high-employment economy would raise labor costs and make it difficult to find workers for menial jobs such as seasonal farmwork.[57] Reflecting these fears, the opposition was led by the National Association of Manufacturers, the Chamber of Commerce, and the American Farm Bureau Federation.[58] The opposition was based on arguments that full employment cannot be guaranteed in a free society, full employment would kill private initiative, full employment would lead to runaway inflation, and government spending would undermine business confidence.[59]

By the time the bill was enacted into law as the Employment Act of 1946, the short, direct promise of full employment was gone. In its place was the following sentence:

> The Congress hereby declares that it is the continuing policy and responsibility of the Federal Government to use all practicable means consistent with its needs and obligations and other essential considerations of national policy with the assistance and cooperation of industry, agriculture, labor, and State and local governments, to coordinate and utilize all its plans, functions, and resources for the purpose of creating and maintaining, in a manner calculated to foster and promote free competitive enterprise and the general welfare, conditions under which there will be afforded useful employment, for those able, willing, and seeking to work, and to promote maximum employment, production, and purchasing power.[60]

The bill made only minimal concrete progress toward the right to a decent job at a decent day's pay. The law endorsed "high" rather than "full" employment and backed off from the promise of institutionalized planning. What survived was a commitment to the goal of "maximum employment."[61] While the Employment Act of 1946 did not go as far as its supporters hoped, it too was a milestone in American economic and political history because it was the first explicit national commitment to promote maximum employment.[62]

Ironically, at the same time that the United States backed away from a guarantee of work to its own citizens, General Douglas MacArthur guided the adoption of the Constitution of Japan of November 3, 1946, which contains, in Chapter III, Article 27, the following right: "All people shall have the right and the obligation to work."[63]

HUMPHREY-HAWKINS FULL EMPLOYMENT AND BALANCED GROWTH ACT OF 1978

Interest in full employment was revived in the 1970s by a broad coalition of civil rights, women's, religious, labor, and senior citizens' organizations that pushed for full employment to replace the policy of maintaining unemployment at politically tolerable levels.[64] What ultimately became the Humphrey-Hawkins Full Employment and Balanced Growth Act was conceived of as a follow-up to the 1946 Employment Act.[65]

The Humphrey-Hawkins Act, while ultimately falling short of the right to employment at a living wage, represented another step forward in the national search for such a right.

From 1946 to the mid-1970s, federal legislation to combat unemployment focused on job training programs and some limited programs of public employment. The training and public employment programs that were enacted, such as the 1962 Manpower Development Training Act, the 1973 Comprehensive Employment and Training Act, and the 1982 Job Training Partnership Act, unfortunately evidenced little substantial impact on employment.[66] Interestingly, during this period some prominent Republicans such as President Richard Nixon and conservative economist Milton Friedman supported a right to a guaranteed income instead of supporting the right to a job.[67]

Part of what drove interest in full employment in the 1970s was growing unemployment. Unemployment, which had held at an average annual rate of 4.7 percent from 1962 to 1973, had risen to 5.2 percent in June 1974, 6.6 percent in November 1974, and 8.2 percent in January 1975, with unemployment among black youths up to 41.1 percent.[68]

The Humphrey-Hawkins Act, as introduced in June of 1974 by its co-author Rep. Augustus Hawkins, described the goal of full employment not as the number-driven goal of prior legislation, but as an enforceable right to work at fair pay:

An authentic full employment policy rejects the narrow, statistical idea of full employment measured in terms of some tolerable level of unemployment—the percentage game—and adopts the more human and socially meaningful concept of personal rights to an opportunity for useful employment at fair rates of compensation.[69]

The right to useful employment at fair wages was a core guarantee of the bill as introduced. The bill proposed "to establish a national policy and nationwide machinery for guaranteeing to all adult Americans able and willing to work the availability of equal opportunities for useful and rewarding employment."[70] The key provision of the Humphrey-Hawkins bill was Section 2(b):

The Congress declares and establishes the right of all Americans able, willing, and seeking work to opportunities for useful paid employment at fair rates of compensation.[71]

As introduced, the federal government would once again become the employer of last resort.[72]

Opponents of the bill stressed the same arguments used against the 1946 Employment Act, including: the negative inflationary impact that they thought full employment, or any reduction of unemployment to minimal levels, would have on the economy;[73] the cost of the bill, saying it would cost $30 to $60 billion annually.[74]

The bill, after extensive changes by its sponsors to meet the objections of opponents, passed in 1978.[75]

Again, instead of a right, Congress enacted a goal:

The Congress . . . declares and establishes as a national goal the fulfillment of the right to full opportunities for useful paid employment at fair rates of compensation of all individuals able, willing, and seeking to work.[76]

When passed as the Humphrey-Hawkins Full Employment and Balanced Growth Act of 1978, it had a five-year target of 3 percent unemployment for individuals over age twenty and 4 percent for individuals over age sixteen, but, unfortunately, no real binding provisions to achieve the goals.[77]

How was the country to achieve this goal?

The purpose of this title is to require the President to initiate, as the President deems appropriate, with recommendations to the Congress where necessary, supplementary programs and policies to the extent that the President finds such action necessary to help achieve these goals.[78]

Gone was the right to employment; gone too was the government as employer of last resort. Like its predecessors, this law resulted in a great goal statement with too little real authority and no systemic change created to achieve those goals.[79]

The Humphrey-Hawkins Act was the most recent legislative attempt to look seriously at the right to employment at decent wages, and, while its ultimate result was disappointing, its passage represents another step forward in the search for an enforceable right to work at a living wage.[80]

The twentieth century's search for the right to work, for a living wage, and for full employment—by FDR in the New Deal and by Congress in the mid-1940s and mid-1970s—is now recognized as a vital part of the American political dynamic, one that will continue to clamor for action as long as Americans value work and opportunity. As social historian Theda Skocpol says:

> Choosing to work for national employment assurance appears likely to remain a potentially popular political choice, although it remains to be seen if any political leadership will soon be forthcoming to devise both the policies and suitably universalistic political alliances needed to work for this goal. Nevertheless, even if little happens soon, the goal of full employment assurance itself—so clearly articulated in 1935 by members of the CES—seems unlikely to fade away. For employment assurance accords with longstanding American values, and it would address the distresses of many groups and regions in our presently unsettled national economy. Sooner or later, therefore, a politics of employment assurance— rather than one of welfare—will surely reappear on the American political scene.[81]

RELIGIOUS SUPPORT

> The community that should arbitrarily shut a man up in prison would not violate his rights more fundamentally than the community or the proprietors who should shut him out from the opportunity of getting a livelihood from the bounty of the earth. In both cases the man demands and has a right to a common gift of God. His moral claim is as valid to the one good as to the other, and it is as valid to both as the claim of his fellows.
> —John A. Ryan, *Economic Justice*

There are those who think that economic forces are beyond human and any other power. The belief in the sanctity of market forces has become their universal belief system. For them, any discussion of economic justice is a waste of time. While to these people it might be a form of blasphemy to suggest that the market can indeed be wrong or unethical in its consequences and effects, some religions and churches still believe that the economy is made for people, rather than the other way around.

Churches do not agree that the market is guided for good by an unseen hand, nor do they believe that the markets are beyond human control for the common good. For example, consider the 1999 statement of Pope Paul II and his criticisms of the global economy:

> The rapid advance towards the globalization of economic and financial systems also illustrates the urgent need to establish who is responsible for guaranteeing the global common good and the exercise of economic and social rights. The free market by itself cannot do this, because in fact there are many human needs which have no place in the market. "Even prior to the logic of a fair exchange of goods and the forms of justice appropriate to it, there exists something which is due to man because he is man, by reason of his lofty dignity."[82]

While everyone must acknowledge that our churches are as deeply flawed as our other institutions, they do have a history of looking at issues from perspectives other than just what is currently fashionable.[83] What do churches think of the need to create an economic system that prioritizes work with dignity for all?

Work has always assumed an important place in Hebrew and Christian scriptures. The Bible has many calls for justice for workers.[84]

Classical texts on charity and justice underscore the importance of giving people in need the opportunity to become self-supporting. For example, more than eight hundred years ago the great Rabbi Moses Maimonides said it was the highest and most meritorious of the eight forms of charity

> to anticipate charity by preventing poverty; namely, to assist the reduced fellow-man, either by considerable gift, or a sum of money, or by teaching him a trade, or by putting him in the way of business, so that he may earn an honest livelihood, and not be forced to the dreadful alternative of holding out his hand for charity—This is the highest step and the summit of charity's golden ladder.[85]

The Catholic Church has repeatedly stressed the importance of giving every person the right to work and to earn a living wage. For example, in 1961, Pope John XXIII called for government and economic systems to ensure that all people had the opportunity to work in order to provide for themselves and their families, and he declared unjust the economic orders that did not provide this opportunity:

> This implies that whatever be the economic system, it allow and facilitate for every individual the opportunity to engage in productive activity. . . .
>
> Consequently, if the organization and structure of economic life be such that the human dignity of workers is compromised, or their sense of responsibility is weakened, or their freedom of action is removed, then we judge such an economic order to be unjust, even though it produces vast amounts of goods, whose distribution conforms to the norms of justice and equity.[86]

Martin Luther King Jr. asked for a "contemporary social and economic Bill of Rights" that included "full employment."[87]

The United Church of Christ has had an ongoing discussion about a proposal for an Economic Bill of Rights to be adopted as an amendment to the U.S. Constitution. Their suggested wording is: "The right of people to access to employment, food, shelter, and health care should not be abridged."[88]

The 1990 Oxford Declaration of members of conservative and evangelical churches recognized that

> Since work is central to God's purpose for humanity, people everywhere have both the obligation and the right to work. . . . The right to earn a living would be a positive or sustenance right. Such a right implies the obligation of the community to provide employment opportunities.[89]

On January 1, 1999, Pope John Paul II issued a decree entitled "Respect for Human Rights: The Secret of True Peace." In it he reaffirmed the importance of the right to work:

> Another fundamental right, upon which depends the attainment of a decent level of living, is the right to work. Otherwise how can people obtain food, clothing, a home, health care and the many other necessities of life? The lack of work, however, is a serious problem today: countless people in many parts of the world find themselves caught up in the devastating reality of unemployment. It is urgently necessary on the part of everyone, and particularly on the part of those who exercise political or economic power, that everything possible be done to resolve this critical situation.[90]

Clearly, there is a solid foundation of popular, political, historical, and religious support upon which to build a right to work.

12   Support for a Right to Living Wages

No business which depends for its existence on paying less than living wages to its workers has any right to continue in this country. By living wages I mean more than a bare subsistence level—I mean the wages of decent living.
—Franklin Delano Roosevelt, Address to Congress, May 24, 1937

THERE IS widespread popular, political, and religious support for the principle that those who work should not still be poor. Living wages are those sufficient to allow a worker and his or her family to be self-supporting.

Advocacy for living wages is not a new concept but rather one that has been discussed for well more than a century.[1] There is growing energy in the living-wage movement because of a series of local victories that resulted in the enactment of a number of living-wage ordinances. More than fifty jurisdictions have enacted living-wage ordinances, and another seventy-five are engaged in ongoing living-wage campaigns.[2] On the federal level, the government has repeatedly discussed the importance of living wages but has not yet made that principle a reality. In the absence of federal leadership, local coalitions of labor and community groups have worked with their local governments across the nation to enact living-wage ordinances. And religious groups have long supported such a right. Each of these efforts has moved us closer as a nation to the goal of living wages for all.[3]

CALCULATING A LIVING WAGE

A living wage is a wage that enables a worker to earn enough to lift the worker and his or her family out of poverty. A living wage allows a worker to become self-supporting and self-reliant. But how much must a worker earn in order to be able to lift a family out of poverty and become self-sufficient? The calculation of a living wage depends in large part on how one calculates what poverty is and how much it costs to become self-supporting.

The discussion must start from the point that a living wage is a whole lot more than the minimum wage.

Full-time minimum-wage work has not been enough to lift most families over the poverty line in well more than a decade. In fact, in 2002, a full-time minimum-wage worker would not have earned enough money to lift a family of four over the official poverty line that was set back in 1984, or a family of three over the line set in 1990.[4]

I propose that a living wage for a single person in 2002 dollars is actually $8.50 an hour if health insurance is provided and $10.50 an hour if it is not.

According to a 2001 report of the Congressional Research Service, if the minimum wage had been adjusted to allow it to retain its 1968 value, in 2001 it would have been about $7.72 per hour.[5] Instead, the 2001 federal minimum wage was $5.15, an hourly wage put into effect September 1, 1997.[6]

If the value of the 1968 minimum wage of $1.60 an hour had kept up with inflation, by 2002 it would have been more than $8 an hour. A bill to raise the minimum wage to $8.15 an hour was introduced into the U.S. House of Representatives in 2001 by seventeen members of Congress. The bill, titled "Minimum Wage Restoration Act, HR 2812," specifically acknowledged that the minimum wage had lost 37 percent of its purchasing power since 1968 and attempted to raise it to $8.15 an hour by January 1, 2003, and index it to the cost of living. Raising the minimum wage to $8.50 would just be giving back to low-wage workers much of what they would and should have had all along if their wages had kept pace with inflation.[7]

One economist pointed out in 2001 that not only was the minimum wage 30 percent lower in real value than the minimum wage in 1968, the economy had become 50 percent more productive in the same time period.[8]

If minimum wage is not the starting point for calculating a living wage, what is?

The lowest possible living wage is calculated by seeing how much a person needs to earn in order to be above the federal poverty guidelines.[9] As discussed in earlier chapters, there are significant problems

with the official poverty guidelines because they seriously underestimate what people need to not be poor, but they remain the barest minimum upon which living wages have been examined.[10]

As I have pointed out, if you look at the example of a single parent
with two children, the official poverty guideline for the year 2002 was
a yearly income of $15,020.[11] For a parent with three kids, the yearly in-
come was $18,100. Working full-time, a parent with two children would
need to make $7.22 per hour and a parent with three children would
need to make $8.70 per hour to at least be lifted over the 2002 official
poverty threshold.

Living wages have been pegged directly to the poverty guidelines
by several cities that have enacted living-wage ordinances, and this remains the starting point for local legislation.[12] However, the problem
with this approach is that in reality $7 to $8 an hour, while a great improvement over minimum wage, is still not enough for a worker to raise
a family. Therefore, other ways to calculate the living wage must be
looked at as well.

One way that some cities calculate living wages is to see what the
federal government defines as needy in other programs for the poor. Because the official poverty threshold is so low, advocates for the working
poor often look to the food stamp guidelines for a more realistic income
to determine what kind of living wage is necessary to lift a family out
of poverty.

Food stamp guidelines are set at 130 percent of the official poverty
thresholds, so a parent with two kids would need $9.38 an hour and a
parent with three kids would need over $11 an hour to lift their families
to 130 percent of the 2002 poverty line.[13]

St. Louis voters used food stamp eligibility guidelines in 2000 when
they set their city's living-wage ordinance at 130 percent of the federal
poverty guideline for a family of three, $8.67 an hour with benefits and
$9.92 without.[14]

Another example of the government recognition that wages much
higher than minimum wage are necessary to raise a family is the Earned
Income Tax Credit program in which workers with two children remain
eligible for some assistance even if they make as much as $14 an hour.[15]

Private groups also recognize that it takes substantial wages for people to be self-supporting. Recall that the Women's Educational and Industrial Union calculated a "self-sufficiency" standard to measure the

real cost of living, including adequate housing, child care, food, transportation, taxes, and medical care; in 2001 the union calculated that it took $43,000—a full-time wage of more than $20 an hour—for a family of four to make it in Boston.[16] Similarly, the Economic Policy Institute calculated what it would cost a family of four to live in Baltimore in 1996. Researchers found that it actually took $34,732.28 to meet basic needs, a full-time wage of more than $16 an hour.[17] That is why some groups, such as the Labor Party, called for a living wage of at least $10 per hour in the late 1990s.[18]

In Chapter 13, I propose calculating a federal minimum living wage by connecting the living wage to a higher and more realistic poverty guideline, with adjustments for health insurance and dependents, and indexing the living wage to rise with inflation.

There are many different ways to calculate a living wage. But reality suggests that wages far higher than minimum wages are needed in order to allow families to become self-supporting and self-sufficient.

POPULAR SUPPORT

The living-wage movement is buoyed by broad public support, and has been since the 1930s.[19]

An April 2000 survey found that 94 percent of the one thousand adults questioned agreed with the statement that "as a country, we should make sure that people who work full-time should be able to earn enough to keep their families out of poverty."[20]

More than half of those polled in June 2001 favored raising the minimum wage by $1.50 an hour over three years.[21] A 2002 poll showed 77 percent of voters favored increasing the minimum wage from $5.15 to $8 an hour. An even higher percentage, 79 percent, favor raising the minimum wage to keep up with inflation.[22]

This support is reflected in a number of recent electoral and legislative victories for living-wage campaigns. Most notable was the nation's highest living-wage ordinance enacted by the Santa Cruz City Council in October 2000; the law mandates that city employees and employees of city contractors be paid at least $11 an hour if they receive health benefits, $12 an hour if they receive no benefits.[23]

Voters in Detroit in November of 1998 passed a living wage ordinance by a four to one margin with support from 80 percent of the voters. The ordinance required contractors doing business with the city to pay their workers a minimum of $7.70 an hour if they provide health insurance and $9.63 an hour if no health insurance is provided. A spokesperson for the Detroit Chamber of Commerce said after the vote, "We knew there was no way we could stop it."[24]

In the fall of 1998, voters in Washington State, by a two to one margin, raised their state minimum wage to $5.70 an hour in 1999, to $6.50 an hour in 2000, and they voted to raise it in future years to keep pace with inflation.[25]

In June 2000, the Alexandria Virginia City Council unanimously passed a living-wage ordinance that requires city contractors to pay $9.84 per hour and provide health insurance to employees on city contracts.[26]

In August 2000, by more than three to one, voters in St. Louis approved a living-wage ordinance setting hourly rates at $8.67 an hour for workers with health benefits, $9.92 for those without.[27]

POLITICAL AND GOVERNMENT SUPPORT ON THE FEDERAL LEVEL

Governments have been regulating wages for quite some time. A brief look at prior wage legislation will place current efforts for living wages in an appropriate historical context.

More than six centuries ago, governmental edict set maximum wages for the working poor. In the very first English statutes where government addressed the situation of poor people, the Statutes of Laborers of 1349–1350, the laws empowered local justices of the peace to set maximum wages in order to protect employers.[28]

The first living wage in England was created when Parliament authorized local justices of the peace to regulate wages. From 1795 to 1834, the justices of the peace in Speenhamland, Berkshire, set the wages of workers to the price of bread and the number of people in a worker's family; whenever the price of wheat rose, wages rose, and if wages did not rise, local authorities supplemented the wage.[29]

Modern minimum-wage regulations were first developed in New Zealand and Australia around the turn of the century; the British Parliament followed in 1909.[30] The first efforts to provide living wages for workers began with a focus on requiring employers to pay at least a minimum wage to workers, usually women workers. In many ways the history of minimum-wage legislation was the history of the rights of women workers who were the lowest paid and had the least legal protection of all of the working poor. At the beginning, the push for a living wage and the push for a minimum wage were related. Those advocating for minimum-wage laws often used the idea of the provision of a living wage as a goal of work.

While minimum-wage legislation did not come to the United States until actions by state legislatures early in the twentieth century, the demand for more than subsistence wages started in earnest after the Civil War. The use of the term "living wage" in these debates dates from the 1870s.[31]

The campaign for a living wage, as opposed to a minimum wage, started with the labor movement both in the United States and in England in the late 1800s.[32] Outside of the labor movement, religious reformers were the first group to call for a living wage, starting with Pope Leo XIII's 1891 papal encyclical to the Catholic bishops of the world entitled "On the Condition of Labor," which recognized the right of every worker to receive wages sufficient to provide for a family.[33]

By the early 1900s, living wages and minimum-wage protections for women and children were beginning to enjoy political support.

The first state minimum-wage law in the United States was enacted in 1912 by Massachusetts and patterned on the British Trade Boards Act of 1909. This law, which covered only minors and women, was not compulsory, and the authorities could only recommended minimum-wage rates that would provide a living wage.[34] Several of these state minimum-wage laws also specifically tried to set their state minimum wage to the "necessary cost of living."[35]

In his 1920 January address to Congress, President Woodrow Wilson proclaimed that workers needed wages sufficient to live in comfort, unhampered by fear of poverty and want in old age.[36] By 1938, when the Fair Labor Standards Act (FLSA), which created the current federal minimum wage, was passed, many states had some form of a minimum-wage law.[37]

Ideas about federal fair-wage legislation were drawn from the same well as the rest of the New Deal but were held up for years because of a 1923 decision by the U.S. Supreme Court that declared minimum-wage laws unconstitutional.[38] The 1923 decision was reaffirmed in 1936, and minimum-wage legislation appeared doomed.[39] When the Court reversed itself in 1937, federal efforts leapt forward.[40]

With a green light from the Supreme Court, President Franklin Roosevelt pushed for passage of the FLSA. As the epigraph at the beginning of this chapter shows, FDR was unrelenting in his view that employers who did not pay adequate wages had no business being in business.[41] He aggressively challenged the business leaders who opposed the law, asking that no one

> let any calamity-howling executive with an income of $1000 a day, who has been turning his employees over to the government relief rolls in order to preserve his company's undistributed reserves, tell you (using his stockholders' money to pay the postage of his personal opinions) that a wage of $11 a week is going to have a disastrous effect on all American industry. Fortunately for business as a whole, and therefore for the nation, that type of executive is a rarity with whom most business executives heartily disagree.[42]

With significant political modifications made necessary to ensure its passage, the Fair Labor Standards Act was signed into law by FDR in 1938. The new law imposed a federal minimum wage of twenty-five cents per hour, which would be raised to forty cents an hour by 1945, on some employees working in interstate commerce.[43]

The FLSA was a significant milestone in progress toward the goal of establishing an enforceable minimum wage, but, as a result of the legislative compromises required for its enactment, it had major deficiencies.[44]

The first major deficiency of the FLSA was that it did not provide a living wage or even a "fair day's pay for a fair day's work" as had originally been intended. After the compromises made in order for the bill to be passed, the FLSA mandated an hourly wage of 25 cents, significantly less than the 34½ cents set by the D.C. Minimum Wage Board twenty years before.[45] The FLSA wage of 25 cents an hour was still a poverty wage in a time when the average hourly wage in the unionized automobile industry in 1937 was 88 cents an hour.[46]

Another major deficiency was that the FLSA excluded millions of workers from its protection, many of whom needed that protection the most. The FLSA was politically crafted in such a way to leave many workers out of its coverage, particularly women and southern African-

American workers, by excluding from the statute's definition of covered employees occupations such as agricultural workers and domestic workers.[47]

Thus, even after the historic enactment of the FLSA, a right to a living wage remained still much more of a hope than a reality for large numbers of workers.

But the push for living wages continued, as can be seen in subsequent actions by FDR and his administration. In December of 1941, the National Resources Planning Board (NRPB), an agency in the Executive Office of the President mandated to consider problems of postwar adjustment, issued several reports, including one titled "Security, Work and Relief Policies."[48] In that report, the NPRB proposed a "New Bill of Rights," which included both a "right to work, usefully and creatively through the productive years" and a "right to fair pay, adequate to command the necessities and amenities of life in exchange for work, ideas, thrift, and other socially valuable service."[49]

Keeping the ideal of a living wage alive, in 1944 FDR proposed a "second Bill of Rights" under which a new basis of security and prosperity could be established for all—regardless of station, race, or creed. This second Bill of Rights included rights "to a useful and remunerative job in the industries or shops or farms or mines of the nation" and "to earn enough to provide adequate food and clothing and recreation."[50]

However, little progress on the enactment of living wages has occurred on the federal level. In fact, the primary challenge for living- and minimum-wage supporters since 1938 has been to raise the minimum wage in the FLSA in order to keep up with the losses inflicted by inflation and to expand the coverage of the law to more low-wage workers.[51]

Despite the ups and downs in the real value of the minimum wage, Congress has repeatedly pledged itself to the goal of a living wage for all workers. For example, in 1989 Congress pointed out that

> the purpose of the [FLSA] was and is to establish a floor below which wages would not fall, a floor which is adequate to support life and a measure of human dignity. It is a laudable legislative effort to ensure a just wage in return for a day's work.[52]

The federal minimum wage has lost its connection to its goal of being a living wage. However, there is another way that the federal government has tried to give some assistance to help make the wages of low-wage workers stretch in the direction of living wages—tax credit subsidies for low-wage workers under the Earned Income Tax Credit (EITC).

The EITC does not directly raise wages for low-wage workers but instead supplements their earnings by giving an extra tax refund. The EITC was added to the tax code during the administration of President Gerald Ford.[53] The credit was increased in 1986, 1990, and 1993 with support from both political parties. The EITC provides assistance in the form of refundable tax credits for low-income, tax-paying workers. It provides a refundable credit for a specified percentage of wages up to a maximum dollar amount. Because it is classified as refundable tax credit, if the amount of the credit exceeds the taxpayer's liability, the taxpayer receives the credit as a cash grant. The EITC is only available to families of people who work.[54]

The EITC is a popular antipoverty strategy because it effectively increases incomes for the working poor without adding burdens to employers. Some commentators consider the EITC the single most effective response this country has made to the impoverishment of low-wage and less-skilled workers.[55]

For fiscal year 2001, Congress estimated that the EITC would provide $30 billion to the working poor and that approximately eighteen million low-income workers would receive the credit, up from six million when the program started in 1975.[56]

In 2001 the EITC worked like this. A worker who made minimum wage and was supporting two or more children at home could qualify for a maximum tax credit of $3,888.[57] The effect is to raise the income of a minimum-wage worker from $5.15 an hour by $1.86 an hour, to income consistent with an hourly wage of $7.01. Once the parents begin making incomes totaling over $12,460, or about $6 an hour for a full-time worker, the credit begins to be reduced.[58]

There is a big problem with the EITC in that the money is not available to low-wage workers except once a year at tax refund time. While there has been an advance EITC payment plan technically in effect since 1979 that allows eligible taxpayers to receive the EITC in their paychecks rather than waiting to claim the refund when they file their tax returns, it is rarely used.[59]

There are other much smaller tax credits also available to workers. The Dependent Care Tax Credit is a nonrefundable credit that allows some workers to deduct child or incapacitated spouse care costs up to

$4,800 if there are two qualifying dependents. The problem with this law at the moment is that it actually provides little relief to low-income families. Internal Revenue Service data indicate that only about 10 percent of this credit goes to families with incomes less than $20,000 per year and nearly half goes to families with incomes over $50,000 annually.[60]

While most of the efforts of the living-wage movement have been dedicated to the enactment of living wages on the local level, there is recent legislative effort on the federal level. In May 2000, Rep. Luis Gutierrez (D-Ill.), along with eighty-three House co-sponsors, introduced the Federal Living Wage Responsibility Act, legislation to require federal contractors to pay workers on federal contracts at least $8.20 an hour.[61] The 2000 legislation specifically keyed hourly wages for employees of federal contracts over $10,000 to an amount sufficient to earn enough to meet the federal poverty threshold for a family of four, which in 2000 was $8.20 an hour. A November 2000 report released by the Economic Policy Institute indicated that more than 162,000 federal contract workers, one in every ten federal contract workers, earn less than a living wage of $8.20 an hour, the amount necessary to lift a family of four above the poverty line.[62] Despite the lack of substantive action so far, this is an area to watch, as it could provide substantial momentum toward living wages if such legislation is enacted.

On the federal level, earnings of workers have not kept up with the goal of providing a living wage. Minimum wages are just that. The EITC does provide help. And it is heartening to see the federal government talk about a living wage for federal contract workers. As we will see in Chapter 13, substantially raising the minimum wage, indexing it to keep up with inflation, expanding the EITC, and providing refundable dependent child and child care credits are all steps that the government can take to provide living wages to workers.

LOCAL LIVING-WAGE LAWS

The real progress in achieving living wages has been on the local government level. As noted earlier, more than fifty jurisdictions have enacted living-wage ordinances, and there are at least another seventy-five active campaigns for ordinances.[63]

These living-wage ordinances, while still small in impact, more than any other action show our nation's real progress toward living wages.

Living-wage ordinances typically work by requiring that private contractors who do business with the government pay their workers a wage that is substantially higher than the minimum wage.

The first sign of progress in the current living-wage movement came in the mid-1990s in Baltimore and emerged from action taken by a coalition of churches and labor organizations.[64]

Fifty churches joined together and approached the American Federation of State, County and Municipal Employees (AFSCME) to join with them to create an organization of labor union members, low-wage service workers, and church members. The churches were seeing an increase in the use by workers of soup kitchens and pantries, and the churches concluded that minimum-wage jobs with no benefits were not helping people escape poverty. AFSCME members were concerned about the privatization of government jobs in areas such as janitorial and food services that replaced better-paying public jobs with low-wage private jobs. The AFSCME concluded that private companies were paying low wages to now-privatized workers in order to win low-bid government contracts. Low-wage workers were often turning to food stamps, publicly financed health care, and private assistance from churches to make up the difference.

This was the municipal subsidization of poverty, concluded coalition members. In response, the coalition created a campaign for a law that would require businesses contracting with the city to pay their workers at least a living wage. Churches and labor contributed people and funds to educate the public about the problem of low wages and to lobby for the living-wage bill. After much hard work, the city enacted the local living-wage law, which went into effect in July 1996.

The Baltimore law required city contractors to pay wages sufficient to lift a family of four over the poverty level. This was $6.10 an hour in 1996, rising in annual increments to $7.70 an hour in 1999. The law was estimated to apply to between two thousand and three thousand government contract workers.[65]

The success of the Baltimore coalition inspired the development of other living-wage coalitions around the country, mostly made up of local labor, community, and religious organizations.

Labor organizations have been pushing living-wage ordinances in order to show their commitment to low-wage workers. They have worked to prevent privatization efforts from replacing decent-paying city

jobs with low-paying private jobs. In these campaigns, labor has rein-
vigorated its efforts to work in coalitions with religious and community
groups.[66]

Community groups have organized around living-wage campaigns
because of a combination of energies from national and local groups and
a continuing national resource support effort by the organizations of
the AFL-CIO, the Association of Community Organizations for Reform
Now (ACORN), and the New Party.[67]

The fifty local living-wage ordinances vary dramatically. While most
of these ordinances apply to businesses in the jurisdictions that have
public contracts with local government, the jurisdictions define a variety of hourly rates as living wages and apply and operate in quite
different ways as well.

The variations in what constitutes a living wage are substantial,
stretching from a low of $6.50 an hour plus benefits ($13,520 a year)
in Duluth, Minnesota, to a high of $11 an hour plus benefits ($22,800) in
Santa Cruz, California.

Living-wage laws also apply to different categories of public contractors. The Baltimore living-wage law applies to businesses with local
public contracts over $5,000,[68] while Miami-Dade requires living wages
by all employers on contracts over $100,000.[69]

Many cities do not restrict their living-wage mandate only to businesses that are parties to local public contracts, but also apply the living-
wage requirements to other businesses that receive governmental benefits. For example, the Los Angeles Living Wage Ordinance requires that
living wages be paid by several types of businesses: firms with service
contracts over $25,000, recipients of bond financing and other subsi-
dies worth at least $1,000,000 a year, and city lessees and licensees with
$200,000 or more in annual revenues and eight or more employees.[70]
The St. Louis law requires that living wages be paid by all city contractors and all companies that receive city tax breaks, grant money, or other
forms of public aid.[71] Parts of the St. Louis law, including the extension
of the law to companies that did not directly contract with the city, were
set aside by a trial court in July of 2001, so this area of the living-wage
laws will have to be carefully watched as the appeals and amendments
unfold.[72] In May 2001, Santa Monica enacted a living-wage law that will
require beginning in July 2002 an hourly wage of at least $10.50 for all
businesses in coastal areas of the community.[73]

Local living-wage laws are not without their critics.[74] One drawback to evaluating current local living-wage ordinances is that so far they apply to relatively few workers, usually less than 1 percent of a city's total workers, or, as of 2001, as few as seventy-five thousand workers nationwide.[75]

Opponents of living wages argue that these ordinances could potentially increase the local poverty rate and cost too much. For example, a survey of more than three hundred economists conducted in 2000 for the Employment Policies Institute, a nonprofit research organization generally opposed to both raising the minimum wage and enacting living-wage ordinances, found that nearly eight in ten of the labor economists surveyed thought living-wage ordinances would result in employers hiring higher-skilled workers. More than 70 percent of respondents said the laws could potentially reduce the number of entry-level jobs and thus increase the local poverty rate.[76] The opposition also suggests that living-wage ordinances increase the cost of governmental contracts. Pasadena, California, estimated that its living-wage ordinance cost about $200,000 for the year 2000; Cambridge, Massachusetts, estimated its cost at $300,000; Madison, Wisconsin, estimated its cost at $47,000.[77]

Supporters of living wages disagree and say that there has been no reported adverse impact to cities or businesses.[78]

Ever since government became involved in wage laws, the economic impact of such laws has been the subject of debate. In mid-2001, Alan Greenspan, chairman of the Federal Reserve, told Congress that he would abolish even the minimum wage if he could because it is "artificial government intervention" that hurts jobs.[79] It is no different for living wages. Clearly, the economic impact of any law varies significantly depending on the wage rate and the scope of coverage.[80] Supporters point to data suggesting that the actual financial impact of local living-wage laws on covered businesses is very small, less than 1 percent of the overall spending of these concerns.[81] Opponents disagree, arguing that living wages put too big a burden on business and actually harm the cause of the working poor by making entry-level employment less available.[82] These economic issues will continue to be debated as long as there are opportunities to do so. Every single time the minimum wage has been raised, people have argued that the increase would wreck the economy and increase the numbers of people in poverty.[83] Our nation has been able to reconcile its social policies with the economy in the past, and it can do so again if it is a priority to do so.

One tactic used by opponents of local living wages is to persuade state legislatures to prohibit local governments from enacting living-wage ordinances, thus launching what I call the "maximum minimums movement."[84] For example, in February 2001 the Utah state legislature passed a law prohibiting local governments from setting a minimum wage higher than the state minimum wage of $5.15 an hour. The main supporter argued that the maximum-minimum wage bill was "one of the most family-friendly pieces of legislation we have passed this session." He argued that the ban on higher municipal minimum wages will make it easier "for young people and people who have just entered this country" to find entry-level work. "We should not allow municipalities to arbitrarily set a wage that denies entry to those trying to get a foothold" in the job market.[85] The Louisiana legislature banned local living-wage laws that raised wages higher than the state minimum just as New Orleans was facing a living-wage ballot initiative.[86] As of 2001, in addition to Utah and Louisiana, Arizona, Colorado, Missouri, and Oregon have each passed legislation at the state level to limit the enactment of local living-wage ordinances.[87]

The opportunity to evaluate fifty different local living-wage ordinances will give all concerned a chance to see which elements in the various approaches work the best. As these local communities collect information from the impact of these relatively new laws, the various hourly rates and the varying thresholds of coverage should provide a wealth of legal and economic experience for the living-wage movement and its opponents to analyze. The variations are a tribute to the willingness of local jurisdictions to allow the law to develop in a way that has not yet appeared possible on the federal or state level.

RELIGIOUS SUPPORT

> Masters, give unto your servants that which is just and equal; knowing that ye also have a Master in heaven. —Colossians 4:1

Religious advocacy for just wages and living wages has been articulated by religious groups for more than a hundred years. Religious groups have gone on record to support the right of all workers to earn living wages, beginning with the Catholic Church in 1891. Protestant churches have gone on record to support living wages since 1908. In 1911, the Milwaukee Federation of Churches joined with local community organizations such as the Consumer's League to push for the first minimum wages for women and children. In 1919, the Federal Council of Churches of Christ in America proclaimed, "The living wage should be the first charge upon industry, before dividends are considered." Other supporters include the Episcopal Church, the Jewish Council for Public Affairs, the Unitarian Universalist Association, and the United Methodist Church.[88]

Indeed, outside of the labor movement, religious reformers were the first group to call for a living wage, starting with Pope Leo XIII's 1891 papal encyclical to the Catholic bishops of the world entitled "On the Condition of Labor," which recognized the right of every worker to receive wages sufficient to provide for a family.[89] Since then, the Catholic Church has repeatedly spoken out for the rights of workers to living wages to support their families. For example, in 1931, Pope Pius XI reaffirmed the principle of the need for a living wage, saying, "In the first place, the worker must be paid a wage sufficient to support him and his family."[90] The U.S. Catholic Bishops spelled out the need for a living wage and exactly how comprehensive a living wage actually is in their 1940 statement:

> The first claim of labor, which takes priority over any claim of the owners to profits, respects the right to a living wage. By the term *living wage* we understand a wage sufficient not merely for the decent support of the workingman himself but also of his family. A wage so low that it must be supplemented by the wage of wife and mother or by the children of the family before it can provide adequate food, clothing, and shelter together with essential spiritual and cultural needs cannot be regarded as a living wage. Furthermore, a living wage means sufficient income to meet not merely the present necessities of life but those of unemployment, sickness, death, and old age as well.[91]

The pope and Catholic bishops have reaffirmed this support for a living wage in statements in 1961, 1963, 1981, 1986, 1991, and 1992.[92]

OPPOSITION TO LOCAL LIVING-WAGE CAMPAIGNS

Not everyone supports living wages. In my experience, people oppose living-wage ordinances for four main reasons: (1) they dislike any government interference in business, (2) they fear job losses in the community, (3) they fear inflation resulting from businesses raising their prices to compensate for higher wage, and (4) they fear that raising wages will reduce the incentives for people to become better educated and improve themselves. Some of these reasons for opposing living wages can be addressed, but some cannot. Opposition based on economics can be contested. Opposition based on job loss can be challenged. Opposition based on an irrational faith in the unseen hand of the market economy is beyond rational discussion.

Many opponents of living wages proclaim that they dislike any government interference in business at all. For many there is an almost religious belief that the "unseen hand" of the market will work to everyone's benefit, that "pursuit of individual self-interest will work to the benefit of the community," and that "what is good for business is good for the nation, and ultimately the world." This view can be illustrated by the words of Paul O'Neill, secretary of the treasury in 2002, who characterized the expansion and implosion of Enron, with all its consequent tragedies for workers, investors, and state economies, as "the genius of capitalism. . . . People get to make good decisions or bad decisions, and they get to pay the consequences or to enjoy the fruits of their decisions. That's the way the system works."[93] Usually, these folks often are opposed to *any minimum wages at all,* be they the inadequate federal minimum wage or any increases in it. They suggest that "the free market" alone ought to be allowed to set wages. For example, the U.S. Chamber of Commerce takes the position that market forces alone should set wage scales: "Instead of allowing market forces to determine pay, living wages put the interests of employees above all other considerations."[94]

Opponents such as the Chamber of Commerce truly believe that having government give a hand to assist working people is wrong. Yet, in my experience, every single one of these business opponents belongs to lobbies and organizations that work furiously year-round in the federal and every state legislature for special government assistance such as tax breaks, improved transportation systems, zoning exemptions, and increased protections from legal responsibility for their errors. Yet they still somehow still think that government helping workers is wrong and antimarket. How they reconcile their relentless quest for special government assistance for businesses yet proclaim themselves as against any government role in commerce is hard to figure. While they oppose all minimum wages, they also fear that giving in on wage issues will lead to further government regulation in areas such as unionization, the environment, and zoning. For these folks, the concept of a "free" market is such a deeply held and almost faith-based belief that there is little chance to have a rational debate about living wages.

Opposition based on fear of job losses in the community is often fanned by the same people who oppose all minimum wages. "I feel every minimum wage, even at the federal level, costs jobs," said a restaurant owner in New Orleans who opposes local efforts to enact a living wage.[95] (If people are constitutionally guaranteed a job at a living wage, this argument would be voided, but it is included as part of the overview of the arguments over local living-wage ordinances.) But for those who are open to discussion and are serious about examining the potential job loss from living wages, there is some useful information available. There obviously is some cost to some business when minimum wages are raised. There are businesses that do not pay any worker minimum wages, so the direct effect on their labor costs are nil. For businesses that do employ low-wage workers, economists such as Professor Robert Pollin point out that increased labor costs due to living wages are minimal and can easily be digested by business or passed on to the general public in the form of very, very small price increases. Pollin points out several ways that raises in wages can be responded to by individual businesses: take less profit (an unlikely response); lay off workers (also unlikely, for presumably the business needs the workers to operate); raise prices a little (very likely); and try to get more productivity as a result of the raises (also very likely).[96] Higher wages also tend to help employers retain workers and cut down the costs to businesses associated with employee turnover. Businesses that pay extremely low wages are also often locale-specific and are not likely to relocate. As a result, job losses, when they occur at all, are very small. Even economists who have been skeptical of living-wage ordinances, such as Professor David Neumark, have come around to conclude that even if slight job losses result from living-wage ordinances, the overall effect on the community is good because of the decrease in poverty among working families. Neumark, an economics professor at Michigan State University, was for years a vocal critic of living-wage laws. After studying the economic impact of living-wage laws across the country, Neumark issued a 149-page report in 2002 for the nonpartisan Public Policy Institute of California that concluded, "Living wages actually reduce poverty. If someone's getting up on a soapbox saying these are a disaster, they may believe it, but there's really no evidence."[97]

Despite this, some critics argue that raises in minimum wages are "job killers." Since the federal minimum wage was enacted in 1938 at twenty-five cents an hour, every single time it has been raised critics have prophesied that the increases would destroy jobs. The minimum wage has been raised eighteen times since its inception, and the jobless rate has been unaffected. In May of 2002, two economists at the Economic Policy Institute, Jared Bernstein and Jeff Chapman, concluded that

> there is little evidence for any negative effect on employment from past increases in the minimum wage, regardless of the business cycle. By analyzing changes in the employment status of affected workers before and after minimum wage increases, economists have rigorously searched for, but generally failed to find, these negative employment effects. The estimates from the empirical literature show that the impact on employment is either statistically insignificant or slightly negative, a finding widely accepted by economists. And even in cases where there is evidence of job losses, the number of workers negatively affected are tiny compared to the number who get an hourly pay raise.[98]

Other opponents of living-wage ordinances fear that the increased labor costs will cause businesses to raise their prices, thus leading to general inflation. What this argument misses is the very, very small increased cost associated with modest raises in the minimum wages of low-wage workers. Pollin and Luce have done the most empirical economic research on the impact of living-wage laws and conclude: "In fact, the wage and benefit increases for most firms due to the living wage requirements will be less than 1 percent of these firms' total spending to produce goods and services." Take the example of fast food. New Orleans voted to raise its minimum wage by a dollar for all employees in the city. Some feared that raising the minimum wage by a dollar would just translate into every hamburger costing a dollar more, thus negating the good effect of the raise for minimum-wage workers and harming everyone else because of raised prices. But a careful look at this example will show why a one-dollar increase in the minimum wage would result in the cost of a hamburger going up one or two cents rather than one dollar. First of all, even in a labor-intensive business such as fast food, not all the costs involved are from low-wage workers. Other big costs are rent, insurance, advertising, and the cost of the hamburger and buns and potatoes and so on. The cost of the workers is only a part of the overall picture. Thus, as economic experts such as Professor Pollin have shown, a one-dollar increase in the minimum wage would translate only into an average 1 to 2 percent rise in the cost of doing business for high-labor employers. Is it worth it for everyone in the community to pay one or two cents more per burger in order to help give those workers up to one dollar more an hour to become more self-sufficient? Many think so. Concerns about inflation can be addressed.[99]

A final fear about living wages is that increases reduce the incentives for people to become better educated and improve themselves. Education is a vitally important part of the overall way our workforce can improve. Do higher minimum wages deter people from going back to school at night to get a degree? I know of no evidence whatsoever that shows that people who get higher than minimum wages go back to school less frequently than others. In my experience, the quest for educational improvement cuts across all economic levels. I know many teachers, police officers, engineers, and even doctors who go back to school. Their wages do not deter them from doing so. In fact, the opposite may well be true. It seems reasonable that with a living wage, which would enable workers to support themselves and their families without having to work a second job, there would be more time for continuing education. There is evidence that this is the case. For example, a 2002 *Time* magazine article on the effect of living-wage ordinances profiled Jerome Gibbons, who, because his pay at the Los Angeles airport was raised from $5.75 to $9.54, was able to drop his second job and now studies at a local college to become a counselor for substance abusers.[100]

Most of these economic considerations will be debated forever between the people who want to keep wages low and those who want to make wages liveable. But, I again remind the reader that it is dishonest and unfair to evaluate only the impact of raising the minimum wage to a living wage and to ignore the tragic daily negative impact of the current system, which condemns millions of people to work that is insufficient to allow them to be self-supporting. Any fair analysis must balance the problems of the current situation with anticipated problems of the solution.

Remember also that the community has a vital stake in this discussion. Low-wage workers still need medical care even if their employer does not provide it or does not pay them enough to afford it. They still need to eat, and they still need a whole lot of help—help that has to come from the community. The U.S. Supreme Court considered this in 1937 when it approved the legality of minimum-wage laws:

> The exploitation of a class of workers who are in an unequal position with respect to bargaining power and are thus relatively defenseless against the denial of a living wage is not only detrimental to their health and well-being but casts a direct burden for their support upon the community. . . . The community is not bound to provide what is in effect a subsidy for unconscionable employers. The community may direct its law-making power to correct the abuse which springs from their selfish disregard of the public interest.[101]

There is substantial support—popular, religious, and political—for a constitutional amendment that guarantees a living wage for every person who is willing to work.

13   How Might a Constitutional Amendment Work?

To provide employment for the poor, and support for the indigent, is among the primary, and, at the same time, not least difficult cares of the public authority.
—James Madison, Letter to Rev. F. C. Shaeffer, January 8, 1820

IN A CHURCH cafeteria where I had just led a brief discussion about establishing a right to a job at a living wage, an older woman came up to me and said, "I like what you say about amending our Constitution. I think everyone should have a chance to work. And I think that everyone who works should be paid enough money to live on. My question to you is, 'How on earth are we going to do that?' " There are several ways that we as a nation can respond to that question.

This book is intended to initiate discussion on the importance of two intertwined principles that are the core of the proposed constitutional amendment: the right of every person who wants a job to have one, and the right of every person who works to earn a living wage. I do not attempt to provide an economic treatise or an offering of all the specific programs or laws that the country might use to fulfill the promise of the constitutional amendment. Others can do that.

This book is an effort to hold up two principles deeply embedded in American thought, to show that we are not currently living up to our principles and that there are ways we can live up to these principles. What I propose here is a process for our nation to strengthen our commitment to end poverty as we know it by allowing every working person the opportunity to support themselves and their families.

The Constitution enshrines the highest goals of this nation. This nation has always valued working to earn enough to secure a dignified living. A constitutional amendment guaranteeing every person the right to

137

work and to earn a living wage simply yet forcefully elevates accepted American principles to protected rights.

It is very important to reaffirm that these two principles must be kept together, for the right to a job without a right to a living wage is just as weak as the right to a living wage without a job. Both rights must remain intact and linked together.

So how might such a constitutional amendment work?

Fortunately for us, our nation has amended its Constitution on other occasions and this amendment would follow the same process. The exact meaning of these rights would be decided by the same combination of constitutional bodies that decide the exact meaning and implementation of our other constitutional rights: Congress, the executive branch, and the judiciary. Implementation of this amendment would operate in the same way as other constitutional obligations, with considerable care, deference, and judgment.

The initial steps of implementation would be the responsibility of the legislative bodies. Congress would be expected to draft and pass appropriate laws consistent with the Constitution. As anyone familiar with the legislative process knows, it is a process that produces unpredictable outcomes. Those with interests in the amendment would be expected to propose ways to make it come alive that would benefit their particular perspective. Some business interests would likely try to get tax relief for their part in providing employment, while others will no doubt try to frustrate and delay implementation and still others will come up with innovative ideas not yet considered. Employees, labor unions, and social welfare organizations will certainly try to influence the legislation in accordance with their own agendas as well. Proposals will be made for public employment, subsidized private employment, higher minimum-wage floors, and tax credits. As in all legislation, compromise will result.

The executive branch would then be called upon to develop the details of administrating the laws and to give oversight of how the new laws are operating. Administration of the laws would likely be by the departments of Commerce, Labor, and the Treasury.

The judiciary would carry out its traditional role of evaluating actions in purpose and practice to ensure they are consistent with the Constitution. Even though judicial interpretation and enforcement of a constitutional right to work for a living wage would be unprecedented, legal scholars point out that enforcing social rights requires the same degree of judicial action as enforcing civil rights.[1]

As a part of the U.S. Constitution, the right to a job at a living wage would be a legally enforceable right for all citizens. What exactly that means would depend on what Congress does, how the laws are implemented, and whether the courts consider the laws constitutional.

Then, most likely, as with all the rest of our constitutional rights, this entire process would start over again as experience demonstrates what works and what does not. Congress, the executive branch, and the judiciary would have this constitutional right on their continuing agenda in the same way as other laws. How we as a nation reconcile our constitutional principles with changing realities occurs every day. For example, Congress, the president, and the judiciary are now grappling with how the First Amendment applies to the internet. Obviously, when our nation enacted the First Amendment, the internet was not contemplated. But we will work out a constitutionally acceptable approach. For the right of every person to a job at a living wage, there would be evolving realities as well: What is most cost effective and what is least. What is most politically palatable and what is less so.

As noted throughout this book, many wise people have already given consideration to a right to a job at a living wage.

Rep. Jesse L. Jackson Jr. has advocated amending the U.S. Constitution to provide a right to a job at a living wage based largely on the excellent analytical work of Gertrude Schaffner Goldberg and Sheila D. Collins and on the agenda of the National Jobs for All Coalition.[2] The Labor Party has been advocating for a constitutional amendment for a right to employment at a living wage of $10 an hour for years.[3]

Professor Charles Black makes some telling observations in the context of his arguments for a constitutional justice of livelihood based on the present Constitution:

> I rather guess that my self-chosen task, for the rest of my years as a constitutionalist, is going to be arguing, in all weathers, the case for the proposition that a constitutional justice of livelihood should be recognized, and should be felt by the president and by Congress as laying upon them serious constitutional duty. In the early phases of this work, I find I am most often asked the question, "How much?" or "Where will you draw the line?" I think it well to try to suggest, at the beginning, that the establishment of a duty is one thing, while the specification of prudent quantities

and means is another—though it must be remembered as well that the decently eligible range of means and measures is one thing when you are under no duty at all to act, and quite another when you are under a serious duty to act effectively.[4]

Once we amend the Constitution, we are under a serious duty to act.

WAYS CONGRESS MIGHT ACT

For Congress, the possible ways of enacting laws in support of this right to a job at a living wage are limitless.

As several professors have noted, this is more about the will than the way:

> Many technical tools are already available to attain full employment and, with a will to do so, others can be discovered. When U.S. elites wanted to send a human being to the moon or to develop high-tech weapons . . . major research efforts were made; when medical scientists lack a cure for an epidemic disease, research funds are provided. But when faced with unemployment, some economists, governments and the corporate interests that they often reflect proclaim it cannot be cured or does not exist or it is "natural."[5]

A constitutional right will give us the will to explore the many technical tools that we can use to achieve full employment.

There are dozens of resources on ideas about how our nation can increase employment and wages for the millions of people who are working but still poor.[6] These ideas range from public job creation to private job subsidies and involve all combinations of raises in the minimum wage, refundable tax credits for the working poor, tax credits for hiring people by private businesses, and wage subsidies for private employers. Full employment at good wages is entirely possible. It is not primarily an economic issue but a political one.[7]

These are thoughtful and creative ideas. But the critical need in America right now is not just for ideas, which many talented people have provided, but for the will and the mechanism to implement these ideas. This constitutional amendment will offer a way for our nation to firmly demonstrate its commitment to the principle that every person who wants to work can, and every person who works full-time will earn enough to be self-supporting.

This section will not attempt to survey the entire field of job creation and wage enhancements. That is much more than an entire book by itself. I will, however, briefly point out a few of the many, many good ideas that are already in circulation to demonstrate that there are ways that Congress can act in order to meet the guarantee of an opportunity for every person to work and earn a living wage.

EXPANDING EMPLOYMENT

Many have given serious thought to how our nation can create more jobs for the millions who need them. Their proposals are the stepping-off point in any discussion of how this right can be implemented. The bottom line remains that every single person who wants to work must have the opportunity. How we provide that opportunity is up to us as a nation to decide, but it can be done.

The right to a job can be implemented by expanding tax subsidies for private employers, granting funds to states to set up private-public partnerships, creating flexible public employment programs, or any combination of the above plus other ways that have undoubtedly not been considered yet.

Congress could introduce new tax incentives to private employers and employees that would support work creation and retention policies. For those who are not employed by the private economy, a state or local public or WPA-type employment corps could help clean and teach and police our nation's communities.

Here is a sampling of some of the ideas already proposed:

- Employment subsidies for private enterprise is the proposal of Edmund Phelps of Columbia University. He suggests that we reward private businesses that hire low-wage workers by providing them continuing tax credits for as many workers as they can employ. Hiring would be increased because of tax incentives, and wages would be raised by wage subsidies that the government would give to employers to help them pay for the workers.[8]
- Lester Thurow of MIT suggests that the federal government create permanent open-ended job programs to guarantee jobs for everyone who wants to work because private enterprise alone is incapable of

it. These must be permanent programs at good wages. They could include both permanent and temporary jobs for people who are unable
to find work. No one who wanted to work would be denied the opportunity.[9]

• Katherine Newman of the Kennedy School of Government at Harvard has outlined several ways to create job opportunities for those
not working. There are small programs already in place that provide
private entities with subsidies and tax credits to hire workers; these
programs should be expanded. Transportation should be subsidized
to match inner-city jobless people with suburban employers who may
be seeking workers. School-to-work programs, including summer job
programs, should allow students to gain realistic work training and
apprenticeship experiences. Leaders should bring together local employers in a consortium to explore recruitment, hiring, and advancement opportunities for workers.[10]

• Rebecca Blank of the University of Michigan is generally not a fan of
most programs to increase job possibilities for lower-skilled workers.
However, she supports targeted job creation in circumstances of high
unemployment, jobs lost through expansion of international trade, and
the integration of new workers, such as mothers who were on welfare,
into the market. In these circumstances she supports public-sector employment, either directly for public institutions or in private nonprofit
settings, and wage subsidies for private employers.[11]

• Broadly targeted wage subsidies for employers of less-skilled workers,
in combination with job development, including assistance in training and job search, show promise in studies conducted by Harvard's
Lawrence F. Katz.[12]

• Timothy Bartik of the W. E. Upjohn Institute for Employment Research
suggests a revival of the New Jobs Tax Credit, which was in effect
in 1977 and 1978. This credit provided subsidies for public and private employers who expand employment. Bartik suggests creation of
a program of employment of the unemployed by small businesses and
small private nonprofits that would provide both direct employment
and opportunities to upgrade work skills in order to transition into
higher-wage work. He points out the successes of focused training programs, aggressive job placements, employment subsidies, and temporary community service work in nonprofit organizations.[13]

• Charles Cerami proposes a Human Employment Tax Credit.[14] This

would give companies a financial incentive to hire and retain workers. Right now, the stock market usually rewards companies that shed
jobs; this credit would do the opposite.[15] Prior tax policies such as
the Investment Credit have given benefits to companies that invest
in machinery (which often resulted in reducing the number of employees), so why not provide credit for investing in people, our most
precious commodity? Some will argue that investing in people rather
than machinery slows down productivity, but others dispute that argument.[16]

• An Employment-Centered Social Policy is proposed by Robert Haveman of the University of Wisconsin. He suggests incentives to make
hiring low-skilled workers more profitable for private businesses than
it is now. For any business, he advocates a tax credit subsidy, mod-
eled on the New Jobs Tax Credit of the 1970s, of 50 percent of the first
$10,000 in wages for the first fifty new workers hired over the employ-
ment level of the previous year.[17]

• According to economist L. Randall Wray of the University of Denver,
it is economically possible for the government to create an economic
safety net by becoming the employer of last resort and offering every
single person who wants to work a job paying above minimum wage.
Thus, instead of using unemployment to fight inflation, the government will be forced to use its tools of spending, taxes, and interest
rates.[18]

• Nancy Rose at California State University suggests that the time is
right for a revival of voluntary government work programs such as the
ones that blossomed in the New Deal. These could create programs in
education, recreation, support for the arts, and construction of transportation and low-cost housing. Special effort must be made to recognize the value of work performed by women and men who care for
children or older dependent family members. Professor Rose reviews
the history of employment programs and suggests that any effort must
incorporate three elements in order to be successful. First, employment
programs must be universally available in order to avoid stigmatizing any one group, such as welfare recipients. Second, the programs
must occur on the federal level because federal programs have historically been more progressive than individual state efforts. Third, the
program must be funded by the federal government rather than individual employers so that all share in the cost.[19]

Look around and see all the human needs that public- or public-private employment programs could fill. What school could not use more teachers, teacher's aides, maintenance people, and hall monitors? What about care after preschool for very young children and after-school programs for older children? What public buildings, playgrounds, parks, and roads could not be better staffed and maintained? How many elderly and disabled could use assistance? How many law enforcement agencies could use extra people to assist in the office and in the field? What about work boarding up or fixing up abandoned houses? Removing lead paint? What libraries are fully staffed and opened all the time? The need is clearly there all across the nation.

When Baltimore operated a public employment program in the 1970s, the city placed the jobless in a variety of work projects: monitoring school truancy and attendance, weatherization and lead paint abatement, library staffing, home health care, beautification projects, nonprofit theater support, tourism promotion, and minor repairs and maintenance in local public housing.[20]

Public-private work partnership programs are key. One example of a successful public-private partnership is shown in the work of the Annie E. Casey Foundation, which has spent several years creating the successful Jobs Initiative program in six cities. Jobs Initiative finds private employers who are able to provide family-supporting wages and career opportunities and links those employers with low-income residents who want jobs. This program found that employers are already concerned about high turnover and labor shortages in skilled entry-level workers and are willing to work as part of a concerted effort involving government agencies, community organizations, low-income residents, and public officials in order to design, implement, and sustain effective employment programs.[21]

A short-lived experimental jobs and wages program called Project Hope in Milwaukee continues to generate good information about how we might proceed. Project Hope, a joint effort of government, private foundations, and nonprofit organizations to lift workers and their families over the poverty line, offered adults who worked at least thirty hours a week significant work incentives such as health insurance, wage subsidies, and child care subsidies. If people could not find a job on their own, the program provided them community service jobs and helped them to find more permanent employment. Participants were chosen at random. They were required to prove at least thirty hours of work a week and hand in paycheck stubs documenting their work efforts. The results of the program, which was offered to more than six hundred workers, are still being analyzed. So far at least, the results are mixed.[22] People enrolled in the program worked more and earned more than people not enrolled in the program, but less than a third worked enough to pull themselves out of poverty. There were definite positive developments for boys whose parents were enrolled in the program. These boys showed better academic performance, stronger study skills, and better behavior than boys not in the program. On the negative side, program staff had difficulty getting participants to understand and follow program rules, and many dropped out. Though the program ended, participants are still being followed to evaluate its long-term effects. So far, it appears that this short-term program of jobs at decent wages was not an instant exit from poverty for each of the poor people chosen at random—not a surprise to those who are familiar with the individual poor person. Poor people are not a group of identical people with the same lives, families, resources, skills, problems, and potential as each other. Poor people are as different from each other as we are from our neighbors and co-workers and friends. The chronic lifelong problems associated with a lack of good jobs and good wages will not be solved overnight. Years of living in the current system have apparently stamped some people as so defeated that they had trouble immediately responding to the opportunities offered.[23] Many more of these types of programs and critical evaluations of them are needed in order to calculate how to best implement a guarantee of a job at a living wage.

Project Quest in San Antonio has been much more successful than Project Hope and may offer some lessons in how the opportunity for good jobs can be better provided. According to respected poverty analyst Mary Jo Bane, Project Quest is "considered by many experts in the field to be one of the best models around."[24] Project Quest was started in 1993 by local community organizations and now operates in partnership with government and business to develop good jobs for the community. The program works directly with businesses to identify real job needs and then makes a two-year commitment to people enrolling in the program to train them and place them in the jobs. While not all people who enrolled in the program have successfully made the transition to living-wage jobs, more than half have. Project Quest continues in operation and has developed the ability to attract new partnerships with the business community. For example, in 2000 Project Quest partnered with Boeing Aerospace to identify and train twenty people on welfare or in low-wage jobs for positions as aircraft structural mechanics paying $9.50 to $10.50 an hour.[25]

There are already several relatively small federal programs that provide some financing for public job creation for welfare recipients as a result of welfare reform, including Temporary Assistance to Needy Families, Welfare to Work Funds, the Workforce Investment Act, and several smaller programs.[26] There are programs to help poor people get and retain good jobs. Results show that even for the hardest-working families who are receiving considerable program assistance, reaching the goal of a family-sustaining wage is much more difficult and takes longer than previously thought.[27] Each of these programs has been subjected to continual evaluation, and there are many ideas about how these and similar programs can be refined and expanded.[28]

For example, the state of Washington has experimented with a number of job creation programs. One private organization, Community Jobs, has enrolled more than five thousand people in small classes and workshops to develop skills in job preparation, job seeking, and job retention. Well over half of those enrolled had moved into nonsubsidized jobs within one year of starting the program.[29] Other Washington job creation programs include even recently released prisoners.[30]

There are numerous other examples across the nation of local job creation initiatives involving governments, businesses, and unions. Indianapolis targeted 750 families on welfare for on-the-job training by the American Federation of State, County and Municipal Employees (AFSCME). Wichita funds a partnership with Cessna Aircraft and the International Association of Machinists union to hire former welfare recipients to work in sheet-metal assembly and blueprint reading. Hennepin County, Minnesota, developed a small pilot project with union and business cooperation to create a six-month training program for low-skilled welfare recipients.[31]

Private-sector jobs should be created with government assistance, according to John E. Schwarz of the University of Arizona. Tax credits for new-job creation, wage subsidies, and other incentives can assist in this effort. If private-sector efforts fail, then public work programs should be instituted.[32]

We must create a system where anyone who wants to work can work and live on what they earn. There have to be living-wage jobs available for every person who wants to work. If the private sector can provide them, with or without government assistance, great. Private employment should be the most important part of this effort. However, if the private sector cannot provide enough jobs for people who want to work, then it is the responsibility of the public sector to provide living-wage jobs in a system of state and local public employment projects.

The private sector provides most of the jobs, and government policies have to support expansion of private-sector employment. Tax deductions and tax credits can provide incentives to the private sector for job creation and retention. There is a long history of these programs on a modest scale. This needs to be expanded. Congress might also consider repealing existing incentives that reward firms for taking jobs out of the country.

Where the private sector does not provide enough living-wage jobs, then it is the responsibility of the public sector to step in and provide those jobs. There are many models of how this can be done. The most politically feasible would be for the federal government to provide block grants to states, with federal oversight, so that each state could create and operate its own living-wage employment programs. The federal government could, however, contract directly with counties or urban areas for job creation programs. This would allow many creative approaches to develop. If the state or local government does not do a good job, then the federal government should step in and run the programs itself or with private contractors. Every community has many needs for jobs that they cannot fill because they do not have the money—aides in public schools, assistants to law enforcement, helpers with public parks and recreation, sitters and readers in hospitals and nursing homes. The possibilities are endless.

The public employment project would act as a clearinghouse for jobs. If people want to work and cannot find a private job, then they would go to their local public employment project and secure a job paying $8.50 an hour, the new federal minimum living wage. If they have dependents, then their wages would be supplemented in the same way as those working in the private sector.

An infinite number of questions are possible about how this right could be implemented, but the answers to those questions will depend on which of the paths Congress chooses to use. There will be significant financial costs involved in giving everyone the right to a job at a living wage—but there are significant financial costs being borne by our communities right now by not giving people opportunities to work at jobs that pay living wages. There will be administrative challenges dealing with problem workers—but we have serious community problems arising out of widespread unemployment and underemployment in our present system right now.

The public has already indicated its support. A 2001 poll showed that more than eight in ten Americans support creating temporary government work programs for the unemployed in needed areas such as school and road construction. This support cuts across all party affiliations—82 percent of Republicans, 90 percent of Democrats, and 83 percent of independents.[33]

In all of this the right to work must remain a right of opportunity. "Every person shall have the right to work" simply means that there must be an opportunity for work for those who seek it. No one would be forced to work, and the voluntarily unemployed would not have to work.

Of course, not all the unemployed are able to work. The Census Bureau reports that between seven million and nine million people are in poverty because of a disability.[34] The poverty rate for adults with disabilities is three times that of the rest of the population.[35] Some of the nonworking poor are unable to work, and for them Social Security Disability and Supplemental Security Income should provide a living income. Surveys, however, show that most of the disabled would work if given the opportunity.[36] They should, if they can, be given the opportunity to work and become self-sufficient.

These examples show that a right to a job for every person is possible. It will be up to Congress to decide how best to proceed to make it a reality.

Creating a Living Wage

As in job creation, there are limitless combinations of ways in which the wages of low-wage workers could be raised to a living wage.

People who work would be entitled under this amendment to receive a living wage for their work. A living wage means compensation sufficient for workers to meet the needs and demands of everyday life, lived in a manner consistent with human dignity.

The bottom line is that those who work full-time should earn enough to support themselves and their families. The precise amount of money that constitutes a living wage will vary over time and with national standards and expectations, but it is intended to cover the commonly accepted living expenses for workers and their dependents. Since it is a living wage, and because it is expected that many workers will be supporting families, the lives of those dependent on the worker must also be included.

The facts show that every person must earn at least the equivalent of double the current minimum wage. Congress can achieve this by raising and indexing the minimum wage, increasing tax credits, providing wage subsidies, or any combination of these and other measures. Wages themselves could be supplemented by tax credits for low-wage workers and expanded for larger families. Most important is to allow working people to become self-supporting. How exactly we do that is up to us.

The key is to scrap the current federal minimum wage and substitute an annually adjusted federal minimum living wage. The new federal minimum living wage would allow people to live at levels consistent with the new federal poverty levels required for self-sufficiency. This is not a wage that is just enough for people to avoid starvation and eviction. A living wage must allow a person and her or his family to live a life of simple dignity. People who work full-time should not have to be dependent on the charity of others or government in order to live fully independent lives. They should not have to be forced into debt through credit cards or other means of borrowing in order to survive. The living wage should be keyed to the revised poverty threshold so that a working person can earn enough to be self-sufficient.

Given a new poverty threshold that is 100 percent higher than the current one, the 2002 living wage for a single person would have to be at least $8.50 an hour for employers who provide health insurance for their workers. For jobs where health care is not provided, the practice among cities around the country when calculating living wages is to insist on an additional $2 an hour to allow the worker to purchase her or his own health insurance. Thus, the federal minimum living wage should be $8.50 an hour for workers who are provided health insurance and $10.50 an hour for workers without health insurance.

If the 1968 minimum wage of $1.60 an hour had only kept up with inflation, by 2002 it would have been more than $8 an hour. In fact, a bill to raise the minimum wage to $8.15 an hour was introduced into the U.S. House of Representatives in 2001 by seventeen members of Congress. The bill, titled "Minimum Wage Restoration Act, HR 2812," specifically acknowledged that the minimum wage had lost 37 percent of its purchasing power since 1968 and attempted to raise it to $8.15 an hour by January 1, 2003, and index it to the cost of living. So, in a sense, raising the minimum wage to $8.50 will be just giving back to low-wage workers much of what they would and should have had all along if the wage had kept pace with inflation.[37]

But the $8.50 an hour minimum wage would only apply to single workers who have no family or kids. This would have to be an annually adjusted absolute floor for any worker. More will be required for workers whose employers do not provide health insurance, as discussed earlier, as well as for workers with families.

Assuming there is employer-provided health insurance, for the two-person household with one working adult and one child, the living wage would have to be $11.48 an hour in 2002 dollars. An hourly rate of $14.44 would be necessary to give a living wage to the sole worker with two children in a three-person household, and so on. These calculations would also be annually adjusted to keep up with changes in the cost of living.

My proposal is to supplement the federal minimum living wage of $8.50 an hour with additional money in each paycheck for workers who need the money to support a family. If there are two minimum-wage workers in the family but no kids, then no wage supplement is necessary. If there is one minimum-wage worker and one high-wage worker, then there is no need for a supplement. But if there is one working parent and two children, then $8.50 an hour is not going to make ends meet, so the paycheck of the parent has to be supplemented up to an equivalent of $14.44 an hour.

This paycheck supplement can operate much like the current Earned Income Tax Credit (EITC), but it must be included in each and every paycheck so that working families can be self-supporting.

As a policy matter, we also should guarantee that two-parent families have the option to have one parent stay at home with children under age six and should give them the option of the federal minimum living wage for the size of their family.

The goal of providing living wages is that workers would no longer have to apply for supplemental assistance to help stretch their wages. For example, food stamps, housing assistance, and other public assistance should not be necessary for workers who are paid living wages.

The public already has indicated support for a much higher floor for wages. A 2002 poll showed that 77 percent of voters favored increasing the minimum wage from $5.15 to $8 an hour. An even higher percentage, 79 percent, favor raising the minimum wage to keep up with inflation.[38]

The fact that more than fifty local governments are already experimenting with living-wage laws offers a tremendous wealth of information to be sifted, analyzed, and argued about to see how living wages can best be implemented.

One option is to raise the minimum wage directly to a realistic level over a period of years and then index it to allow it to keep up with inflation. Raising the minimum wage to living-wage levels must key the minimum wage to a more realistic poverty line.

Another option is to raise the tax benefits for low-wage workers beyond current assistance levels provided by the EITC and other tax credits. Ways to improve the EITC include modifications to allow low-wage workers to get their credits on a regular basis instead of just at tax time. Recall that while there has been an advance EITC payment plan technically in effect since 1979, it is rarely used.[39]

The Dependent Care Tax Credit, currently a nonrefundable credit that primarily helps middle- and upper-income workers, if expanded and made refundable could also provide some assistance to low-wage workers.[40] By a two to one margin, voters polled in 2001 favored making this credit refundable for low-income families.[41] The 2001 tax law made some changes—including expansion of the child tax credit and changing the EITC to include expansion for married families—to assist low-income working families. But, according to Robert Greenstein of the Center on Budget and Policy Priorities, because the overall bill is so costly, until its future plans are modified it will sharply reduce the potential for other social welfare programs.[42]

Probably some combination of raising wages and granting tax credits would be called for, or perhaps what would work best is some other more innovative method not yet in widespread use.

Part of the political calculation that Congress will consider depends in part on where the cost of raising wages is imposed. Raising the minimum wage to living-wage levels would impose the cost of this social policy directly on the employers who benefit from the workers. Increasing tax credits or other indirect supplements to low-wage workers would spread out the cost of this social policy to all taxpayers.

Here are some of the current proposals for raising low wages to more decent levels and making work pay:

• John E. Schwarz of the University of Arizona notes that the stall in compensation levels for workers in the United States since 1973 has coincided with the decline in the power of labor unions and their ability to press wages upwards. Therefore, his ideas for better wages start with the need to bring more balance to the laws that allow workers to organize to press for their own interests. To this he adds increases in the minimum wage, expansion of the EITC, and provisions for health and child care.[43]

• The EITC could continue to be a part of the effort to lift low-wage workers to living-wage levels if the program was changed in three ways, according to economists Robert Cherry and Max B. Sawicky.[44] First, increase the coverage within the program to allow more low-wage workers to receive more benefit. Second, modify the program's marriage penalty. And third, simplify the filing process. Cherry and Sawicky propose a Universal Unified Child Credit for working families that would expand and combine the EITC and other tax credits into one mechanism.[45]

• Robert Pollin and Stephanie Luce of the University of Massachusetts have written extensively on the need to lift minimum wages to the level of living wages.[46]

• Increases in the minimum wage coupled with expansion of the EITC, along with strengthening the opportunities for workers to bargain collectively, would assist the working poor tremendously, suggests Katherine Newman. When unions are strong they can create union-management partnerships for better wages, increase advancement, and reduce turnover. Newman also recognizes that child care and health care, if not universally provided, have to be incorporated into the definition of a decent wage.[47]

• Isabel Sawhill and Adam Thomas of the Brookings Institution suggest a modest three-part work support program that combines increasing the minimum wage by one dollar, strengthening the EITC, and increasing the child care credits, which they think could assist more than 20 million families in the bottom third of incomes and lift 4.6 million people out of poverty.[48]

- To achieve living wages, Rebecca Blank of the University of Michigan recognizes the importance of expanding the EITC, raising the minimum wage, and providing wage subsidies for employers, but she also points out the need for increased attention to child care subsidies and health care insurance. Both child care and health care make substantial demands on the ability to work and the wages earned, and they have nearly universal application. They can be and need to be a part of any solution.[49]

- Harvard's Theda Skocpol also stresses the importance of access to universal health care and child care in combination with repeatedly raising the minimum wage and fortifying the EITC in order to make work pay and allow families to escape poverty. These can be achieved by tax credits or subsidies directly to workers and their families and to institutions that care for them.[50]

- The Employment-Centered Social Policy proposed by Robert Haveman of the University of Wisconsin includes a wage subsidy for workers, something along the lines of an expanded EITC, that would bring their incomes up to the equivalent of a living wage.[51]

- Professors Barry Bluestone and Bennett Harrison suggest raising and indexing the minimum wage, increasing the value of the EITC, and strengthening labor laws to allow employees to exert more equal pressure on wages.[52]

- Raising the minimum wage, assisting part-time employees with proportional and portable benefits and more realistic wages, and subsidizing community-based employment are some of the suggestions offered by Stephen Herzenberg, John Alic, and Howard Wial. Can these steps and others increase employment and raise wages without causing unsolvable problems? These authors state, "Without trivializing the technical and political challenges of avoiding unemployment while raising wages, we believe the existing situations in Europe and the United States hardly span all possible ways of organizing a postindustrial economy."[53]

These examples show that the right to a living wage is possible. It will be up to Congress to decide how best to proceed to make this idea a reality.

COST

What about cost? No doubt, there will be substantial cost involved in implementing a constitutional, just right to a job at a living wage. But please never forget that we are already paying a significant cost to maintain our current unjust system.

When we consider the cost of guaranteeing every person a job, we must first compare that cost to the cost of not giving people jobs. That will help us understand the real costs involved. Each 1 percent of unemployment costs the federal budget between $70 billion and $100 billion each year.[54]

Also understand that there are resources out there—they will just have to be redistributed a little.

The rich have definitely been getting quite richer. From 1983 to 1998, the richest 20 percent of Americans received 91 percent of the total growth in wealth, most of that (53 percent) going to the top 1 percent, according to Professor Edward N. Wolff, an economist at New York University. From 1983 to 1998, the richest 1 percent accumulated 53 percent of the total gain in wealth; the next 19 percent received another 39 percent.[55]

Even the most modest estimates show that executive pay has risen to heights unseen even in among late-eighteenth-century robber barons. The 1965 ratio of CEO pay to average worker was 20 to 1, in 1978 it was 28 to 1, in 1989 it was 60 to 1, and by 1999 it was 106 to 1. Some say the disparity is much higher, as much as 500 to 1 in 2001.[56]

According to an April 2002 report of Citizens for Tax Justice, just closing corporate tax loopholes and assistance to corporations could save $170 billion each year![57]

Estimates on costs vary depending on the details and breadth of the programs proposed.

- Philip Harvey calculated that in 1997 our nation could have given every unemployed person a job paying $8.50 an hour, and it would have cost a little more than a 12 percent increase in Social Security tax rates.[58]

- Isabel Sawhill and Adam Thomas of the Brookings Institution suggest that a dollar carefully spent on work-support programs such as an increase of $1 in the minimum wage, strengthening the EITC, and increased child care credits would cost about $25.8 billion annually but for each dollar spent would generate more than a dollar in income.[59]
- John E. Schwarz of the University of Arizona calculates that a comprehensive public-private sector program resulting in good-paying jobs for all who need them, health insurance, child care, retraining of low-skilled workers, and a comprehensive skills-training program for high school students would ultimately cost about $180 billion annually. This is, as he points out, a substantial investment in America, but as a part of personal income it comes to about four cents out of every dollar.[60]
- Edmund Phelps of Columbia University estimates that his suggested low-wage employment subsidy would cost $125 billion a year, offset by some savings in public assistance programs.[61]
- Timothy Bartik of the W. E. Upjohn Institute for Employment Research estimates that the cost of creating and maintaining a program for 5.5 million new jobs at $8 an hour would average around $42 billion a year.[62]

While these new rights undoubtedly have financial implications, some suggest that the cost of raising wages may in fact be offset by improvements in the nation's productivity because of reduced turnover in low-wage industries.[63]

There will also be savings by giving everyone who wants it the opportunity to become self-supporting. Who pays for the living costs of low-wage workers and the unemployed now? If low-wage workers or the unemployed need food and rental assistance and medical treatment, who pays for that now? Or do they go without? The cost of low-wage workers and the unemployed is already being paid for by family members, friends, churches, and all levels of government.[64] The Congressional Budget Office estimated that a 1 percent rise in unemployment over a five-year period costs the U.S. Treasury more than $400 billion.[65]

Additionally, our nation is likely now paying substantial costs in crime prevention because of high unemployment among those ages sixteen to twenty-four. One recent study found that the decline in unemployment during the mid-1990s may have explained 30 percent of the fall in crime rates. The unemployment rate among those ages sixteen to twenty-four was 26 percent in 1999, compared to 4.2 percent overall.[66] While employment and decent wages will never by themselves deter people from engaging in criminal activity, our nation obviously pays a huge price for crime, and investing in improved work opportunities will certainly help.[67]

Protests against a constitutional right to employment and a living wage will certainly arise from those who are benefiting the most from our current economic system. This amendment, they will argue, violates the natural rules of the economic system and is too inflationary.

There is no "natural" economic system. Our economic system has been and still is constantly manipulated to the advantage of certain segments of society. As any tax lawyer, legislator, or businessperson will admit, our government is already deeply involved in assisting middle- and upper-income wage earners because of policies in our current economic system. For example, the home mortgage deduction costs the federal government some $100 billion a year. The bigger the home, the larger the deduction. But who argues that this huge tax expenditure violates the natural laws of economics? It is a social decision that we as a nation have made to support certain values, often to benefit the very well off. This is not to suggest that we give up the home mortgage deduction, but that we use the same type of creative government policy to allow every person in our country who wants to work the opportunity to earn a living wage.[68]

- Professor James K. Galbraith of the University of Texas assures us that our nation can have full employment and still keep inflation under control by redirecting our national monetary policy.[69] He also argues that we can significantly raise the minimum wage, by more than $2 an hour over a few years, without inflation or loss of employment.[70] As he notes, the 1996 raises in the minimum wage were vehemently criticized as both inflationary and as job destroyers, yet "the rise in the federal minimum wage in 1996 proved to be one of the great economic nonevents of all time."[71]

- L. Randall Wray of the University of Denver agrees. It is economically possible for the government to create an economic safety net by becoming the employer of last resort and offering every single person who wants to work a job paying above minimum wage. Instead of using unemployment to fight inflation, the government will be forced to use its other tools of spending, taxes, and the interest rate.[72]

• Lester Thurow of MIT says that we can guarantee a public job at decent wages to every person who needs one. Such a guarantee would reflect our determination to make the United States a society that truly values the work ethic. This would involve an economic restructuring of our economy with attendant cost.

What would such a program cost? Payments for labor, materials, and capital might be high, but with all economic projects, the costs would depend on the difference between the value of the output produced and the payments made to factors of production. If care is shown in project selection, there is no reason the projects could not generate substantial net benefits. If you are employing idle economic resources (workers without jobs), their real economic costs (opportunity costs) would be substantially less than the monetary costs.[73]

Supporters of these changes should note that when the British Parliament tried to establish fair wages, business interests were severely critical and accused Parliament of interfering in commerce. Parliament was unpersuaded by the criticisms that businesses might close if they had to pay a decent wage. A 1908 committee of Parliament studying low-wage employment concluded:

> It is doubtful whether there is any more important condition of individual and general well-being than the possibility of obtaining an income sufficient to enable those who earn it to secure, at any rate, the necessaries of life. If a trade will not yield such an income to average industrious workers engaged in it, it is a parasite industry, and it is contrary to the general well-being that it should continue.[74]

Traditional thought will analyze the implications of a right to a job by merely superimposing the right to work on the current situation and focusing on all the difficulties it can cause.

Some will say, as President Warren G. Harding said in 1921:

> There has been vast unemployment before and there will be again. There will be depression and inflation just as surely as the tides ebb and flow. I would have little enthusiasm for any proposed remedy which seeks either palliation or tonic from the Public Treasury.[75]

But, our own individual well-being and the well-being of our nation are tied up with the poor who live and work in our midst who now earn poverty-level wages. If our well-being is at stake, then we will face the problem and figure out financially responsible ways to take the steps that are in our own best interest.

Amending the Constitution enshrines our common commitment to the principles that every person who wants to work should have that chance and that every person who works should be able to be self-supporting. By virtue of this amendment, these principles that are so widely held will move to the top of our national agenda and remain there as we as a nation move forward.

These are principles we agree with. This is the opportunity to align our national commitments with our principles. Amending the Constitution is a big step, but it is not unprecedented and the ways that it will work are familiar to all branches of government. There is no reason not to begin.

These are but a few of the answers to some of the practical problems of guaranteeing a right to a job at a living wage to each citizen. This is possible if there is the political will. The key is the national commitment to employment at living wages. A constitutional amendment would re-frame the debate from whether we can do it to how to do it. Any method chosen by Congress will be less than perfect—it will contain mistakes and will have to be modified, like all other human actions.[76] Will such an amendment cause problems? Absolutely. All efforts toward progress cause problems.[77]

In light of this nation's history, however, movement toward economic justice is possible. In light of this nation's history, it is time to take another step to advance the possibility that the American dream of self-sufficiency is indeed possible for every person willing to work.

14   The Way to End Poverty as We Know It

The time has arrived for us to take further action to extend the frontiers of social progress. . . . Our Nation so richly endowed with natural resources and with a capable and industrial population should be able to devise ways and means of insuring to all our able-bodied working men and women a fair day's pay for a fair day's work.
—Franklin D. Roosevelt, Address to Congress, May 24, 1937

MOST PEOPLE realize that our current system does not work very well for poor people, especially poor working people. We recognize that millions of people are working but are still poor. We want everyone to have the opportunity to work. And we want everyone who works to earn enough to support themselves and their families. But while most of us would like these things to happen, we do not know how to make them happen.

We know there are some problems for those trying to find work, but most people do not know there are approximately fifteen million people who are either out of work altogether or working part-time but would like to be working full-time. We know there are working poor people, but most people do not know there are thirty million people who are working but earning poverty-level wages. We know that the working poor have kids, and we are concerned about them and their families. There is a solution for these more than forty million people—a solution that will benefit all of the nation.

A constitutional amendment that guarantees every person the right to a job at a living wage can help our nation end poverty as we know it. Keep in mind that our Constitution is a living, changing promise to each other. It has been amended in the past, and it can be amended again.

Giving a job that pays a living wage to everyone who wants to work is a tall order, even if a majority of the people want to do it.

No one should underestimate the amount of work involved. Changing our current system to guarantee a job at a living wage to everyone who wants one will be a major undertaking. There are economic costs involved, and there will be lots of problems: administrative problems, political problems, and economic problems.

No one should underestimate the amount of conflict involved. Many powerful and influential people and institutions are quite comfortable with current economic arrangements because they benefit from them. Others are fearful of any significant change. Questioning the fairness and justice of the present system will prompt powerful counter-response, as it does in all campaigns for change.

Some will say it is unrealistic to expect social change in today's political and moral climate.

To those who say it is unrealistic to expect significant social change, I say, remember our history. If we take a quick look around, we may be discouraged. But if we take a longer look around, we can see that progress has been made. As Martin Luther King Jr. often said, quoting the abolitionist preacher, Theo Parker: "The arc of the moral universe is long, but it bends towards justice."[1]

Look what was achieved in the twentieth century. At the beginning of the twentieth century, young children labored in our nation's factories; today child labor is mostly prohibited. At the beginning of the twentieth century, our workers got paid whatever amount their employers would give them; today we have a minimum wage. At the beginning of the twentieth century, workers permanently injured on their jobs were fired, and they and their families were left to fend for themselves; today we have workers' compensation. At the beginning of the twentieth century, our parents and grandparents received no pensions or health care and had to rely on younger family members and charities to live; today we have Social Security and Medicare. At the beginning of the century, laws freely discriminated against the disabled, women, minorities, and people's religious beliefs; now our laws prohibit much of that.

Some will say that government should not be involved—government is not the problem, and government is not the solution. But, as historian Stephen Ambrose said, "The government was surely a solution in the Depression and in World War II and on the civil rights front and on providing a decent life for old folks in this country."[2]

All ideas for progress start out being dismissed as unrealistic, but if the arc of history does indeed bend toward justice, then we are indeed bending toward the right to a job at a living wage. We have made a national commitment to end welfare and push people to work. The next step is to guarantee people the right to a job at a living wage.

A guarantee of a right to work and earn a living wage will not end all poverty nor eliminate the need for all social and educational programs. There will still be people too disabled to work. New investment in education is very necessary to help people develop skills that will keep them out of the at-risk category of low-skilled workers.

But the fact that this amendment will not end all poverty does not mean it will not end poverty as we know it. It will end poverty as we know it. And the fact that there is still much to do in education and assistance for those unable to work does not mean we should not take the steps necessary to provide real work opportunities at living wages for those who can work.

Some people will say this idea will cost too much or violates the laws of economics. That is exactly what some people said when the end of slavery was called for. That is what people said when Social Security was first discussed. That is what people said when the child labor laws, minimum wage, unemployment insurance, Medicare, and protection for people with disabilities were first proposed. These ideas were called unrealistic, idealistic, impractical, and impossible. But, after thinking about it, Americans decided that getting government involved to help out was the right thing to do. And after some years of thought and debate, Congress made these ideas into law.

Progressive developments in law and government policy prove what President Woodrow Wilson observed: "Government is not a machine, but a living thing. It is accountable to Darwin, not Newton."[3]

So, what can one person do about ending poverty for the working poor?

First, think. We must allow ourselves to think. The most powerful act any of us can engage in is to allow ourselves to think in new ways. Is a guarantee of a job at a living wage consistent with our vision of what America should be about? Think about it.

Second, we must each learn more about ending poverty by giving everyone the opportunity to work their way out of it. Most people really do not realize the extent of poverty in this country, especially among those who work. We need to face up to that poverty and explore innovative ways to end it. Finances are also important. This book presented the thinking of respected economists who indicate that our economic system can accept the idea of full employment and living wages without wrecking our economic lives. But others will certainly dispute this. Because of my experiences as a lawyer, I know there are always other "experts" who, for a fee or for free, will dispute any opinion of any another expert. We must be willing to listen and learn.

Third, we must be prepared to engage in a thoughtful national debate about this idea. Certainly any change such as the one I have proposed will be provocative. Some will say it is long overdue. Others will say it is impossible and will wreck our nation and our economy. If history is any indicator, I expect that over time the public will slowly come to a majority consensus about the wisdom or folly of this idea. If we are serious about allowing people to work their way out of poverty, then this constitutional amendment makes sense. Others will think this is crazy. Working it out will take patience. Many people fear any change, however good or bad it may appear. Their fear will prompt them to try to scare others away from even considering this idea. Others are heavily invested in maintaining the current system where there is no right to a job or a living wage. They, too, will try to derail any real discussion. There will be dissension even among those who support the idea. Some will want to implement it immediately, others will want to proceed much more slowly. Thoughtful debate takes time, openness to considering new and different ideas, and a commitment to listening. That is a challenge for all of us.

Fourth, we must be prepared to take action. If, after engaging in thoughtful consideration and debate, the idea rings true, then the steps to make it happen must begin. The process of amending the Constitution is time-consuming, but for good reason. State and federal representatives must be convinced that amending the Constitution is in our national interest. Amending the Constitution is not a step they take lightly, nor should they. But it is a step that should be taken and will be taken once there is enough citizen support.

Once the right to a job at a living wage becomes a part of our national promise to one another, we will labor together to live up to our promise. Since we are all human beings, and our government is made up of people like us, our progress will take time and we will make mistakes. Success will not be instantaneous or immediate. But as we make the opportunity for a job at a living wage a reality, we can again take pride in our country's willingness to try to fulfill the promise of the American dream. The ability of people to support themselves and provide for their families will strengthen our local communities and our nation.

The time has arrived. We can, if we are willing, devise ways of ensuring that all our people have the opportunity to earn a fair day's pay for a fair day's work.

With a constitutional amendment guaranteeing a job earning a living wage to each person who is willing to work, we will end poverty as we know it for millions upon millions of American men, women, and children.

Notes

CHAPTER 1: WHY A RIGHT TO A JOB AT A LIVING WAGE?

1. Rose Gutfeld, "The Real Cost of Living: 'Self-Sufficiency' May Be the Next Frontier for U.S. Welfare Reform," Ford Foundation Report, Winter 2001, <www.fordfound.org/publications/ff_report/view_ff_report_detail.cfm? report_index=261>.

2. Kathryn H. Porter and Allen Dupree, "Poverty Trends for Families Headed by Working Single Mothers, 1993 to 1999," Table 3, Center on Budget and Policy Priorities, August 2001. A copy of the report is available at <www.cbpp.org/8-16-01wel.pdf>.

John Iceland, "Poverty among Working Families: Findings from Experimental Poverty Measures," September 2000, U.S. Census Bureau, Economics and Statistics Administration, Current Population Reports P23-203. Under other poverty guidelines, the percentage of poor people who live in working families increases.

3. U.S. Department of Agriculture, Food and Nutrition Service, Rules on Income Limits, <www.fns.usda.gov/fsp/applicant_recipients/income.htm>.

4. U.S. Department of Health and Human Services, 2002 HHS Poverty Guidelines, <www.aspe.hhs.gov/poverty/02poverty.htm>.

5. William Sloane Coffin, *A Passion for the Possible* (Knox, 1997), 36.

6. The 2001 poll was a national survey conducted by Lake Snell Perry & Associates in October 2001 for Jobs for the Future. Available through Richard Kazis at Jobs for the Future, (617) 728-4446, or Susan Kannel at Lake Snell Perry & Associates, (202) 776-9066.

The 2002 poll was conducted by Lake Snell Perry & Associates in January 2002 for the Ms. Foundation for Women. Available through Judith Selzer at Ms. Foundation for Women, (212) 742-2300.

7. "Brief History of Social Security," Social Security Online, <www.ssa.gov/history/briefhistory3.html>, and Ann Shola Orloff, *The Politics of Pensions: A Comparative Analysis of Britain, Canada, and the United States, 1880–1940* (University of Wisconsin Press, 1993), 158.

8. Statement of Franklin D. Roosevelt, 89 Cong. Rec. 4960 (1937).

CHAPTER 2: MYTHS AND FACTS
ABOUT POVERTY AND WORK

1. Lawrence Mishel, Jared Bernstein, and John Schmitt, *The State of Working America, 2000/2001* (Cornell University Press, 2001), 318.

According to researchers at George Washington University, in the 1990s 5.5 million poor people lived in families where there was at least one full-time, year-round worker; 14.5 million poor people, nearly 60 percent of all the nation's poor, lived in families where someone worked at least part-time; nearly 9.3 million workers were poor; of the working poor, 2 million worked full-time, year-round. Sar A. Levitan, Frank Gallo, and Isaac Shapiro, *Working but Poor: America's Contradiction* (Johns Hopkins University Press, 1993), 15–19, 46.

2. Bradley R. Schiller, *Economics of Poverty and Discrimination*, 7th ed. (Prentice Hall, 1998), 59–60.

3. Amy Waldman, "Long Line in the Bronx, But for Jobs, Not the Yankees," *New York Times*, October 20, 1999.

4. The official employment and unemployment figures are published monthly by the Bureau of Labor Statistics, U.S. Department of Labor, <www.bls.gov/schedule/schedule/2003/month_sched.htm>. The *Monthly Labor Review* is published by the Bureau of Labor Statistics (BLS) of the U.S. Department of Labor. In the "Notes on Current Labor Statistics," at the beginning of each month's report, the BLS advises that it does not count within its definition of employed or unemployed "discouraged workers, defined as persons who want and are available for a job and who have looked for work sometime in the last 12 months (or since the end of their last job if they held one within the past 12 months) but are not currently looking, because they believe there are no jobs available or there are none for which they could qualify."

The real numbers of unemployed people are usually reported in full on the web site of the National Jobs for All Coalition, <www.njfac.org/jobnews.html>.

For more on "discouraged workers" and others outside the labor force who want to work, see Monica D. Castillo, "Persons Outside the Labor Force Who Want a Job," *Monthly Labor Review* 121(7) (July 1998): 34. Castillo reported that in 1997, 4.9 million people fit this category.

5. See official poverty guidelines at the web site of the U.S. Department of Health and Human Services, <www.aspe.hhs.gov/poverty/01poverty.htm>.

6. Edith Rasell, Jared Bernstein, and Heather Boushey, "Step Up, Not Out: The Case for Raising the Federal Minimum Wage for Workers in Every State," Economic Policy Institute, Issue Brief #149, February 7, 2001, p. 2.

Other research organizations arrive at similar figures. For more information see the web sites of the Economic Policy Institute, Minimum Wage Facts at a Glance, <www.epinet.org/Issueguides/minwage/minwagefacts.html>, and Making Wages Work, <www.financeprojectinfo.org/mww/minimum.asp#strategies>.

7. Mishel, Bernstein, and Schmitt, *State of Working America, 2000/2001*, 325, Table 5.19.

8. In 1995, there were 36.4 million people in poverty in the United States. *Statistical Abstract of the United States, 1997*, 477, Table 741. According to the 1997 *World Almanac*, the populations of the countries mentioned, in millions, are: El Salvador, 5.8; Haiti, 6.7; Honduras, 5.6; Ireland, 3.5; New Zealand, 3.5; Nicaragua, 4.2.

9. In 1995, there were 36.4 million people in poverty in the United States. *Statistical Abstract of the United States, 1997*, 477, Table 741. The populations of the states mentioned, in millions are: Alabama, 4.2; Arkansas, 2.5; Iowa, 2.8; Kansas, 2.5; Kentucky, 3.8; Maine, 1.2; Minnesota, 4.7; Mississippi, 2.7; Nebraska, 1.6; North Dakota, .6; Oregon, 3.2; South Dakota, .7; Tennessee, 5.3. *Statistical Abstract of the United States, 1997*, 28, Table 26.

10. *Statistical Abstract of the United States, 2000*, 475, Table 754. In 1998, more than forty-six million people (17 percent of all people in the United States) lived below 125 percent of the poverty level. The number was as high as fifty-one million—a full 20 percent of the population—in 1993.

11. The additional populations of these states are, in millions: Delaware, .7; Hawaii, 1.1; Montana, .9; New Hampshire, 1.2; New Mexico, 1.7; Rhode Island, .9; Vermont, .6; West Virginia, 1.8; Wyoming, .5. *Statistical Abstract of the United States, 1997*, 28, Table 26.

12. Mishel, Bernstein, and Schmitt, *State of Working America, 2000/2001*, 325, Table 5.19.

13. "Summary: A Status Report on Hunger and Homelessness in American Cities—1998," U.S. Conference of Mayors. Available at <www.usmayors.org/uscm/homeless/hhsummary.html>.

14. *Statistical Abstract of the United States, 2001*, 441, Table 676.

15. "Study: Media Portrays Poor as Black," Associated Press, August 19, 1997, as cited in Gwendolyn Mink, *Welfare's End* (Cornell University Press, 1998), 161n58.

16. William Julius Wilson, *When Work Disappears: The World of the New Urban Poor* (Knopf, 1996), 66.

17. For example, in 1994, the median income for white families was $39,308; for black families it was $21,548. *Statistical Abstract of the United States, 1995*, 48, Table 49. For both whites and blacks, median income fell from 1990 to 1994: for whites it fell from $41,922 to $39,308; for blacks it fell from $23,550 to $21,548. *Statistical Abstract of the United States, 1995*, 48, Table 49. For Hispanic families, the 1992 median income was $23,912. *Statistical Abstract of the United States, 1995*, 51, Table 53. For American Indians the 1989 median family income was $21,619. *Statistical Abstract of the United States, 1995*, 50, Table 52.

Black men earned less, on average, in 1989 ($14,182) than in 1979 ($14,619), while the average earnings of white men increased (from $20,564 to $21,361), according to data from the U.S. Census Bureau. Lisa Saunders, "Relative Earnings of Black Men to White Men by Region, Industry," *Monthly Labor Review* 118(4) (April 1995): 68.

18. Relative income of African-American households held steady at about 60 percent of white income in the 1980s, but the relative wealth position of most black families deteriorated. In 1983, the median white family had eleven times the wealth of the median nonwhite family. By 1989, this ratio had grown to twenty. Middle-class blacks did succeed in narrowing the wealth gap with whites, but most nonwhite families moved even farther behind. More than one in three nonwhite households now have no positive wealth at all, in contrast to one in eight households. Edward N. Wolff, *Top Heavy: A Study of the Increasing Inequality of Wealth in America* (Twentieth Century Fund Press, 1995), 2.

19. *Statistical Abstract of the United States, 2000*, 475, Table 755. Since 1970, the poverty rate among all children in the United States has ranged from a low of 14.9 percent in 1970 to a high of 22 percent in 1993. In 1998, the child poverty rate was 18.3 percent.

20. *Statistical Abstract of the United States, 2000*, 475, Table 755.

Since 1970, the poverty rate among white children has ranged from a low of 10 percent in 1970 to a high of 17 percent in 1993. In 1998, the poverty rate among white children was 14.4 percent.

Since 1970, the poverty rate among African-American children has ranged from a low of 36.4 percent in 1998 to a high of 46.3 percent in 1992.

Since 1970, the poverty rate among Hispanic children has ranged from a low of 27.2 percent in 1978 to a high of 41.1 percent in 1994. In 1998, the rate was 33.6 percent.

21. Robert Pear, "Infant Mortality Rate Drops but Racial Disparity Grows," *New York Times*, July 10, 1995, p. A8.

22. *Statistical Abstract of the United States, 2000*, 476, Table 758. The poverty level for African Americans over age sixty-five was 26.4 percent in 1998 and for Hispanics over age sixty-five 21 percent.

23. Mishel, Bernstein, and Schmitt, *State of Working America, 2000/2001*, 306, Table 5.11, analyzed Census Bureau data and found that the poverty rate among female-headed households in the last year for which data was available was 33.1 percent. See also *Statistical Abstract of the United States, 1997*, 478, Table 742.

24. Jennifer Gardener and Diane Herz, "Working and Poor in 1990," *Monthly Labor Review*, 115(12) (December 1992): 20, note that while the working poor include more men than women, the poverty rate for women in the labor force was higher than that for men. The higher rate for women was largely the result of two factors: women were much more likely to head families on their own, and, on average, women supported their families with lower earnings than did men.

25. Paulette Thomas, "Success at a Huge Personal Cost," *Wall Street Journal*, July 26, 1995, p. B1.

In 1999, working women earned 76.9 percent of what working men did. Mishel, Bernstein, and Schmitt, *State of Working America, 2000/2001*, 127.

26. *Statistical Abstract of the United States, 2000*, 437, Table 752.

The gender-pay gap (defined as the ratio of women's to men's median annual earnings for full-time, year-round workers) has closed considerably in the past several decades. Paul Ryscavage, "Gender-Related Shifts in the Distribution of Wages," *Monthly Labor Review,* 117(7) (July 1994): 3, 6, footnote 15 (citing *Money Income,* B-37, Table B-10).

27. Jonathan R. Veum, "Interrelation of Child Support, Visitation, and Hours of Work," *Monthly Labor Review,* 115(6) (June 1992): 40. The composition of families has changed significantly over the past fifteen to twenty years. Families headed by women grew from 21.1 percent in 1970 to 31.1 percent in 1988. The growth in the number of such families is occurring for two reasons: there has been a large increase in marital separation and divorce, and there has been a rise in the number of unwed mothers. Research shows that young mothers who receive child support payments are more likely to work than nonrecipients and are apt to work longer hours and have higher earnings if their children are visited by their father; young fathers who pay child support are more likely than nonpayers to visit their children.

28. *Statistical Abstract of the United States, 2000,* 475, Table 755. In 1998, the child poverty rate was 18.3 percent.

29. *Statistical Abstract of the United States, 2000,* 476, Table 758. The poverty level of people over age sixty-five was 10.5 percent in 1998.

30. *Social Security Bulletin,* 1995 Annual Statistical Supplement, 163, Table 3E2. In 1995, 10.5 percent of the elderly were poor. *New York Times,* September 27, 1996, p. A11.

Older Americans are now the chief beneficiaries of federal money, receiving about a third of federal outlays, roughly $13,000 per person over age sixty-five per year. Robert J. Samuelson, *The Good Life and Its Discontents: The American Dream in the Age of Entitlement, 1945–1995* (Times Books, 1995), 143, 161.

31. *2000 Green Book,* U.S. House of Representatives Committee on Ways and Means, 1293, Table H-8.

32. Linda F. Alwitt and Thomas D. Donley, *The Low-Income Consumer: Adjusting the Balance of Exchange* (Sage Publications, 1996), 7.

33. "There have been significant changes in the welfare system, yet a rise in child poverty rates is now a real risk in the US." Jeff Madrick, Economic Scene, *New York Times,* June 13, 2002.

34. This is despite the tremendous widening of the gap between nations. "In 1820, the richest country had only three times as much income per person as the poorest; today, the richest nation has 30 times the income." Jeff Madrick, Economic Scene, *New York Times,* November 1, 2002.

To illustrate, one American or European consumes as much in food, goods, and services as forty-three Rwandans. John L. Allen Jr., "Make Globalization User-Friendly Is Catholic Plea," *National Catholic Reporter,* July 27, 2001.

More than one-fifth of the world's population, 1.3 billion people, live on less than a dollar a day. United Nations, *Human Development Report 2000* (Oxford University Press, 2000), 4.

35. Loretta E. Bass and Lynne M. Casper, "Are There Differences in Registration and Voting Behavior Between Naturalized and Native-Born Americans?" U.S. Census Bureau, Population Division Working Paper No. 28, February 1999, Table 1, Reported Voting and Registration among Citizens, by Nativity Status: November 1996. Available at <www.census.gov/population/www/documentation/twps0028/twps0028.html>.

CHAPTER 3: OUR HISTORY SHAPES OUR THINKING

1. Michael B. Katz, *In the Shadow of the Poorhouse: A Social History of Welfare in America* (Basic Books, 1986), 3–109; David J. Rothman, *The Discovery of the Asylum: Social Order and Disorder in the New Republic* (Little, Brown & Co., 1971), 180–205.

2. For a more detailed history of these English laws, see William P. Quigley, "Five Hundred Years of English Poor Laws, 1349–1834: Regulating the Working and Nonworking Poor," *Akron Law Review* 30(1) (Fall 1996): 73–128.

3. Statute of Laborers, 1349, 23 Edward 3rd (Eng.), Chapter 7, reprinted in *Statutes at Large,* Vol. 2, ed. Danby Pickering (London, 1762), 26, 29.

4. Quigley, "Five Hundred Years," 88.

5. Ibid., 92–98, discussing 22 Henry 8th, Chapter 12 (1531), and 27 Henry 8th, Chapter 25 (1536).

6. Children between the ages of five and fourteen who "live in idleness, and be taken begging, may be put to service . . . to husbandry, or other crafts or labours." Quigley, "Five Hundred Years," 97.

7. Ibid., 96.

8. English laws about poor people were codified in a comprehensive way in 1601 under Queen Elizabeth. Quigley, "Five Hundred Years," 100–103, discussing 43rd Elizabeth, Chapter 2 (1601).

9. William P. Quigley, "Backwards into the Future: How Welfare Changes in the Millennium Resemble Poor Law of the Middle Ages," *Stanford Law & Policy Review* 9 (1998): 101–13.

10. Those wishing more details on poor laws in these times should look, for starters, at: Walter I. Trattner, *From Poor Law to Welfare State: A History of Social Welfare in America,* 5th ed. (Free Press, 1994), and Sidney and Beatrice Webb, *English Local Government—English Poor Law Policy,* Volume 10, 1910, reprinted 1963.

My other works on the poor laws predating this time period include "Five Hundred Years"; "Work or Starve: Regulation of the Poor in Colonial America," *University of San Francisco Law Review* 31 (1996): 35; "Reluctant Charity: Poor Laws in the Original Thirteen States," *University of Richmond Law Review* 31 (1997): 111; "The Quicksands of the Poor Law: Poor Relief Legislation from 1790 to 1820," *Northern Illinois University Law Review* 18 (1997): 1; and "Rumblings of Reform: Northern Poor Relief Legislation in Antebellum America, 1820–1860," *Capital University Law Review* 26 (1997): 739.

11. See Joel F. Handler, *The Poverty of Welfare Reform* (Yale University Press, 1995); Michael B. Katz, *The Price of Citizenship: Redefining the American Welfare State* (Metropolitan Books, 2001); and Frances Fox Piven and Richard A. Cloward, *The New Class War: Reagan's Attack on the Welfare State and Its Consequences* (Pantheon Books, 1985).

CHAPTER 4: CURRENT OFFICIAL DEFINITION OF POVERTY

1. *Jacobellis v. State of Ohio*, 84 S. Ct. 1676, 1683 (1964), Stewart concurring.

2. See Theda Skocpol, *Protecting Soldiers and Mothers: The Political Origins of Social Policy in the United States* (Belknap Press, 1992), 105. See also William P. Quigley, "The Earliest Years of Federal Social Welfare Legislation: Federal Poor Relief Prior to the Civil War," *University of Detroit Mercy Law Review* 79 (2002): 157.

The government had promised pensions as incentives to soldiers who signed up for the war and stayed in the service. The pensions given by the federal government were modest and inadequate to support those who had been wounded so badly that they could no longer work. Therefore, in 1792 the federal government expanded the system of pensions for poor veterans and created our nation's first social welfare system. But, since many more people applied for these pensions than Congress had anticipated, a new federal law had to be quickly enacted to determine who among the veteran applicants was really poor and who was not. Thus, in 1792, we enacted our nation's first reform of its federal laws for the poor.

3. Pensions for life were authorized for those "disabled in the actual service of the United States, during the late war, by wounds or other known cause." 1 Stat. 243, Chapter 11, Section 2, March 23, 1792.

4. 1 Stat. 324, Chapter 17, February 28, 1793.

5. The law required medical certification by two court-appointed physicians or surgeons of "the nature of the said disability, and, in what degree, it prevents the claimant from obtaining his livelihood, by labor" and additional proof of the continuation of the claimed disability. Section 1, para. 3, p. 325.

6. Skocpol, *Protecting Soldiers and Mothers*, 67–152.

7. See the history of discussions about how many were poor, who was poor, and why in James T. Patterson, *America's Struggle Against Poverty, 1900–1994* (Harvard University Press, 1994), 78–125.

8. For more in-depth discussion of the many attempts to define poverty before Orshansky, see Gordon M. Fisher, "From Hunter to Orshansky: An Overview of (Unofficial) Poverty Lines in the United States from 1904 to 1965," available at <www.census.gov/hhes/poverty/povmeas/papers/hstorsp4.html>. A seven-page summary of the report is available at <www.aspe.hhs.gov/poverty/papers/htrssmiv.htm>.

9. Constance Citro and Robert Michael, eds., *Measuring Poverty: A New Approach* (National Academy Press, 1995), 24–25; Patricia Ruggles, *Drawing the*

Line: Alternative Poverty Measures and Their Implications for Public Policy (Urban Institute Press, 1990), 4–5. Orshansky used two prior government surveys. Federal researchers had surveyed families, learning that in prior years families generally spent about one-third of their income on food. Conducting surveys in 1955, the U.S. Department of Agriculture calculated the food-buying patterns of lower-income families and came up with four food plans. Of these the lowest cost was the "Economy Food Plan," which was designed for "temporary or emergency use when funds are low." The Social Security Administration (SSA) then multiplied the dollar figure for the lowest cost of the four plans by three and came up with an estimate of what income was required for a family to earn enough to eat. Initially, adjustments were made for the size of the families, the gender of the family head, the ages of the people in the family, and whether they lived in the city or the country; the SSA figured that country people did not need as much as city people because they could grow some of their own food.

10. Louis Uchitelle, "Devising New Math to Define Poverty," *New York Times,* October 18, 1999. The formula was based on a food budget intended to provide barely sufficient nutrition—and then only if "the housewife is a careful shopper, a skillful cook and a good manager who will prepare all the family's meals at home."

11. Rebecca M. Blank, *It Takes a Nation: A New Agenda for Fighting Poverty* (Princeton University Press, 1997), 10–12; Thesia I. Garner et al., "Experimental Poverty Measurement for the 1990s," *Monthly Labor Review* 121(3) (March 1998): 39, 40; Citro and Michael, eds., *Measuring Poverty,* 17, 24–31; Ruggles, *Drawing the Line,* 32–35.

12. See U.S. Department of Health and Human Services, <www.aspe.os. dhhs.gov/poverty/01poverty.htm>.

13. 2002 HHS Poverty Guidelines, <www.aspe.os.dhhs.gov/poverty/ 02poverty.htm>. There are slightly higher numbers for Alaska and Hawaii.

14. National Survey of American Attitudes towards Low-Wage Workers and Welfare Reform, conducted by Lake Snell Perry & Associates polling 1,001 Americans age eighteen and older, April 27–30, 2000. For more information about the poll contact Richard Kazis, Jobs for the Future, (617) 728-4446.

15. NPR/Kaiser/Kennedy School Poll, "Poverty in America," at <www.npr. org/programs/specials/poll/poverty>.

16. Uchitelle, "Devising New Math."

17. NPR/Kaiser/Kennedy School Poll, "Poverty in America," at <www.npr. org/programs/specials/poll/poverty>.

18. Press release, Ms. Foundation for Women, "Strong Majority of Americans Say Raise Minimum Wage to $8 and Agree Government Has Responsibility to End Poverty," February 12, 2002. Lake Snell Perry & Associates poll conducted January 2002. Available at <www.ms.foundation.org/press-021202.html> on the Ms. Foundation web site.

19. Jared Bernstein, Chauna Brocht, and Maggie Spade-Aguilar, *How Much*

Is Enough? Basic Family Budgets for Working Families (Economic Policy Institute, 2000), 2–3.

20. Greg Schrock, a researcher for the council, which works to attract companies and new jobs to Indiana, said, "We have to understand where the economy is moving in terms of job creation, and it is unrealistic to think that we will move away from the creation of lower-wage jobs in the service and hospitality industries." Uchitelle, "Devising New Math."

21. Ralph Ranalli, "Bill Offers New Gauge for Poverty: Backers Insist US Benchmark Doesn't Reflect Mass, Realities," *Boston Globe,* May 8, 2001.

22. Sidebar, *New York Times Magazine,* June 7, 1998, p. 75.

23. Uchitelle, "Devising New Math."

24. Blank, *It Takes a Nation,* 10–12; Thesia I. Garner et al., "Experimental Poverty Measurement," 39, 40; Citro and Michael, eds., *Measuring Poverty,* 17, 24–31; Patricia Ruggles, *Drawing the Line,* 32–35; Bernstein, Brocht, and Spade-Aguilar, *How Much Is Enough?,* 10–46.

25. John E. Schwarz, "The Hidden Side of the Clinton Economy," *Atlantic Monthly* 282(4) (October 1998): 8.

26. Ibid.

27. Ibid.

28. Ibid.

29. *2000 Green Book,* U.S. House of Representatives Committee on Ways and Means, 957–58.

30. Ibid., 958, Table 15–34.

31. 42 USC 2996 et seq; 45 CFR 1611.3, 1611.4 and 1611.5.

32. *2000 Green Book,* 808, Table 13–12.

33. Citro and Michael, eds., *Measuring Poverty,* 39–96.

34. Ibid., 247–92.

35. Garner et al., "Experimental Poverty Measurement," 39, 56.

The *New York Times* reported the views of the Census Bureau authorities: " 'It is certainly our opinion, and the opinion of every researcher we have talked to, that something should be done to update the poverty measure,' " said Edward Welniak, chief of the Census Bureau's Income Statistics Branch. The Census Bureau has started an experiment with a new poverty line that would have raised the 1999 income threshold for living above poverty to $19,500 for a family of four, from the official figure of $16,600 per family. As a result, 46 million Americans, or 17 percent of the population, could be recognized as officially below the line. "Sociologists and economists who analyze what people should earn to escape poverty in our country put the line even higher than the Census Bureau's measures. Published in July [of 1999], the Census Bureau's measures are already triggering a national debate. They set the threshold for a family of four somewhere between $21,000 and $28,000. The bureau's criteria rely heavily on a study by the National Academy of Sciences. Unfortunately, they don't allow cash for emergencies—auto repair, for example, or fixing a leaky roof, or health emergencies." Uchitelle, "Devising New Math."

CHAPTER 5: A NEW DEFINITION OF POVERTY

1. The oft-quoted line in the epigraph is taken from Adam Smith's 1776 *The Wealth of Nations*, where he discusses the differences between taxes on necessary consumable commodities and luxury consumables. The entire quote is worth noting, as it instructs on the changing understanding of the definition of poverty:

> By necessaries I understand, not only the commodities which are indispensably necessary for the support of life, but whatever the custom of the country renders it indecent for creditable people, even of the lowest order, to be without. A linen shirt, for example, is, strictly speaking, not a necessary for life. The Greeks and Romans lived, I suppose, very comfortably, though they had no linen. But in the present times, through the greatest part of Europe, a creditable day-labourer would be ashamed to appear in public without a linen shirt, the want of which would be supposed to denote that disgraceful degree of poverty, which, it is presumed, no body can well fall into without extreme bad conduct.

Adam Smith, *The Wealth of Nations* (1776; Modern Library Edition, 1937), Book 5, Part II, Article 4, pp. 821–22.

2. Patricia Ruggles, *Drawing the Line: Alternative Poverty Measures and Their Implications for Public Policy* (Urban Institute Press, 1990), xv.

3. Declaration of Independence, July 4, 1776, para. 2.

4. Universal Declaration of Human Rights, United Nations General Assembly Resolution 217A (III), December 10, 1948, Article 1.

5. Ibid., Article 22.

6. Ibid., Article 23, Sec. 1.

7. Pope John XXIII, "Peace on Earth," April 11, 1963, reprinted in *The Gospel of Peace and Justice: Catholic Social Teaching Since Pope John*, ed. Joseph Gremillion (Orbis, 1976), para. 11, p. 203; para. 18, p. 205; para. 20, p. 205.

8. Poll conducted January 2002 by Lake Snell Perry & Associates for the Ms. Foundation for Women. Available through Judith Selzer at Ms. Foundation for Women, (212) 742-2300.

9. The National Research Council suggested recalculating the poverty threshold upward to a range that is 9 to 53 percent higher than official current lines. Constance Citro and Robert Michael, eds., *Measuring Poverty: A New Approach* (National Academy Press, 1995), 154. In my view, these estimates are still too modest because they did not really look at what it costs to become self-sufficient and do not truly try to cover the costs of really living in simple dignity in this very rich nation.

10. Housing costs were based on the estimates of fair market rents given by the U.S. Department of Housing and Urban Development and varied dramatically in different parts of the country. Fair market rents include utilities (except telephone and cable) and are generally set at the fortieth percentile level of rents in the area—that is, 40 percent of rental units of this size would be less expensive and 60 percent would be more expensive. The 2002 HUD fair market rents

for a two-bedroom are $543 in Birmingham, $823 in Los Angeles, $873 in New Haven, $878 in Atlanta, $668 in Colorado Springs, and $616 in Kankakee, Illinois. That is approximately $6,500 to $10,000 a year in rental costs. (For more see <www.huduser.org/datasets/fmr.html.>)

Food costs were developed on the basis of the federal government's Low Cost Food Plan, which is about 25 percent higher and, according to the authors, more realistic than the Thrifty Food Plan, which is the basis for calculation of food stamps and the federal poverty threshold. No cost for takeout or fast food is included at all.

Child care costs were calculated on statewide surveys of the costs of licensed child care providers.

Transportation costs assume that the family will use public transportation if it is available. If not, HUD assumes that working adults need a car to get to work and thus transportation costs include gas, insurance, and a small allowance for maintenance, but not the cost of purchasing a car.

Health care costs assume that the worker is covered by employer health insurance. Costs include the employee's share of the health insurance premiums and out-of-pocket costs such as prescriptions, co-payments, and deductibles.

See <www.sixstrategies.org/sixstrategies/selfsufficiencystandard.cfm> for more information about how these self-sufficiency standards are calculated.

11. See Arizona self-sufficiency budget at <www.sixstrategies.org/states/stateproject.cfm?strStateProject=AZ>.

12. See California self-sufficiency budget at <www.sixstrategies.org/states/stateproject.cfm?strStateProject=CA>.

13. See Kentucky self-sufficiency budget at <www.sixstrategies.org/states/stateproject.cfm?strStateProject=KY>.

14. See New York self-sufficiency budget at <www.sixstrategies.org/states/stateproject.cfm?strStateProject=NY>.

15. See Texas self-sufficiency budget at <www.sixstrategies.org/states/stateproject.cfm?strStateProject=TX>.

16. Heather Boushey et al., *Hardships in America: The Real Story of Working Families* (Economic Policy Institute, 2001), available at <www.epinet.org/books/hardships.pdf>.

17. Connecticut General Statute Sec. 4-66e sets out the process for determining self-sufficiency, and Connecticut General Statute 31-111(10) defines the underemployed worker as a person whose education and skill limit their capacity to earn 100 percent of the self-sufficiency standard.

CHAPTER 6: THE EXTENT OF UNEMPLOYMENT AND UNDEREMPLOYMENT

1. "When the underemployed and those not statistically recognized are added, such as the disheartened who have abandoned the search for work, and the

homeless, perhaps one-eighth of the work force is directly adversely affected by unemployment." David L. Gregory, "Catholic Labor Theory and the Transformation of Work," *Washington and Lee Law Review* 119 (1988): 124.

2. John E. Schwarz, "The Hidden Side of the Clinton Economy," *Atlantic Monthly* (282)(4) (October 1998): 8.

3. Lawrence Mishel, Jared Bernstein, and John Schmitt, *The State of Working America, 2000/2001* (Cornell University Press, 2001), 221–22.

4. Official employment and unemployment figures are published monthly by the Bureau of Labor Statistics, U.S. Department of Labor. At the beginning of each month's reports, the BLS advises that they do not count within their definition of employed or unemployed "discouraged workers, defined as persons who want and are available for a job and who have looked for work sometime in the last 12 months (or since the end of their last job if they held one within the past 12 months) but are not currently looking, because they believe there are no jobs available or there are none for which they could qualify."

The real numbers of people unemployed are usually reported in full on the web site of the National Jobs for All Coalition (<www.njfac.org/jobnews.html>).

5. Robert M. Solow, *Work and Welfare* (Princeton University Press, 1998), 27.

6. Mishel, Bernstein, and Schmitt, *State of Working America, 2000/2001*, 220.

7. Rebecca M. Blank, "The Employment Strategy: Public Policies to Increase Work and Earnings," in *Confronting Poverty: Prescriptions for Change*, ed. Sheldon H. Danziger, Gary D. Sandefur, and Daniel H. Weinberg (Harvard University Press, 1994), 168, 170.

8. John D. Kasarda, "Jobs, Migration, and Emerging Mismatches," in *Urban Change and Poverty*, ed. Michael McGeary and Laurence E. Lynn Jr. (National Academy Press, 1988), 192. He goes on to note: "It is both an irony as well as a tragedy that we have such huge surpluses of entry-level labor in the inner cities at the same time suburban businesses are facing serious entry-level labor shortages" (192).

What can be done in the interim while the right to employment at a living wage is being considered? Kasarda sees a long-term solution of increased education but recognizes that such a solution will provide little benefit to those currently unemployed. He sees potential reversal of the economic and cultural isolation of the inner-city jobless with the adoption of the following strategies: "(1) computerized job opportunity network providing up-to-date information on available jobs throughout the metropolitan area, the region, and the nation; (2) partial underwriting of more distant job searches by the unemployed; (3) need-based temporary relocation assistance, once a job has been secured; (4) housing vouchers for those whose income levels require such assistance, as opposed to spatially fixed public housing complexes; (5) stricter enforcement of fair-housing and fair-hiring laws; (6) public-private cooperative efforts to van pool unemployed inner-city residents to suburban businesses facing labor shortages; and (7) a thorough review of all public assistance programs to ensure that they are not inadvertently anchoring those with limited resources to distressed areas in which there are few prospects for permanent or meaningful employment" (193).

9. "Working Hard, Earning Less: The Story of Job Growth in America," National Priorities Project 1999, p. 12. Available through the National Priorities Project, (413) 584-9566, or Jobs with Justice, (202) 434-1106.

10. Kasarda, "Jobs, Migration," 148, 189.

11. William Julius Wilson, *The Truly Disadvantaged: The Inner City, the Underclass, and Public Policy* (University of California Press, 1987), 43.

12. William Julius Wilson, *When Work Disappears: The World of the New Urban Poor* (Knopf, 1996), 19.

13. Leon H. Keyserling, "The New Deal and Its Current Significance," *Washington Law Review*, 59 (1984): 795, 797–98.

14. Glenn C. Loury, "Tenuous Trickle-Down," *New York Times*, May 29, 1999.

15. Lani Guinier and Gerald Torres, *The Miner's Canary: Enlisting Race, Resisting Power, Transforming Democracy* (Harvard University Press, 2002), 11–14.

16. Paul Offner and Harry Holzer, "Left Behind in the Labor Market: Recent Employment Trends among Young Black Men," released April 2001 by the Brookings Institution Center on Urban and Metropolitan Policy. The full report is available at <www.brook.edu/dybdocroot/es/urban/publications/offnerholzer.pdf>.

17. "Working Women Count: A Report to the Nation," U.S. Department of Labor, Women's Bureau, 1994; Mishel, Bernstein, and Schmitt, *State of Working America, 2000/2001*, 127.

18. Pat Swift, "A Way to Figure What the Pay Gap Will Cost You," *Buffalo News*, September 12, 1998.

19. Jacqueline Jones, *Labor of Love, Labor of Sorrow: Black Women, Work, and the Family from Slavery to the Present* (Vintage Books, 1985), 324. See also Jacqueline Jones, *The Dispossessed: America's Underclass from the Civil War to the Present* (Basic Books, 1992), 284–90.

20. Gwendolyn Mink, "TANF Reauthorization: An Opportunity to Invest in America's Future," Issue Brief No. 13, December 10, 2001. This presentation by Dr. Mink to the ADA Economic Policy Committee is available at <www.adaction.org/TANF.htm>.

21. For examples, see Guinier and Torres, *Miner's Canary*, 131–67.

22. Rebecca M. Blank, *It Takes a Nation: A New Agenda for Fighting Poverty* (Princeton University Press, 1997), 59–60.

23. In New Orleans, the city I live in, there are 5.1 low-skill people for each low-skill job available. Bruce Alpert and Bill Walsh, "Few Low-Skill Jobs," *Times-Picayune*, June 21, 1998.

24. Bradley R. Schiller, *Economics of Poverty and Discrimination*, 7th ed. (Prentice Hall, 1998), 59–60.

25. Amy Waldman, "Long Line in the Bronx, but for Jobs, Not the Yankees," *New York Times*, October 20, 1999.

26. Philip Harvey, *Securing the Right to Full Employment: Social Welfare and the Unemployed in the United States* (Princeton University Press, 1989), 14. Contrast this with Sweden, where the median rate of unemployment for the twenty-seven-year period from 1959 to 1986 was 2 percent, or West Germany where the median for the same period was 1.5 percent, or Japan where the median was 1.6 percent. Ibid., 13, Table 1.1.

27. Michael B. Katz, *In the Shadow of the Poorhouse: A Social History of Welfare in America* (Basic Books, 1986), 6.

28. Lester C. Thurow, *The Zero-Sum Society: Distribution and the Possibilities for Economic Change* (Basic Books, 1980), 203.

29. Solow, *Work and Welfare*, 24–32.

30. James Tobin, "Poverty in Relation to Macroeconomic Trends, Cycles, and Policies," in *Confronting Poverty: Prescriptions for Change*, ed. Sheldon H. Danziger, Gary D. Sandefur, and Daniel H. Weinberg (Harvard University Press, 1994), 147, 162.

31. William Vickrey, "Today's Task for Economics," *American Economic Review* (83) (March 1993): 1–10, cited in Sheila Collins, Helen Lachs Ginsburg, and Gertrude Schaffner Goldberg, *Jobs for All: A Plan for the Revitalization of America* (Apex, 1994), 10.

32. Herbert J. Gans, *The War against the Poor: The Underclass and Antipoverty Policy* (Basic Books, 1995), 133–34. Gans observes, and this author agrees, that all these projections could prove to be wrong, and if so, no one would be more pleased. See also Jeremy Rifkin, *The End of Work: The Decline of the Global Labor Force and the Dawn of the Post-Market Era* (G. P. Putnam, 1995).

33. Robert J. Samuelson, *The Good Life and Its Discontents: The American Dream in the Age of Entitlement, 1945–1995* (Times Books, 1995), 11.

34. Evelyn Nieves, "California Counties Pay Jobless to Move Away," *New York Times*, June 18, 2001.

35. N. R. Kleinfield, "The Company as Family No More," *New York Times*, March 4, 1996.

36. Christopher Farrell and Michael Mandel, "The Cold War's Grim Aftermath," *Business Week*, February 24, 1992.

37. Louis Uchitelle and N. R. Kleinfield, "On the Battlefields of Business, Millions of Casualties," *New York Times*, March 3, 1996.

38. Nina Munk, "Finished at Forty," *Fortune*, February 1, 1999, p. 50. This is not new. As Lawrence Mishel, Jared Bernstein, and John Schmitt show in *The State of Working America, 1996–97* (M. E. Sharpe, 1997), 19, in the period 1991–1993, during an economic recovery, 5 percent of the male workforce and 4 percent of the female workforce were permanently displaced from their jobs because of downsizing, closure of facilities, or permanent layoff. Most of these people found other jobs, but a fourth of those who had health insurance in their old jobs did not have it in their new ones. At the same time, middle-income families have seen their net wealth decline in the early 1990s, leaving less savings to cushion layoffs and periods of unemployment.

39. There is a good discussion of this problem in Gertrude Schaffner Gold-

berg and Sheila D. Collins, *Washington's New Poor Law: Welfare "Reform" and the Roads Not Taken, 1935 to the Present* (Apex Press, 2001), 222–26.

40. Jacqueline Jones, *The Dispossessed: America's Underclass from the Civil War to the Present* (Basic Books, 1992), 89–95.

41. Labor Department Report on Employment, April 2002, Table A-4. Selected employment indicators show part-time workers. Remember that Table A-10 tells the number of unemployed people who want to work but are not counted as part of the unemployed; in this monthly report they are another 4.5 million people.

42. Barry Bluestone and Bennett Harrison, *Growing Prosperity: The Battle for Growth with Equity in the 21st Century* (Houghton Mifflin, 2000), 91–92.

43. John Iceland, "Poverty among Working Families: Findings from Experimental Poverty Measures, 1998." U.S. Census Bureau, Economics and Statistics Administration, Special Studies, Current Population Report No. P23–203, September 2000. Under other poverty guidelines the percentage of poor people who live in working families increases.

44. Connecticut defines underemployed persons as workers earning wages that are not enough to allow them to become self-sufficient. See Connecticut General Statutes Sec. 4-66e and Connecticut General Statute 31-111(10).

45. Uchitelle and Kleinfield, "On the Battlefields of Business."

46. Michael B. Katz, *The Price of Citizenship: Redefining the American Welfare State* (Henry Holt, 2001), 317–40.

47. Solow, *Work and Welfare*, 35. See also ibid., 33–39.

48. Mark Weisbrot, "From Welfare to Poverty," *Sunday Journal* (Suburban D.C.), December 21, 1997, p. 8. Also available at <www.cepr.net/columns/weisbrot/welfare_reform.htm>

49. William Julius Wilson and Andrew J. Cherlin, "The Real Test of Welfare Reform Still Lies Ahead," *New York Times*, July 13, 2001.

50. Peter Edelman, "The Worst Thing Bill Clinton Has Done," *Atlantic Monthly* 279(3) (March 1997): 43.

CHAPTER 7: THE COST OF UNEMPLOYMENT AND UNDEREMPLOYMENT

1. Leslie Eaton, "Changing to Meet the Job Market," *New York Times*, October 20, 1999.

2. James Tobin, "Poverty in Relation to Macroeconomic Trends, Cycles, and Policies," in *Confronting Poverty: Prescriptions for Change*, ed. Sheldon H. Danziger, Gary D. Sandefur, and Daniel H. Weinberg (Harvard University Press, 1994), 147, 162.

3. William Vickrey, "Today's Task for Economics," *American Economic Review* (83) (March 1993): 1–10, cited in Sheila Collins, Helen Lachs Ginsburg, and Gertrude Schaffner Goldberg, *Jobs for All: A Plan for the Revitalization of America* (Apex, 1994), 10.

4. Philip A. Harvey, *Securing the Right to Full Employment: Social Welfare Policy and the Unemployed in the United States* (Princeton University Press, 1989), 51–52.

Unemployment is bad for those thrown out of work, who lose income and the nonpecuniary benefits of work. It is bad for society in general because of the loss of production. It saps people's confidence in the economic system when, as often happens during a depression, idling plants and unemployed workers coexist. Jon Elster, "Is There (or Should There Be) a Right to Work?" in *Democracy and the Welfare State*, ed. Amy Gutmann (Princeton University Press, 1988), 52.

5. Helen Lachs Ginsburg et al., "The Challenge of Full Employment in the Global Economy," 21. Available from the National Jobs for All Coalition, New York, (212) 870-3449.

6. Jared Bernstein and Ellen Houston, *Crime and Work: What We Can Learn from the Low-Wage Labor Market* (Economic Policy Institute, 2000), vii–viii.

7. Harvey, *Securing the Right*, 51–53, suggests the cost for the income maintenance programs for the unemployed is $1,000 per household per year, with another $1,600 per household annually in lost production and an incalculable amount for the suffering that results from lack of work.

8. "Economic Justice For All: Pastoral Letter on Catholic Social Teaching and the U.S. Economy" (U.S. Catholic Conference, 1986), 15.

Chapter 8: The Working Poor

1. Mishel Lawrence, Jared Bernstein, and John Schmitt, *The State of Working America, 2000/2001* (Cornell University Press, 2001), 129. The "poverty level wage" for 1999, the amount needed to earn at least the official poverty line for a family of four, was $8.19 an hour. Not every one of these workers is officially classified as poor, because there may be two earners in the family or there may be less than four people in the household.

2. Ibid., 129–32, Tables 2.10 and 2E.

3. Chapter 6 on unemployment and underemployment estimates that about 15 million people were out of work or working part-time but wanted full-time work. See Chapter 6, note 4.

4. See also John E. Schwarz, "The Hidden Side of the Clinton Economy," *Atlantic Monthly* 282(4) (October 1998): 8.

5. Eileen Appelbaum, ed., *Balancing Acts: Easing Burdens and Improving the Options for Working Families* (Economic Policy Institute, 2000). Also available at <www.lights.com/epi/virlib/Studies/2000/balancinga/entirebook.PDF>.

6. Dana Milbank, "Working Poor Fear Welfare Cutbacks Aimed at the Idle Will Inevitably Strike Them, Too," *Wall Street Journal*, August 9, 1995, A10. Who are the working poor? Fifty-six percent of people in poverty are in working-poor households; 20 percent of food-stamp recipients are from working-poor households; 43 percent of children on Medicaid are from working-poor families.

7. "The American Dream, Update," Summer 1999, published by Second Harvest. This twenty-page report is available by calling Second Harvest, (312) 263-2303.

8. Barbara Ehrenreich, *Nickel and Dimed: On (Not) Getting By in America* (Metropolitan Books, 2001), 16.

9. According to the Fair Labor Standards Act, employers are not required to pay more than this to tipped employees unless their total earnings fall below the minimum wage. Then the employer has to make up the difference. 29 CFR Sec. 531.59. See William P. Quigley, "Primer on Minimum Wage and Overtime Issues under the Fair Labor Standards Act for Low-Wage Workers and Their Advocates," *Clearinghouse Review* 925 (February 1996): 29.

10. Ehrenreich, *Nickel and Dimed*, 25.

11. Ibid., 25–26.

12. Ibid., 221.

13. "A Profile of the Working Poor, 1999." U.S. Department of Labor, Bureau of Labor Statistics, February 2001, p. 1, <www.bls.gov/cps/cpswp99.pdf>. In estimating the number of people who are both working and poor, the Department of Labor counts only those who worked more than twenty-seven weeks in the year and reports 6.8 million people.

14. Ibid., 5, Table 1, reports 5.387 million people worked fifty to fifty-two weeks and were still below the poverty level.

15. Ibid., 5, Table 1, reports 9.666 million total in the labor force but still below the poverty level, 6.796 million worked twenty-seven weeks or more, and 5.387 million worked fifty to fifty-two weeks.

16. Ibid., 2.

17. Mishel, Bernstein, and Schmitt, *State of Working America, 2000/2001*, 318. According to researchers at George Washington University in the 1990s: 5.5 million poor people lived in families where there was at least one, full-time, year-round worker; 14.5 million poor people, nearly 60 percent of all the nation's poor, lived in families where someone worked at least part-time; nearly 9.3 million workers were poor; of the working poor, 2 million worked full-time, year-round. Sar A. Levitan, Frank Gallo, and Isaac Shapiro, *Working but Poor: America's Contradiction*, rev. ed. (Johns Hopkins University Press, 1993), 15–19, 46.

It is also true, as noted earlier in Chapter 6, that millions of the poor do not work. Remember, half of the poor are children and elderly. Mishel, Bernstein, and Schmitt, *State of Working America, 2000/2001*, 318.

18. "Profile of the Working Poor, 1999," BLS, 1. While the majority of the working poor are white (70 percent), the rate of white workers (4.3 percent) who were both working and poor was significantly lower than for black (10.2 percent) and Hispanic (10.7 percent) workers. And working women (5.9 percent) were more likely to be working and poor than working men (4.4 percent).

19. Molly Ivins, "Old Issue of Pay Inequity for Women Just Won't Go Away," *Buffalo News*, May 8, 1999.

20. Shannon McCaffrey, "Minimum Wage Can't Pay Rent," *Wisconsin State Journal,* September 21, 2000. HUD, which calculates "fair market rents" for every region of the country, says people should not spend more than 30 percent of their income on rent. Using that standard, no full-time minimum-wage worker can afford an average rent in any county in the USA.

21. Michelle Krupa, "In Search of a Home: Crisis of the Working Poor," *Beacon News,* September 6, 1999.

22. Nina Bernstein, "With a Job, Without a Home," *New York Times,* March 4, 1999.

23. Jennifer Mena, "Poor Renters Find Shelter on Floors," *Orange County Register,* May 17, 1999.

24. Rick Wartzman, "How Minimum Wage Lost Its Status as a Tool of Social Progress in the U.S.: Washington Now Considers the Minimum Wage Law a Drag on Employment; Two Shifts for Pat Williams," *Wall Street Journal,* July 19, 2001.

25. Fran Quigley, "24 Hours of Welfare Reform," *NUVO Weekly,* January 13, 2000.

26. Deborah Leff, "Food for Thought, Update," published by Second Harvest, Summer 1999. For a copy of this report, contact Second Harvest, (312) 263-2303.

27. "The American Dream, Update," Summer 1999, published by Second Harvest. This twenty-page report is available by calling Second Harvest, (312) 263-2303.

28. Steven Greenhouse, "Low-Wage Jobs Leading Gains in Employment," *New York Times,* October 1, 2000.

29. Ibid.

30. Louis Uchitelle, "The Quiet Help of Family Members," *New York Times,* October 24, 1999.

31. Ibid.

32. Rebecca M. Blank, *It Takes a Nation: A New Agenda for Fighting Poverty* (Princeton University Press, 1997), 5.

33. "Summary: A Status Report on Hunger and Homelessness in American Cities—1998," published by the U.S. Conference of Mayors. Available online at <www.usmayors.org/uscm/homeless/hhsummary.html>.

34. Mishel, Bernstein, and Schmitt, *State of Working America, 2000/2001,* 129.

35. Jennifer M. Gardener and Diane E. Herz, "Working and Poor in 1990," *Monthly Labor Review* 115(12) (December 1992): 20. According to the 1990 census, the working poor were 5.5 percent of all persons in the labor force; 6.6 million workers in the labor force lived in families whose income fell below the current official poverty level. For about 3.4 million full-time wage and salary workers, their earnings were not enough to bring their family income above the poverty threshold.

Bruce W. Klein and Philip L. Rones, "A Profile of the Working Poor," *Monthly Labor Review* 112(10) (October 1989): 3–13, define the "working poor" as "persons who devoted more than half of the year to working or looking for work and who lived in families with incomes below the official poverty level" (4). They identified three major labor market problems that help create the numbers of working poor: unemployment, involuntary part-time work, and low earnings.

Levitan, Gallo, and Shapiro, *Working but Poor,* 15, cite working-poor data for 1991 that indicated 2.6 percent of all full-time, year-round workers were poor and another 7 percent of those with any work experience lived in poverty.

36. Joel F. Handler and Yeheskel Hasenfeld, *We the Poor People: Work, Poverty, and Welfare* (Yale University Press, 1997), 11.

37. "School Lunch and Breakfast Programs," *2000 Green Book,* U.S. House of Representatives Committee on Ways and Means, pp. 957–59.

38. *2000 Green Book,* U.S. House of Representatives Committee on Ways and Means, 958, Table 15-34.

39. Ibid., 376, Table 7-4.

40. Ibid., 247, Table 3-12.

41. "Profile of the Working Poor, 1999," BLS, 2. See also Mishel, Bernstein, and Schmitt, *State of Working America, 2000/2001,* 314–27.

42. Levitan, Gallo, and Shapiro, *Working but Poor,* 31.

43. "Economic Report of the President to Congress, 1998," *Transmittal to the Congress, February 1998* (U.S. Government Printing Office, 1998), 37.

44. Rick Wartzman, "How Minimum Wage Lost Its Status as a Tool of Social Progress in the U.S.: Washington Now Considers the Minimum Wage Law a Drag on Employment; Two Shifts for Pat Williams," *Wall Street Journal,* July 19, 2001.

45. In 1995 there were 22 million part-time workers, 4.5 million of whom wanted full-time work and couldn't get it, while nationwide the number of temporary workers tripled in a decade to 2.1 million. Peter T. Kilborne, "Even in Good Times, It's Hard Times for Workers," *New York Times,* July 3, 1995.

46. See Chapter 6, note 4 above.

47. Mishel, Bernstein, and Schmitt, *State of Working America, 2000/2001,* 318.

48. Robert J. Samuelson, *The Good Life and Its Discontents: The American Dream in the Age of Entitlement, 1945–1995* (Times Books, 1995), 11.

49. Louis Uchitelle and N. R. Kleinfield, "On the Battlefields of Business, Millions of Casualties," *New York Times,* March 3, 1996.

50. Over a ten-year period, from 1986 to 1996, the assets of Chase Manhattan grew by 38 percent, from $87.7 billion to $121.2 billion, while its workforce shrank by 28 percent, from 44,450 employees to 33,500. N. R. Kleinfield, "The Company as Family No More," *New York Times,* March 4, 1996.

51. "Working Hard, Earning Less: The Story of Job Growth in America," National Priorities Project 1999, p. 2. Available through the National Priorities Project, (413) 584-9566, or Jobs with Justice, (202) 434-1106.

52. Shera Dalin, "Rights Group Says New Jobs Don't Pay Living Wage," *St. Louis Post-Dispatch,* December 9, 1998, C1.

53. Ted Rohrlich, "Living Wage Movement Targets County Government,"

Los Angeles Times, November 4, 1998, B1. The county also recognized that these low-wage workers were using government services like free medical care and thus the government was subsidizing low-wage employers.

54. Professor Krueger found that workers who use computers on the job earn 10 to 15 percent higher wages than similar workers who don't and that women are more likely to be using them on the job than men. Alan B. Krueger, "How Computers Have Changed the Wage Structure: Evidence from Microdata, 1984–1989," *Quarterly Journal of Economics* 108(1) (February 1993): 33–60.

Median wages for high school graduates fell by 6 percent, adjusted for inflation, from 1980 to 1996 while those for college graduates rose 12 percent. Peter Passell, "Benefits Dwindle along with Wages for the Unskilled," *New York Times,* June 14, 1998, A1.

In real terms, the earnings of men who didn't graduate from high school declined by nearly 20 percent between 1979 and 1989, and by nearly 25 percent relative to college graduates. Maury Gittleman, "Earnings in the 1980's: An Occupational Perspective," *Monthly Labor Review* 117(7) (July 1994): 16.

Every year more than 20 percent of American youths drop out of high school before graduation, and overall drop-out rates top 40 percent. "The Parents Agree," *Wall Street Journal,* July 7, 1995, A8.

Lack of education is a factor, with workers having limited education falling farther and farther behind those with more education. In 1980, the typical male college graduate earned 80 percent more than the typical high school graduate; by 1990, that gap had nearly doubled. Robert B. Reich, *The Work of Nations: Preparing Ourselves for 21st Century Capitalism* (Addison-Wesley, 1992), 206.

Also, among men, the percentage of year-round, full-time workers in 1992 with low earnings was 31 percent for those without a high school diploma, and just 5 percent among those with a bachelor's degree. "The Earnings Ladder: Who's at the Bottom? Who's at the Top?" Bureau of the Census Statistical Brief, SB/94-3RV, June 1994, p. 2.

55. Rebecca M. Blank, "The Employment Strategy: Public Policies to Increase Work and Earnings," in *Confronting Poverty: Prescriptions for Change,* ed. Sheldon H. Danziger, Gary D. Sandefur, and Daniel H. Weinberg (Harvard University Press, 1994), 173.

56. Mishel, Bernstein, and Schmitt, *State of Working America, 2000/2001,* 152–60.

57. Peter T. Colborne, "Even in Good Times, It's Hard Times for Workers," *New York Times,* July 3, 1995, A1.

58. Nelson Lichtenstein, *State of the Union: A Century of American Labor* (Princeton University Press, 2002), x.

59. For examples of good campaigns that combine efforts of union organizing and racial justice, see Lani Guinier and Gerald Torres, *The Miner's Canary: Enlisting Race, Resisting Power, Transforming Democracy* (Harvard University Press, 2002), 131–67.

60. Lichtenstein, *State of the Union,* 246–76.

61. Ken Matheny and Marion Crain, "Making Labor's Rhetoric Reality," *Green Bag* 5 (Autumn 2001): 17.

62. Lichetenstein, *State of the Union,* 13, 16; U.S. Bureau of Labor Statistics, Bureau of Labor Statistics, <www.bls.gov/news.release/union2.nr0.htm>.

63. U.S. Department of Labor, Bureau of Labor Statistics, <www.bls.gov/news/release/union2.nr0.htm>.

64. Annette Bernhardt, Laura Dresser, and Catherine Hill, "Why Privatizing Government Services Would Hurt Women Workers," October 2000 report of Institute for Women's Policy Research. Available at <www.gao.gov/a76panel/hill1.pdf>.

The AFL-CIO reports that women union members earn 40 percent more than nonunion women. See "Working Women: Equal Pay—Facts about Working Women" at <www.aflcio.org/yourjobeconomy/women/factsaboutworking women.cfm>.

65. Barry Bluestone and Bennett Harrison, *Growing Prosperity: The Battle for Growth with Equity in the 21st Century* (Houghton Mifflin, 2000), 237–63; Jacqueline Jones, *The Dispossessed: America's Underclass from the Civil War to the Present* (Basic Books, 1992), 288–90.

66. William Julius Wilson, *When Work Disappears: The World of the New Urban Poor* (Knopf, 1996), 25–50.

67. Jones, *Dispossessed,* 284–85. See also Jacqueline Jones, *American Work: Four Centuries of Black and White Labor* (W. W. Norton, 1998), 369–82.

68. Jared Bernstein, Lawrence Mishel, and Chauna Brocht, "Any Way You Cut It: Income Inequality on the Rise Regardless of How It Is Measured." Briefing paper, Economic Policy Institute, September 2000, <www.epinet.org/briefingpapers/inequality/inequality.html>.

Not only did the gap between low-wage workers and high-wage workers widen, but the percentage of workers in the middle of the distribution thinned out, resulting in larger percentages of workers at the bottom and top. Wages for middle-income people have also leveled off. In 1999, according to MIT economics professor Lester C. Thurow, median family incomes hadn't risen since the early 1970s despite the fact that the average wife in a two-parent household was working fifteen more weeks a year than she did in the 1970s and real wages for 80 percent of the male workforce remained below where they used to be. Lester C. Thurow, "The Boom That Wasn't," *New York Times,* January 18, 1999, A19.

See also Paul Ryscavage, "Gender-Related Shifts in the Distribution of Wages," *Monthly Labor Review* 117(7) (July 1994): 3.

69. "Working Hard, Earning Less: The Story of Job Growth in America," National Priorities Project 1999, p. 11. Available through the National Priorities Project, (413) 584-9566, or Jobs with Justice, (202) 434-1106.

70. In 1996 the average CEO paycheck was 209 times that of a low-wage factory employee. Jennifer Reingold, "Executive Pay," *Business Week,* April 21,

1997. Compensation information for chief executives is available at <www.paywatch.org>.

71. Mishel, Bernstein, and Schmitt, *State of Working America, 2000/2001*, 208–12.

72. Steven Greenhouse, "A Rising Tide, but Some Boats Rise Higher Than Others," *New York Times*, September 3, 2000. In 1977 the richest 1 percent averaged $234,700 in after-tax income; in 1999 it was $515,600.

73. Blank, *It Takes a Nation*, 53–54. The oft-quoted phrase that "a rising tide lifts all boats" is attributed to President John F. Kennedy.

74. Glenn C. Loury, "Tenuous Trickle-Down," *New York Times*, May 29, 1999.

CHAPTER 9: LOW-WAGE WORK

1. Edith Rasell, Jared Bernstein, and Heather Boushey, "Step Up, Not Out: The Case for Raising the Federal Minimum Wage for Workers in Every State," Economic Policy Institute, Issue Brief No. 149, February 7, 2001, p. 2. Other research organizations arrive at similar figures. For more information see Economic Policy Institute, Minimum Wage Facts at a Glance, <www.epinet.org>, and Making Wages Work, <www.financeprojectinfo.org/MWW/asp>. In Louisiana, 13.3 percent of workers, or more than 226,000 people, would get a raise; in Mississippi, 12.3 percent of workers, or more than 137,000 people, would get a raise. State-by-state breakdowns of how many would have their wages raised are available in Rasell, Bernstein, and Boushey, "Step Up, Not Out," 4, Table 2.

2. Rick Wartzman, "How Minimum Wage Lost Its Status as a Tool of Social Progress in the U.S.: Washington Now Considers the Minimum Wage Law a Drag on Employment; Two Shifts for Pat Williams," *Wall Street Journal*, July 19, 2001.

3. 29 USC 206, PL 104–188, Sec. 2104(b).

4. William G. Whittaker, "RL30690: Minimum Wage and Related Issues Before the Congress: A Status Report," Congressional Research Service, January 24, 2001, available at <carper.senate.gov/acrobat%20files/rl30690.pdf>.

5. Economist Robert Pollin quoted in column by Alexander Cockburn, "Bill and Al Joust across a Moral Divide," *Seattle Times*, February 15, 2001. Robert Pollin and Stephanie Luce, *The Living Wage: Building a Fair Economy* (New Press, 1998), 1. Rasell, Bernstein, and Boushey, "Step Up, Not Out."

6. Wartzman, "How Minimum Wage."

7. For more on the minimum wage, its history, and its problems, see William P. Quigley, "'A Fair Day's Pay for a Fair Day's Work': Time to Raise and Index the Minimum Wage," *St. Mary's Law Journal* 27 (1996): 513.

The first state minimum-wage law in the United States was enacted in 1912 by Massachusetts and patterned on the British Trade Boards Act of 1909. Vivien

Hart, *Bound by Our Constitution: Women, Workers, and the Minimum Wage* (Princeton University Press, 1994), 14–62. For a brief history of the Massachusetts campaign to enact the minimum-wage law, see ibid., 66–72. Willis J. Norlund, *The Quest for a Living Wage: The History of the Federal Minimum Wage Program* (Greenwood Press, 1997), 11–14.

By 1938, the year the Fair Labor Standards Act (FLSA) was passed, many states had some form of a minimum-wage law.

Keith B. Leffler, "Minimum Wages, Welfare, and Wealth Transfer to the Poor," *Journal of Law and Economics* 21 (1978): 345, 346. Twenty-five states had in effect some form of minimum-wage regulation at the effective date of the FLSA. These states were: Arizona, Arkansas, California, Colorado, Connecticut, Illinois, Kansas, Kentucky, Louisiana, Massachusetts, Minnesota, Nevada, New Hampshire, New Jersey, New York, North Dakota, Ohio, Oklahoma, Oregon, Pennsylvania, Rhode Island, South Dakota, Utah, Washington, and Wisconsin. "Comment: The Federal Wages and Hours Act," *Harvard Law Review* 52 (1939): 646, 673, fn 203, citing 2 Wage & Hour Rep. 17–21 (Jan. 9, 1939).

8. Quigley, "Fair Day's Pay," 549–55.

9. Sar A. Levitan, Frank Gallo, and Isaac Shapiro, *Working but Poor: America's Contradiction,* rev. ed. (Johns Hopkins University Press, 1993), 49–50, calculate that 2.9 million outside sales workers and 10.8 million private nonsupervisory employees are outside the protection of the FLSA. Of these, 2.4 million workers paid by the hour earned less than minimum wage in 1991.

In 1984, 1.8 million people were reported as earning less than the minimum wage. These 1.8 million were estimated to be in industries such as outside sales work, low-volume retail trade and service firms, and seasonal amusement establishments. Earl F. Mellor and Steven E. Haugen, "Hourly Paid Workers: Who They Are and What They Can Earn," *Monthly Labor Review* 109(2) (February 1986): 20, 23.

10. Press release, Ms. Foundation for Women, "Strong Majority of Americans Say Raise Minimum Wage to $8 and Agree Government Has Responsibility to End Poverty," February 12, 2002. Lake Snell Perry & Associates poll conducted January 2002. Available at <www.ms.foundation.org/press-021202.html> on the Ms. Foundation web site.

11. Shannon McCaffrey, "Minimum Wage Can't Pay Rent," *Wisconsin State Journal,* September 21, 2000.

12. The 2001 poverty guidelines can be found at the web site of the U.S. Department of Health and Human Services. <www.aspe.hhs.gov/poverty/01poverty.htm>.

13. The Economic Policy Institute calculates "poverty-level wages" as those that would still leave a full-time year-round worker earning less than the poverty threshold for a family of four. In 1999 that meant that full-time year-round workers earned poverty-level wages if they made less than $8.19 an hour. In 1999, 26.8 percent of all workers—more than 30 million workers—earned less

than that. Lawrence Mishel, Jared Bernstein, and John Schmitt, *The State of Working America, 2000/2001* (Cornell University Press, 2001), 325, Table 5.19.

14. Marlene Kim, "Women Paid Low Wages: Who They Are and Where They Work," *Monthly Labor Review* 23(9) (September 2000): 26.

15. Food stamp eligibility guidelines are available on the web site for the U.S. Department of Agriculture. <www.fns.usda.gov/fsp/faqs.htm#6>.

16. "Summary: A Status Report on Hunger and Homelessness in American Cities—1998," published by the U.S. Conference of Mayors. Available online at <www.usmayors.org/uscm/homeless/hhsummary.html>.

17. For more information on EITC eligibility guidelines see <www.irs.gov/individuals/article/0,,id=96406,00.html> on the IRS web site.

18. It is estimated that workers spend 30 percent of their income on housing. In a survey of fair market rents for two-bedroom apartments nationwide released in the fall of 2000, the National Low Income Housing Coalition found that a worker would need to work ninety-seven hours a week at the 2000 minimum wage of $5.15 an hour to afford rent and other basic necessities, or earn a living wage of $12.47 an hour. "Out of Reach: The Growing Gap between Housing Costs and Income of Poor People in the United States," Report of National Low Income Housing Coalition, Fall 2000, can be found at <www.nlihc.org/oor2000>

19. Michelle Krupa, "In Search of a Home: Crisis of the Working Poor," *Beacon News,* September 6, 1999.

20. Women's Educational and Industrial Union, <www.weiu.org/index.php?page=9>.

21. Steven Greenhouse, "Low-Wage Jobs Leading Gains in Employment," *New York Times,* October 1, 2000. Analysis of job growth in New York City by the Working Group on the New York City Low-Wage Labor Market, a team of economists from government and nonprofit groups, found the number of jobs paying less than $25,000 rose 22 percent, nearly four times as much as jobs paying $25,000 to $75,000.

22. William Julius Wilson and Andrew J. Cherlin, "The Real Test of Welfare Reform Still Lies Ahead," *New York Times,* July 13, 2001, note that many of the people who left welfare have traded one type of poverty—nonworking—for working poverty.

23. In 1834 the English Parliament enacted another reform of the poor laws, the Poor Law Amendment Act of 1834. This act made many fundamental changes in the English system of poor relief.

24. "Study Says Welfare Switch Slighted Young," *New York Times,* April 16, 2002. A three-state study found that mothers who left welfare now earn more than while on welfare but still remain in poverty.

Jodi Wilgoren, "After Welfare, Working Poor Still Struggle, Report Finds," *New York Times,* April 25, 2002. Twenty-four studies covering seven midwestern states found that the states shrunk their welfare rolls but that former recipients remained mired in poverty.

See also Sheldon Danziger et al., "Does It Pay to Move from Welfare to Work?" Joint Center for Poverty Research Policy Brief 4(4) (2002). This can be found at <www.jcpr.org/policybriefs/vol4_num4.html>.

Chapter 10: A Constitutional Amendment

1. William P. Quigley, "The Right to Work and Earn a Living Wage: A Proposed Constitutional Amendment," *New York City Law Review* 2 (1998): 139. See also William P. Quigley, "The Right to Work and Earn a Living Wage: A Proposed Amendment to the U.S. Constitution," *Blueprint for Social Justice* 50 (May 1997).

2. Adolph Reed Jr., "A New Minimum: $10 an Hour," *Progressive* 61(4) (April 1, 1997); Adolph Reed Jr., "A Right to a Job—By Constitutional Amendment," *People's Tribune*, June 1998, <www.lrna.org/league/PT/PT.1998.06/PT.1998.06.3.html>.

3. David G. Gil, "Full Employment: The 'Supreme Law of the Land,'" National Jobs for All Coalition, May 1995, <www.njfac.org/us6.htm>; Philip Harvey, *Securing the Right To Employment: Social Welfare Policy and the Unemployed in the United States* (Princeton University Press, 1989); Philip Harvey, "Employment as a Human Right," in *Sociology and the Public Agenda*, ed. William Julius Wilson (Sage Publications 1993), 351–74; Philip Harvey, "Fashioning a Work-Based Strategy for Welfare Reform Based on International Human Rights Doctrine," *Journal of Public Health Policy* 16 (1995): 269.

4. Jesse L. Jackson Jr. and Frank E. Watkins, *A More Perfect Union: Advancing New American Rights* (Welcome Rain Press, 2001), 252–84; Gertrude Schaffner Goldberg and Sheila D. Collins, *Washington's New Poor Law: Welfare "Reform" and the Roads Not Taken, 1935 to the Present* (Apex Press, 2001), 290–312; Helen Lachs Ginsburg et al., "The Challenge of Full Employment in the Global Economy," available from National Jobs for All Coalition, (212) 870-3449.

5. Herbert J. Gans, *The War against the Poor: The Underclass and Antipoverty Policy* (Basic Books, 1995), unpaginated.

6. Alexander Hamilton, *The Federalist* No. 78 at 2:296 (1788), in Fred R. Shapiro, *Oxford Dictionary of American Legal Quotations* (Oxford University Press, 1993), 58.

7. *Cohens v. Virginia*, 19 U.S. (6 Wheat.) 264, 389 (1821).

8. U.S. Constitution, Article V.

9. Dale Bumpers, "How the Sunshine Harmed Congress," *New York Times*, January 3, 1999, p. 9.

10. After *Reynolds v. Simms*, 377 U.S. 533 (1964) and *Baker v. Carr*, 369 U.S. 186 (1962), thirty-two states, only two fewer than necessary under Article V, petitioned Congress to call a convention for the purpose of overruling the decisions. David R. Dow, "When Words Mean What We Believe They Say," *Iowa Law Review* 76 (1990): 41.

Judith Elder, "Article V, Justifiability, and the Equal Rights Amendment," *Oklahoma Law Review* 31 (1978): 63; Ruth Bater Ginsburg, "Ratification of the Equal Rights Amendment: A Question of Time," *Texas Law Review* 57 (1979): 919.

When the Supreme Court ruled in *Texas v. Johnson*, 488 U.S. 884 (1989) that flag burning constituted protected speech, calls for amending the Constitution were raised. On June 28, 1995, the U.S. House of Representatives, by a vote of 312 to 120, reversed an earlier vote in 1990 and endorsed a proposed constitutional amendment that would permit Congress and the states to outlaw physical desecration of the American flag. The amendment reads: "The Congress and the states shall have the power to prohibit the physical desecration of the flag of the United States." The amendment was supported by resolutions from all states except Vermont. Kenneth J. Cooper, "House Approves Amendment on Flag Desecration," *Washington Post*, June 29, 1995, A7.

11. Charles Brown, "A Constitutional Amendment for a Right to Earn a Living," *Guild Practitioner* 56 (1999): 109, suggests that such an amendment will take a mass movement to implement.

12. Those who wish to search further into these questions should look at the following articles: Akhil Reed Amar, "The Consent of the Governed: Constitutional Amendment Outside of Article V," *Columbia Law Review* 457 (1994): 94; Akhil Reed Amar, "Philadelphia Revisited: Amending the Constitution Outside Article V," *University of Chicago Law Review* 1043 (1988): 55; Michael Stokes Paulsen, "A General Theory of Article V: The Constitutional Lessons of the Twenty-Seventh Amendment," *Yale Law Journal* 677 (1993): 103; and Dow, "When Words Mean," 76.

13. Kathleen M. Sullivan, "What's Wrong with Constitutional Amendments?" in *New Federalist Papers: Essays in Defense of the Constitution,* ed. Alan Brinkley, Nelson Polsby, and Kathleen M. Sullivan (1997), 64–65.

14. Michael Novak, "What Wealth Gap?" *Wall Street Journal,* July 11, 1995, A14.

15. "What is at stake here is the different perceptions of human rights that seem to prevail in the North and the South. Westerners tend to afford special prominence to civil and political rights—at the expense of economic, social and cultural rights and of the right to development. Civil and political rights are the ones that were initially identified by Western political philosophers. They were the rights that were known when the United States was established and which found their way into the American Bill of Rights. Economic, social, and cultural rights, on the other hand, traditionally received special emphasis in socialist countries and—to add to Western skepticism—are often referred to as 'red rights.'" Johan D. van der Vyver, "Book Review: Human Rights in the Twenty-First Century: A Global Challenge," *Emory International Law Review* 787 (1993): 799.

16. Robert E. Rodes, *Law and Liberation* (University of Notre Dame Press, 1986), 12–13.

17. Professor Tribe, after noting the debt owed to Professor Frank Michelman for groundbreaking effort to define such a doctrine in Michelman, "The Supreme Court, 1968 Term—Foreword: On Protecting the Poor through the Fourteenth Amendment," *Harvard Law Review* 7 (1969): 83, suggests:

> I am convinced that, despite its difficulties, a doctrine will ultimately emerge that recognizes under the fifth and fourteenth amendments constitutional rights to decent levels of affirmative governmental protection in meeting the basic human needs of physical survival and security, health and housing, employment and education.

Laurence H. Tribe, "Unraveling National League of Cities: The New Federalism and Affirmative Rights to Essential Governmental Services," *Harvard Law Review* 90 (1977): 1065, 1065–66.

"[T]he basic principle that would have to be established is that the liberty protected by due process includes a right to a job; or . . . more concretely, that the citizenry have property rights in jobs." Arthur Miller, "Toward Recognition of a Constitutional Right to a Job," in *Politics, Democracy and the Supreme Court: Essays on the Frontier of Constitutional Theory* (Greenwood Publishing, 1985), 330.

18. See, e.g., Peter B. Edelman, "The Next Century of Our Constitution: Rethinking Our Duty to the Poor," *Hastings Law Journal* 39 (1987): 1 (substantive due process and equal protection); Charles Black, "Further Reflections on the Constitutional Justice of Livelihood," *Columbia Law Review* 86 (1986): 1103 (Declaration of Independence, Preamble to the Constitution, and the Ninth Amendment); Laurence H. Tribe, *American Constitutional Law* (Foundation Press, 1978), 573–1178; Michelman, "The Supreme Court," 7.

Kenneth L. Karst, in "Foreword: Equal Citizenship under the Fourteenth Amendment," *Harvard Law Review* 91 (1997): 1, and *Belonging to America: Equal Citizenship and the Constitution* (Yale University Press, 1989), 125–46, suggests a denial of equal citizenship by chronic unemployment and poverty.

For examples of the opposite view, see Ralph K. Winter Jr., "Poverty, Economic Equality, and the Equal Protection Clause," in *Supreme Court Review 1972*, ed. Philip B. Kurland (University of Chicago Press, 1973), 41; and Robert H. Bork, "Commentary: The Impossibility of Finding Welfare Rights in the Constitution," *Washington University Law Quarterly* (Summer 1979): 695.

19. "Experience suggests that in fact there will be a systematic bias in judicial choice of fundamental values, unsurprisingly in favor of the values of the upper-middle, professional class from which most lawyers and judges, and for that matter most moral philosophers, are drawn. . . . But watch most fundamental-rights theorists start edging toward the door when someone mentions jobs, food, or housing: these are important, sure, but they aren't fundamental." John Hart Ely, *Democracy and Distrust: A Theory of Judicial Review* (Harvard University Press, 1980), 58–59.

For a more detailed overview of the history of an understanding of the right to work, see William E. Forbath, "Why Is This Rights Talk Different from All Other Rights Talk? Demoting the Court and Reimagining the Constitution,"

Stanford Law Review 46 (1994): 1771, 1793–804. See also Theda Skocpol, *The Missing Middle: Working Families and the Future of American Social Policy* (W. W. Norton, 2000), 234.

20. Gil, "Full Employment." Professor Gil argues that the 1945 ratification of the UN charter makes the charter's right to employment part of the "Supreme Law of the Land."

For more discussion of the importance of employment and human rights, see Richard Lewis Siegel, *Employment and Human Rights* (University of Pennsylvania Press, 1994), and Joseph Wronka, *Human Rights and Social Policy in the 21st Century* (University Press of America, 1992).

21. See Chapters 11 and 12 on governmental and political support for a right to a job and a right to living wages.

22. These approaches include legislation seeking improvements in education for children so present trends can be reversed, cutting social programs off for those who do not work, increased minimum wages and/or income support for those who work, training for unemployed adults, incentives for private employers to hire the unemployed, more rigorous enforcement of civil rights laws in the area of housing and hiring, and public employment. See Rebecca M. Blank, *It Takes a Nation: A New Agenda for Fighting Poverty* (Princeton University Press, 1997), 199–204; Gans, *War against the Poor*, 135–47; John D. Kasarda, "Jobs, Migration, and Emerging Mismatches," in *Urban Change and Poverty*, ed. Michael McGeary and Laurence E. Lynn Jr. (National Academy Press, 1988), 188–95; William Julius Wilson, *The Truly Disadvantaged: The Inner City, the Underclass, and Public Policy* (University of Chicago Press, 1987), 180–87.

CHAPTER 11: SUPPORT FOR A RIGHT TO A JOB

1. "The Fortune Survey," *Fortune* 12(1) (July 1935): 67.

2. Robert Y. Shapiro et al., "The Polls—A Report: Employment and Social Welfare," *Public Opinion Quarterly* (51) (1987): 268, 274. In 1956, 56 percent agreed; in 1958, 57 percent agreed; in 1960, 58 percent agreed; in March 1976, 67 percent agreed; in April 1976, 69 percent agreed; and in May 1976, 70 percent agreed.

3. The first question asked by the pollsters was: "As you may know, there is talk about giving every family an income of at least $3,200 a year, which would be for a family of four. If the family earns less than this, the government would make up the difference. Would you favor or oppose such a plan?" This was rejected by 58 percent who said "no," with 36 percent saying "yes" in June 1968. In January 1969, 62 percent said "no" and 32 percent said "yes."

The second question was: "Another proposal is to guarantee enough work so that each family that has an employable wage earner would be guaranteed enough work each week to give him a wage of about $60 a week, or $3,200 a year. Would you favor or oppose such a plan?" This was supported by 78 percent (with 18 percent opposed) in June 1988 and 79 percent (with 16 percent opposed) in January 1969. *Gallup Opinion Index,* No. 38 (July 1968): 23–24, and *Gallup Opinion Index,* No. 43 (January 1969): 20–21. The $3,200 figure was the poverty threshold for a family of four in 1965.

4. E. J. Dionne, "Poll Finds Reagan Support Down but Democrats Still Lacking Fire," *New York Times,* December 1, 1987, A1.

5. Robert Shapiro and J. T. Young, "Public Opinion and the Welfare State: The United States in Comparative Perspective," *Political Science Quarterly* 104 (1989): 59–87, as cited in Lawrence Bobo and Ryan A. Smith "Antipoverty Policy, Affirmative Action, and Racial Attitudes," in *Confronting Poverty: Prescriptions for Change,* ed. Sheldon H. Danziger, Gary D. Sandefur, and Daniel H. Weinberg (Harvard University Press, 1994), 367.

6. "Opinion Outlook," *National Journal* (June 20, 1992): 1486, as cited in Sar A. Levitan, Frank Gallo, and Isaac Shapiro, *Working but Poor: America's Contradiction,* rev. ed. (Johns Hopkins University Press, 1993), 144, footnote 3.

7. *The Gallup Poll Monthly,* Number 351, page 33, December 1994. In April 1994, 60 percent approved, and in December 1994, 54 percent approved.

8. A national survey conducted by Lake Snell Perry & Associates in October 2001 for Jobs for the Future. Available through Richard Kazis at Jobs for the Future, (617) 728-4446, or Susan Kannel at Lake Snell Perry & Associates, (202) 776-9066.

9. 27 Henry 8, Chapter 25, Section 1 (Eng.) (1536), reprinted in *Statutes at Large,* Vol. 4, ed. Danby Pickering (London, 1762), 387. For more see William P. Quigley, "Five Hundred Years of English Poor Laws, 1349–834: Regulating the Working and Nonworking Poor," *Akron Law Review* 30 (1996): 96–98. Even poor beggar children under fourteen years of age could "be put to service . . . to husbandry, or other crafts or labors." 27 Henry 8, Chapter 25, Section 6 (Eng.) (1536), *Statutes at Large,* Vol. 4, ed. Danby Pickering (London, 1762).

Some social welfare scholars suggest this was the first crude creation of a public works project. Walter I. Trattner, *From Poor Law to Welfare State: A History of Social Welfare in America,* 6th ed. (Free Press, 2001), 9.

10. Those who were too disabled to work were to be supported by local government. These were "the lame, impotent, old, blind and such other among them, being poor and unable to work." Those who were poor and unemployed but able to work were to be set to work by local government. Taxes were to be levied to provide materials such as "flax, hemp, wool, thread, iron, and other necessary ware and stuff" so that the local unemployed could have work to do. 43 Elizabeth, Chapter 2 (Eng.) (1601), *Statutes at Large,* Vol. 7, ed. Danby Pickering (London, 1762), 37. See Quigley, "Five Hundred Years," 100–103.

11. Order of 1636, 1 Massachusetts Bay Records 186 (Shurtleff ed. 1853), as cited in Stefan A. Riesenfeld, "The Formative Era of American Public Assistance," *California Law Review* 43 (1955): 175, 206.

12. See discussion in William P. Quigley, "Work or Starve: Regulation of the Poor in Colonial America," *University of San Francisco Law Review* 31 (1996): 35–54.

13. Thomas Paine, *The Rights of Man* (1791), Part 2, Chapter 5, reprinted in Michael Foot and Isaac Kramnick, eds., *The Thomas Paine Reader* (Penguin Books, 1987), 339–40. For Paine's plan, see p. 340.

14. See specific state laws described in William P. Quigley, "Reluctant Charity: Poor Laws in the Original Thirteen States," *University of Richmond Law Review* 31 (1997): 111, 152–60.

15. Leah Hannah Feder, *Unemployment Relief in Periods of Depression: A Study of Measures Adopted in Certain American Cities, 1857 through 1922* (Russell Sage Foundation, 1936), 31.

This is not at all new to the United States. Others have suggested that there are grounds for thinking the Pyramids and the Temple of Jerusalem were public works projects to cope with joblessness. Peter Kelvin and Joanna E. Jarrett, *Unemployment: Its Social Psychological Effects* (Cambridge University Press, 1985), 1.

16. Theda Skocpol, *Social Policy in the United States: Future Possibilities in Historical Perspective* (Princeton University Press, 1995), 234.

17. Feder, *Unemployment Relief*, 288.

18. John R. Commons, *The Distribution of Wealth* (Macmillan, 1893; reprinted 1905), 80.

19. For more details see Philip Harvey, *Securing the Right to Employment: Social Welfare Policy and the Unemployed in the United States* (Princeton University Press, 1989), and sources cited in William P. Quigley, "The Right to Work and Earn a Living Wage: A Proposed Constitutional Amendment," *New York City Law Review* 2 (1998): 139, 143–66.

20. Josephine Chapin Brown, *Public Relief: 1929–1939* (Henry Holt, 1940), 64–65.

21. James T. Patterson, *America's Struggle against Poverty 1900–1994* (Harvard University Press, 1994), 53.

22. Bonnie Fox Schwartz, *The Civil Works Administration, 1933–1934: The Business of Emergency Employment in the New Deal* (Princeton University Press, 1984), gives an excellent well-documented overview of the CWA and FERA. See also Nancy E. Rose, *Put to Work: Relief Programs in the Great Depression* (Monthly Review Press, 1994).

23. Trattner, *From Poor Law*, 286–87; Schwartz, *Civil Works Administration*, 213. Schwartz points out that "Not until 1971 would a mere tenth of the 4 million jobless [employed by the CWA] enjoy the status of public employees" (vii–ix).

24. "In February 1934, the FERA, the CWA, and the CCC assisted about 8 million households with 22 million people or 22.2 percent of the American population." Brown, *Public Relief*, 160–61, 254–62. Trattner, *From Poor Law*, 285–87.

25. Harvey, *Securing the Right to Employment*, 99.

A companion program, the Civilian Conservation Corps (CCC), provided jobs to millions of young people from 1933 to 1942. The CCC, authorized in March 1933, put unemployed young people to work on reforestation and flood and fire control. Michael B. Katz, *In the Shadow of the Poorhouse: A Social History of Welfare in America* (Basic Books, 1986), 224.

By 1939, 0.8 million young Americans were working for the National Youth Administration and the Civilian Conservation Corps (CCC), and another 2.3 million workers were on the rolls of the WPA. Patterson, *America's Struggle*, 57. Skocpol, *Social Policy*, 169.

26. Annual Message to Congress on the State of the Union, January 4, 1935, 79 Cong. Rec. 94, 95–96.

27. Patterson, *America's Struggle*, 63. The WPA was given $1.39 billion in funding out of the total $4.54 billion allocated for relief.

The name of the WPA was changed to the Work Projects Administration in 1939. See history of the WPA in Katz, *In the Shadow of the Poorhouse*, 228–34. Patterson, *America's Struggle*, 63–64, puts the annual total on WPA jobs at a high of 3.5 million, around 30 percent of the 8 to 10.7 million unemployed.

28. Marvin Olasky, *The Tragedy of American Compassion* (Regnery Publishing, 1992), 158–59, notes that the WPA was known by its critics as "We Piddle Around" and "We Pay for All." Olasky, a severe critic of most contemporary social assistance programs, looks comparatively fondly on the WPA and finds evidence that it was both "benefit and boondoggle." He admires its attempts to "stress work and worthiness over relief" and its conscious attempts to work within "American values toward work and dependency" (159–61).

Patterson, *America's Struggle*, 63, notes that the WPA's "theater, arts, and writers' projects were bold ventures in government support of cultural activities."

Katz, *In the Shadow of the Poorhouse*, 230–34, details the criticisms of the supporters and detractors of the work relief programs. The administrative problems of putting millions of people to work in a very short time with no prior programs to learn from was an incredible challenge. The goals of the programs were mixed, including immediately putting people to work, many of whom were unskilled, but also employing people for constructive public projects, which demand planning and skilled workers. Since all could not be helped, should the programs help those most desperate (and least skilled) or those with skills who needed but a temporary job? Wages had to be above relief levels but could not politically challenge private wage levels. And these are but a few of the challenges faced.

29. Katz, *In the Shadow of the Poorhouse*, 229. In a 1939 executive reorganization, the WPA was folded into a new Federal Works Agency. Skocpol, *Social Policy*, 172. The CCC was ended by Congress in 1942, and after the 1942 election FDR called for the end of the WPA. Ibid., 174–75.

30. Trattner, *From Poor Law*, 289.

31. "Since then we have tried to walk on one leg only, only to hobble along with half a social welfare system." Harvey, *Securing the Right to Employment*, 20.

32. *The Report on the Committee on Economic Security of 1935, and Other Basic Documents Relating to the Development of the Social Security Act*, Fiftieth Anniversary Edition (Washington, D.C.: National Conference on Social Welfare, 1985), 23–24, quoted in Skocpol, *Social Policy*, 1995, at 229–30.

33. *Fortune*, July 1935 poll.

34. Skocpol, *Social Policy*, 236.

35. President Franklin Roosevelt, in his message asking for the enactment of the Fair Labor Standards Act. 81 Cong. Rec. 4960, May 24, 1937.

36. Alan Brinkley, *The End of Reform: New Deal Liberalism in Recession and War* (Knopf, 1996), 245–50; Steven Kemp Bailey, *Congress Makes a Law: The Story behind the Employment Act of 1946* (Columbia University Press, 1950), 26.

37. Brinkley, *End of Reform*, 249.

38. Bailey, *Congress Makes a Law*, 27, citing *New York Times*, March 11, 1943, 12. The list of all the rights includes:

> 1. The right to work, usefully and creatively through the productive years.
> 2. The right to fair pay, adequate to command the necessities and amenities of life in exchange for work, ideas, thrift, and other socially valuable service.
> 3. The right to adequate food, clothing, shelter and medical care.
> 4. The right to security, with freedom from fear of old age, want, dependency, sickness, unemployment and accident.
> 5. The right to live in a system of free enterprise, free from compulsory labor, irresponsible private power, arbitrary public authority, and unregulated monopolies.
> 6. The right to come and go, to speak and to be silent, free from the spying of secret police.
> 7. The right to equality before the law, with equal access to justice in fact.
> 8. The right to education, for work, for citizenship, and for personal growth and happiness.
> 9. The right to rest, recreation and adventure, the opportunity to enjoy and take part in an advancing civilization.

39. The NRPB, like previous New Dealers, regarded public works and public employment as the solutions to the unemployment problem. For those in need of steady work that the private economy could not provide, the federal government should provide a job. Skocpol, *Social Policy*, 174.

40. Harvey, *Securing the Right to Employment*, 106; citing U.S. National Resources Planning Board, National Resources Development Report for 1943, 78th Cong., 1st Sess., 1943, Doc. No. 128, Part 1, Post War Plan and Program, p. 17.

41. Skocpol, *Social Policy*, at 173–75.

42. 87 Cong. Rec. 46, January 6, 1941.

43. 87 Cong. Rec. 46–47, January 6, 1941.

44. State of the Union Address, 90 Cong. Rec 55, 57, January 11, 1944.

45. 90 Cong. Rec. 57, January 11, 1944. The complete "second bill of rights" proposed by FDR includes:

> The right to a useful and remunerative job in the industries or shops or farms or mines of the Nation;
> The right to earn enough to provide adequate food and clothing and recreation;
> The right of every farmer to raise and sell his products at a return which will give him and his family a decent living;
> The right of every business man, large and small, to trade in an atmosphere of freedom from unfair competition and domination by monopolies at home or abroad;

The right of every family to a decent home;

The right to adequate medical care and the opportunity to achieve and enjoy good health;

The right to adequate protection from the economic fears of old age, sickness, accident, and unemployment;

The right to a good education.

90 Cong. Rec. 57, January 11, 1944.

46. "Unemployment has been practically abolished twice in the lives of most of us—in the last war and in this war. Why does war solve the problem of unemployment which is so unsolvable in peace?" William H. Beveridge, *The Pillars of Security* (New York, 1943), 51, cited in Bailey, *Congress Makes a Law*, 9, footnote 13.

47. Activating the government to make sure everyone had a job was an idea that was increasingly being considered by elected officials and economists in the United States and Great Britain. William H. Beveridge, *Full Employment in a Free Society* (Great Britain, 1944).

48. "The Democratic Party stands on its record in peace and war. To speed victory, establish and maintain peace, guarantee full employment and provide prosperity." *New York Times*, July 21, 1944, 12, quoted in Bailey, *Congress Makes a Law*, 41.

49. "Gov. Dewey's Address in San Francisco Asking for Political Freedom with Security," *New York Times*, September 22, 1944, 13.

50. By late 1944, a coalition of people representing the interests of Senator James Murray of Montana, Senator Harley Kilgore of West Virginia, the National Farmers Union, and various governmental agencies began drafting a Full Employment Bill. Bailey, *Congress Makes a Law*, 36–59.

51. Section 2(a) of proposed Full Employment Act of 1945, 91 Cong. Rec. 377, January 22, 1945, 79 Cong., 1st Sess., S. 380.

S. 380 was introduced into the U.S. Senate on January 22, 1945, by Senator James E. Murray. Cong. Rec., 79th Cong., 1st Sess., January 22, 1945, p. 377. S. 380 is profiled in Bailey, *Congress Makes a Law*, 47.

52. Remarks of Senator Murray on the occasion of introducing the proposed Full Employment Act of 1945, 91 Cong. Rec. 377, 381, January 22, 1945.

For more on the 1946 Full Employment Act, see Bailey, *Congress Makes a Law*.

53. Full Employment Act of 1945, 91 Cong. Rec. 377–78. Brinkley, *End of Reform*, 261.

Harvey, *Securing the Right*, 108, sees the original bill as a reflection of the growing ascendancy of a more conservative Keynesian economists over the liberal New Deal strategies contained in the NPRB plan, i.e., "Postwar Keynesianism promised full employment without the need to tamper with the microeconomic structure of the economy" (108).

54. Questions and Answers on the Full Employment Bill, Question 2, 91 Cong. Rec. 378, January 22, 1945. Also, in his remarks to the Senate, Murray noted:

The bill recognizes that these Americans are entitled to opportunities for "useful, remunerative, regular, and full-time employment."

The right to a job does not mean guaranteeing John Jones a given job carrying a set salary and a definite social standing. It is not the aim of this bill to provide specific jobs for specific individuals. However, I believe nobody will deny that our economic system of free enterprise must offer opportunities for jobs for all who are able and want to work. Our American system owes no man a living but it does owe every man an opportunity to make a living. That is the proper interpretation of the "right to work."

91 Cong. Rec. 381, January 22, 1945.

55. Bailey, *Congress Makes a Law*, 86–87.

Unfortunately, the support of organized labor was initially less than totally enthusiastic because of concentration on other issues such as minimum wage, unemployment compensation, and the continuation of the Fair Employment Practices Commission. Bailey, *Congress Makes a Law*, 82, 92–96; Harvey, *Securing the Right*, 108–9.

Also, the rest of these groups had little political ability to organize the grass-roots support the bill needed for passage.

Bailey, *Congress Makes a Law*, 180–81, points out that 69 percent of those polled in Chicago during July 1945, seven months after the bill was introduced, had never even heard of any full employment bill.

The pollsters then asked a follow-up question, loosely based on the bill. "What would you think about a bill like this? First, the Congress would find out each year how many jobs there are going to be for the coming year. Then, if there are not enough jobs for everyone, Congress would give financial help to private business so that it could provide more jobs. Then, if there were still too few jobs, the government would give contracts to private business to build public works to help make up the balance of the jobs needed." The response was 83 percent for, 12 percent against, 5 percent doubtful.

56. Brinkley, *End of Reform*, 262.

57. Ibid.

58. Bailey, *Congress Makes a Law*, 129–49.

59. Ibid., 130–32.

Opponents were helped by developments in the postwar economic and political climate. An anticipated postwar depression did not occur, and antilabor opposition was energized by a wave of postwar strikes. Helen Ginsburg, "Full Employment as a Policy Issue," in *Employment and Labor-Relations Policy*, ed. Charles Bulmer and John L. Carmichael Jr. (Lexington Books, 1980), 15, 17.

60. Employment Act of 1946, Pub. L. 79-304, 60 Stat. 23, February 20, 1946.

Section 2 of the Employment Act of 1946, Pub. L. No. 79-304, 60 Stat. 23 (1946), p. 23. See also Brinkley, *End of Reform*, 263.

61. Section 2 of the Employment Act of 1946, 60 Stat. 23. Ginsburg, "Full Employment," 15, 17. Skocpol, *Social Policy*, at 231.

Harvey, *Securing the Right*, 109–10, notes the comment of Senator Robert Taft (R-Ohio), a leader of the opposition: "I don't think any Republicans need fear voting for the bill . . . because there is no employment bill anymore."

But see Leon H. Keyserling, "The New Deal and Its Current Significance," *Washington Law Review* 59 (1984): 795, 824–30. Keyserling, who chaired the Council of Economic Advisors from 1949 to 1953, said there were serious efforts to follow the 1946 Employment Act and design policies to achieve full employment until a new administration appointed a new Council of Economic Advisors whose prime, and almost exclusive, focus was switched to fighting inflation.

62. Harvey L. Schantz and Richard H. Schmidt, "Politics and Policy: The Humphrey-Hawkins Story," in *Employment and Labor-Relations Policy*, ed. Charles Bulmer and John L. Carmichael Jr. (Lexington Books, 1980), 25, 26. "[T]he Employment Act of 1946 is generally looked upon as a milestone in the economic history of the United States" (26).

63. See 1946 Constitution of Japan, Chapter III, Article 27 <www.solon.org/Constitutions/Japan/English/english-Constitution.html#CHAPTER_III>. See J. M. Roberts, *The Penguin History of the World* (Penguin USA, 1992), 1018.

64. Margaret Weir, *Politics and Jobs: The Boundaries of Employment Policy in the United States* (Princeton University Press, 1992), 132–43; Helen Ginsburg, "Full Employment," 5, 21.

65. Kenneth M. Casebeer, "Holder of the Pen: An Interview with Leon Keyserling on Drafting the Wagner Act," *University of Miami Law Review* 42 (1987): 285, 318. He is described as the "ghost writer" for much of the amendments to the Humphrey-Hawkins Act (296).

66. Rebecca M. Blank, "The Employment Strategy: Public Policies to Increase Work and Earnings," in *Confronting Poverty: Prescriptions for Change*, ed. Sheldon H. Danziger, Gary D. Sandefur, and Daniel H. Weinberg (Harvard University Press, 1994), 188–91.

The 1962 Manpower Development and Training Act (MDTA) was designed to train and educate workers in order to transition them into employment in the private sector. From 1963 to 1978, MDTA reportedly enrolled nearly 700,000 persons in training; of these, about 450,000 people completed the training, and about 400,000 people secured employment within a year of training. Timothy A. Canova, "Monologue or Dialogue in Management Decisions: A Comparison of Mandatory Bargaining Duties in the United States and Sweden," *Comparative Labor Law Journal* 12 (1991): 257, 263, footnote 23.

The 1973 Comprehensive Employment and Training Act (CETA) was geared toward the economically disadvantaged, the unemployed, and the underemployed. CETA provided job training, education, counseling, and public service jobs. CETA's impact on unemployment was slight and symbolic. David Cohen, "Labor Market Policy in Sweden and the United States: The Cooperative State vs. Enduring Notions of Capitalism," *Comparative Labor Law Journal* 15 (1993): 55, 77. During its years of operation, CETA funding averaged between 0.3 and 0.4 percent of the GNP; at its height, CETA served only about one-sixth of the six million officially jobless. Contrast Sweden, which provided relief work to 45 percent of its unemployed in the recession of 1978.

Mary K. Marvel, "The Social and Political Consequences of Manpower Training Programs: The Case of CETA," in *Employment and Labor-Relations Policy,* ed. Charles Bulmer and John L. Carmichael Jr. (Lexington Books, 1980), 41, 56–57, found that mere participation in CETA was not necessarily of itself a positive accomplishment. CETA participants thought little of the program and the impact on their lives. Rather, learning a skill and employing that skill appeared to achieve much more. CETA was dismantled by the Reagan administration in the 1980s and replaced with the 1982 Job Training Partnership Act (JTPA). Cohen, "Labor Market Policy," 76.

The JTPA avoided the public-sector job creation of the CETA program and looked instead to the private sector. It gave private employers some control over the program and reduced the Washington, D.C., oversight of the Labor Department with local regulation.

67. Milton Friedman, *Capitalism and Freedom* (University of Chicago Press, 1962), 190–95. See also Patterson, *America's Struggle,* 185–94.

68. Schantz and Schmidt, "Politics and Policy," 25, 26.

69. Hawkins' bill was HR 15476 and was initially called the Equal Opportunity and Full Employment Bill. Hawkins described the goal of the bill in the *Congressional Record,* 93rd Congress, June 26, 1974, 21278–21283. Senator Hubert Humphrey sponsored an identical bill in the Senate, S. 50, and from then on the various versions of the bills came to be known as the Humphrey-Hawkins bill. 122 Cong. Rec. 6610, March 16, 1976.

70. Remarks of Senator Humphrey, 122 Cong. Rec. 6610, March 16, 1976. Senator Humphrey noted that the goal of the bill was to reduce "unemployment to 3 percent of the adult labor force as promptly as possible, but within no more than 4 years after the date of enactment of this act." 122 Cong. Rec. 6611, March 16, 1976.

71. Section 2(b), 122 Cong. Rec. 6616, March 16, 1976.

72. Section 104 of the proposed act, 122 Cong. Rec. 6616, mandated "priority policies and programs that comprise a full employment program"; Title II, Section 201 of the proposed act, 122 Cong. Rec. 6617, established "employment policies to create jobs in both the private and public sectors of the economy"; and Section 206(d) of the proposed act, 122 Cong. Rec 6619, guaranteed that "Insofar as adult Americans able, willing, and seeking work are not provided with job opportunities [under other provisions of the act], such opportunities shall be provided by the President through reservoirs of federally operated public employment projects and private nonprofit employment projects approved by the Secretary of Labor."

73. Schantz and Schmidt, "Politics and Policy," 25, 27–28. See also Minority Views, House Report 95-895, p. 37.

Unfortunately for the bill, the Carter administration economic officials even testified that 4 percent unemployment would most likely be inflationary. Schantz and Schmidt, "Politics and Policy," 25, 29.

74. Ibid., 25, 30.

75. The legislative history of Humphrey-Hawkins is summarized at Schantz and Schmidt, "Politics and Policy," 25, 27–34. It passed the House 257 to 162 on March 16, 1978, and the Senate 70 to 19 on October 13, 1978.

76. Section 102 (b). Full Employment and Balanced Growth (Humphrey-Hawkins) Act of 1978, Pub. L. 95-523, 92 Stat. 1887 (codified as amended at 15 U.S.C. 3101–3152).

77. Section 4(b)(1). Full Employment and Balanced Growth Act of 1978, Pub. L. 95-523, 92 Stat. 1887, 15 U.S.C. 3101, October 27, 1978. Skocpol, *Social Policy*, 232.

Section 4(b)(1) of the bill said that the unemployment rate was to be reduced to 4 percent within five years. Section 4(c)(1) said that full employment and a balanced budget should be achieved "as soon as practicable."

The statute also set other goals of reducing inflation, increasing real income, and balancing the federal budget. Section 2(c).

78. Section 201. Full Employment and Balanced Growth (Humphrey-Hawkins) Act of 1978, Pub. L. 95–523, 92 Stat. 1887 (codified as amended at 15 U.S.C. 3101–3152).

79. Forrest Chisman, "An Effective Employment Policy: The Missing Middle," in *Rethinking Employment Policy,* ed. D. Lee Bawden and Felicity Skidmore (Urban Institute Press, 1989), 251.

In fact, almost immediately after the act was passed by Congress, President Carter announced a new anti-inflationary policy that called for voluntary wage and price guidelines and cutbacks in federal hiring, and, in his Annual Economic Report to Congress in January 1979, projected an increase in unemployment to 6.2 percent.

As two commentators sympathetic to the goals of full employment noted:

Passage of Humphrey-Hawkins, then, has not resolved, even temporarily, differences over the direction of national economic policies. Although a major piece of goal-setting legislation has been placed on the statute books, the essential economic debate continues.

Schantz and Schmidt, "Politics and Policy," 25, 36.
See also Weir, *Politics and Jobs*, 138–40.
80. Ginsburg, "Full Employment," 15, 21:

For the first time a process is established for formulating national economic policies openly and in a comprehensive, coordinated, and consistent basis in the pursuit of full employment. (21)

After the passage of the Humphrey-Hawkins bill, political priorities changed. Fighting inflation, even if that meant accepting some unemployment, became more of a concern than full employment. While the federal government continued to support unemployment insurance and other benefits for the unemployed, there was growing political popularity for blaming government for all problems. There was also a significant decline in the power of labor to influence legislation. As a consequence, there were really no new federal initiatives to create employment opportunity during the administrations of Carter, Reagan, Bush, or Clinton.

Weir, *Politics and Jobs,* 141–79.

81. Skocpol, *Social Policy,* 249.

82. John Paul II, "Respect for Human Rights: The Secret of True Peace," January 1, 1999, para. 9, <www.vatican.va/holy_father/john_paul_ii/messages/peace/documents/hf_jp-ii_mes_14121998_xxxii-world-day-for-peace_en.html>.

83. Ann Pettifor, director of the Jubilee 2000 Coalition in London, which is calling on the prosperous nations of the world to cancel the outstanding debt of impoverished nations, spoke of the support her organization was looking for in unions, doctors' organizations, and churches. Churches, she said, were often the only places where "one can have a discussion based on nonmarket values." Gustav Niebuhr, "Forgive Them Their Debts, World Council Says," *New York Times,* December 15, 1998, A10.

84. Genesis 3:19; Leviticus 19:13; Deuteronomy 24:15; Jeremiah 22:13; James 5:4.

85. The Eight Degrees of Charity, as set down by Maimonides, theologian, philosopher, and physician (1135–1204), found in David M. Schneider, *The History of Public Welfare in New York State, 1609–1866* (University of Chicago Press, 1938), unpaginated inside cover. See also <www.sephardicsages.org/8.html>.

86. "Mater et Magister, On Christianity and Social Progress," May 15, 1961, paras. 56 and 82, in David J. O'Brien and Thomas A. Shannon, *Catholic Social Thought* (Orbis Books, 2001), 93.

This call was the latest in a line of support for the rights of workers by leaders of the Catholic Church. David L. Gregory, "Catholic Social Teaching on Work," *Labor Law Journal* 49 (March 1998): 912–19. See also David L. Gregory, "Breaking the Exploitation of Labor?" *Fordham Urban Law Journal* 25 (1997): 1, 30–35.

In the early 1900s, Fr. John A. Ryan preached, wrote, and taught that there is clear religious support for a right to work and a right to a living wage. John A. Ryan, *Economic Justice: Selections from Distributive Justice and a Living Wage,* ed. Harlan R. Beckley (Westminster John Knox, 1996), 113–16. Fr. Ryan found these rights arising from four basic principles: first, all persons have an intrinsic worth that gives each an equal claim to the earth's resources; second, the way people stake their claim to the earth's resources is by working; third, every person who wants to work must be given the opportunity to work so they can access their equal claim to the earth's resources; fourth, every person who works has an inborn right to sustenance from the earth, and to refuse to give it to the worker is to deprive him or her of access to a livelihood on reasonable terms.

The Catholic bishops in "Economic Justice For All: Pastoral Letter on Catholic Social Teaching and the U.S. Economy" (U.S. Catholic Conference, 1986), pointed out that economic inequalities must be evaluated in light of the twin priorities of meeting the basic needs of the poor and increasing the level of participation by all members of society in the economic life of the nation. According to those criteria, they found the current "disparities of income and wealth in the United States to be unacceptable" (para. 185, p. 92). Their pastoral letter issued a strong call for serious, comprehensive change: "Justice requires that all members of our society work for economic, political, and social reforms that will decrease these inequities" (para. 185). The bishops understood and appreciated the direct contributions made by so many to help the poor and struggling but said that "private charity and voluntary action are not sufficient" (para. 189, p. 93). They called on people of good will to provide "employment opportunities at just wages for all who are able to work" (para. 196a, p. 97).

87. Martin Luther King Jr., *Where Do We Go From Here: Chaos or Community?* (Beacon Press, 1967), 163, 193, 200.

88. "Christian Faith and Economic Life, United Church of Christ," in *On Moral Business: Classical and Contemporary Resources for Ethics in Economic Life*, ed. Max L. Stackhouse et al. (William B. Eerdmans, 1995), 454–65.

89. "Villars Statement on Relief and Development," in *On Moral Business: Classical and Contemporary Resources for Ethics in Economic Life*, ed. Max L. Stackhouse et al. (William B. Eerdmans, 1995), paras. 25–26, p. 476. The Oxford Declaration, as an international document, recognizes that in some countries resources for full employment may be inadequate, and in those countries, justice may only require them to seek the highest possible level of employment. No one has ever suggested that the United States does not have the resources for full employment; it has only been a question of priority.

90. John Paul II, "Respect for Human Rights: The Secret of True Peace," January 1, 1999, para. 8, <www.vatican.va/holy_father/john_paul_ii/messages/peace/documents/hf_jp-ii_mes_14121998_xxxii-world-day-for-peace_en.html>.

CHAPTER 12: SUPPORT FOR A RIGHT TO LIVING WAGES

1. Seth Harris, "Conceptions of Fairness and the Fair Labor Standards Act," *Hofstra Labor & Employment Law Journal* 18 (2000): 19, 39 et seq. Harris points to the existence of theorists and advocates for just wages dating back to 1750 (39–46) and state and local efforts to enact living wages that reach back to the early 1900s (46–69).

2. "Minimum Wage: Santa Cruz Adopts 'Living Wage' Measure of $12 Hourly for City and Contract Employees," *BNA Daily Labor Report*, October 26, 2000. Santa Cruz joins fifty-five other cities and counties requiring contractors who receive contracts of $10,000 or more to pay a living wage to workers. Campaigns are under way in another seventy-five cities and counties to enact a living wage.

See also Carolyn Hirschman, "Paying Up," *HR Magazine* 45(7) (July 1, 2000).

3. My most recent effort to inquire into the state of living wages was published as "The State of the Living Wage Movement," *University of Mississippi Law Journal* 70 (2001): 889.

Those interested in more about the living wage movement should consult the web sites <www.epinet.org/Issueguides/minwage/minwage.html> and <www.umass.edu/peri/lwlinks.html> for a list of publications as well as David Card and Alan B. Krueger, *Myth and Measurement: The New Economics of the Minimum Wage* (Princeton University Press, 1995); Seth Harris, "Conceptions of Fairness"; Vivien Hart, *Bound by Our Constitution: Women, Workers and the Minimum Wage* (Princeton University Press 1994); Willis J. Norlund, *The Quest for a Living Wage: The History of the Federal Minimum Wage Program* (Greenwood Press, 1997); John A. Ryan, *A Living Wage* (Macmillan, 1920); Holly Sklar, Laryssa Mykyta, and Susan Wefald, *Raise the Floor: Wages and Policies That Work for All of Us* (South End Press, 2002); J. M. Spectar, "Pay Me Fairly, Kathie Lee! The WTO, the Right to a Living Wage, and a Proposed Protocol," *New York Law School Journal of International & Corporate Law* 20 (2000): 61; and Jerald Waltman, *The Politics of the Minimum Wage* (University of Illinois Press, 2000).

Organizations providing information about living wage issues include: ACORN, an organization committed to supporting living wage ordinances <www.livingwagecampaign.org>; AFSCME, a union supporting living wage ordinances, <www.afscme.org/livingwage>; the Economic Policies Institute, supportive of living wage ordinances, <www.epinet.org>; and the Employment Policies Institute, a comprehensive source for information opposing raising the minimum wage or enacting living-wage ordinances, <www.epionline.org>. See also <www.makingwageswork.org>.

4. *2000 Green Book,* U.S. House of Representatives Committee on Ways and Means, 1284, Table H-2.

5. William G. Whittaker, "RL30690: Minimum Wage and Related Issues Before the Congress: A Status Report," Congressional Research Service, January 24, 2001, available at <carper.senate.gov/acrobat%20files/rl30690.pdf>.

6. 29 USC 206, PL 104-188, Section 2104(b).

7. HR 2812, Minimum Wage Restoration Act, 107th Congress, August 2, 2001, co-sponsored by Representatives Sanders, Kucinich, Lee, McKinney, Owens, Brown (Fla.), Brown (Ohio), Clayton, Costello, Davis (Ill.), Filner, Kildee, Norton, Serrano, Solis, Stark, and Weiner.

The Congressional Research Service (CRS) estimated in 2001 that the 1968 federal minimum wage, if it had been adjusted for inflation, would have been $8.05. William G. Whittaker, "Fair Labor Standards Act: Wage/Hour and Related Issues before the 107th Congress," April 1, 2002, Congressional Research Service Report RL30993. Available at <www.senate.gov/~hutchinson/Business8.pdf+william+whittaker+RL30993&hl=en&ie=UTF-8>.

Additionally, Sklar, Mykyta, and Wefald, *Raise the Floor,* 53, estimate that the value of the 1968 minimum wage would have been $7.92 in the year 2000.

8. Economist Robert Pollin quoted in a column by Alexander Cockburn, "Bill and Al Joust across a Moral Divide," *Seattle Times,* February 15, 2001. Robert Pollin and Stephanie Luce, *The Living Wage: Building a Fair Economy* (New Press, 1998), 1. Edith Rasell, Jared Bernstein, and Heather Boushey, "Step Up, Not Out:

The Case for Raising the Federal Minimum Wage for Workers in Every State," *Economic Policy Institute*, Issue Brief No. 149, February 7, 2001, p. 2.

9. See Chapter 4 on official poverty levels. The current poverty guidelines can be found at the web site of the U.S. Department of Health and Human Services, <www.aspe.hhs.gov/poverty/02poverty.htm>.

10. See discussions in Chapters 4 and 5 about the problems with the current poverty guidelines that are really much too low.

11. See note 9 above.

12. See list of municipalities with living wages in William P. Quigley, "State of the Living Wage Movement," *University of Mississippi Law Journal* 70(3) (2001): 889.

13. Food stamp eligibility guidelines are available at <www.fns.usda.gov> on the web site for the U.S. Department of Agriculture.

14. The ordinance, which sets hourly wages for city contractors and companies that receive city tax breaks, grant money, or other forms of aid, was approved by St. Louis voters by a vote of 26,311 to 7,794. Kip Betz, "Minimum Wage: St. Louis Voters Approve 'Living Wage' Requirement for City Contract Workers," *BNA Daily Labor Report*, August 11, 2000.

15. For more information on EITC eligibility guidelines see <www.irs.gov/individuals/article/0,,id=96406,00.html> on the IRS web site.

16. Ralph Ranalli, "Bill Offers New Gauge for Poverty: Backers Insist US Benchmark Doesn't Reflect Mass, Realities," *Boston Globe*, May 8, 2001.

17. Jared Bernstein, Chauna Brocht, and Maggie Spade-Aguilar, *How Much Is Enough? Basic Family Budgets for Working Families* (Economic Policy Institute, 2000), 2–3.

18. See William P. Quigley, "The Right to Work and Earn a Living Wage: A Proposed Constitutional Amendment," *New York City Law Review* 2 (1998): 139. Adolph Reed, "A New Minimum: $10 an Hour," *Progressive*, April 1, 1997, p. 16. Dick Meister, "A Right to a Job and a Living Wage: Campaigns for a Constitutional Amendment," *Sacramento Bee*, August 5, 1997, B7.

19. See Waltman, *Politics of the Minimum Wage*, 48–68.

When the minimum wage was first introduced in the 1930s, Americans backed it by a 3-to-2 margin. In the decades since that time, there has been "heavy public backing for increasing the minimum wage," according to Gallup polls. George Gallup, "Support for Higher Minimum Wage," *San Francisco Chronicle*, May 28, 1987. Opinion polls taken over the last ten years have consistently shown overwhelming support among both Democrats and Republicans for raising the minimum wage. See, for example, "Polls Suggest Americans Know Little about Policy Issues," *Fort Worth Star-Telegram*, February 26, 1995, and Robert Shogan and Doyle McManus, "Campaign Gears Up," *Los Angeles Times*, May 15, 1995.

20. Linda Roeder, "Minimum Wage: Survey Shows Support for Living Wage, Economists Say at Washington Summit," *BNA Daily Labor Report*, Thursday, May 25, 2000. The survey was prepared in connection with a conference spon-

sored by Jobs for the Future, "Low Wage Workers in the New Economy: Strategies for Opportunity and Advancement." The survey was conducted for Jobs for the Future which generally supports living wage ordinances. Copies of the survey results are available from Jobs for the Future, (617) 728-4446, or at Lake Snell Perry & Associates, (202) 776-9066.

National Survey of American Attitudes towards Low-Wage Workers and Welfare Reform, conducted by Lake Snell Perry & Associates polling 1,001 Americans age eighteen and older, April 27–30, 2000. For more information about the poll contact Richard Kazis, Jobs for the Future, (617) 728-4446.

21. Richard L. Berke and Janet Elder, "Bush Loses Favor Despite Tax Cut and Overseas Trip," *New York Times*, June 21, 2001.

22. Poll conducted January 2002 by Lake Snell Perry & Associates for the Ms. Foundation for Women. Available by contacting Judith Selzer at Ms. Foundation for Women, (212) 742-2300.

23. "Minimum Wage: Santa Cruz Adopts 'Living Wage' Measure of $12 Hourly for City and Contract Employees," *BNA Daily Labor Report*, October 26, 2000.

24. Charles Hurt, "Living Wage Foes Make Plans," *Detroit News*, November 5, 1998.

25. "Local News: Election Results," *Seattle Times*, November 21, 1998. There were 1,259,456 "yes" votes (66 percent) to 644,749 "no" votes (34 percent).

While many states have set higher minimum wages than the federal level, Washington is the first state to annually raise the minimum wage based on the rate of inflation.

26. "Minimum Wage: City in Alexandria, Virginia, Approves New Living Wage Ordinance for City Contractors," *BNA Daily Labor Report*, June 20, 2000.

Frederick Kunkle and Craig Thomas, "Alexandria Officials Aim to Defend Living Wage," *Washington Post*, February 1, 2001. Alexandria requires city contractors to pay $9.84 per hour (including insurance) to employees on city contracts. An effort is under way in the state legislature to preempt the law.

27. Betz, "Minimum Wage."

28. Workers were at a premium because of the devastation of the Black Plague (1348–1349), which killed almost a third of England's population. Those workers who survived were demanding higher wages because of the shortage of help. The Statutes of Laborers rolled back maximum wages for workers to pre–Black Plague levels and imposed criminal penalties on workers and employers who violated the law. Statute of Laborers, 1349, 23 Edward 3; Statute of Laborers, 1350, 25 Edward 3. See discussion in William P. Quigley, "Five Hundred Years of English Poor Laws, 1349–1834: Regulating the Working and Nonworking Poor," *Akron Law Review* 30 (1996): 73, 82–92.

Because of these, "the precedent of government involvement in labor standards regulation dates at least six centuries." Willis J. Norlund, "A Brief History of the Fair Labor Standards Act," *Labor Law Journal* 39 (1988): 715–16.

29. Karl de Schweinitz, *England's Road to Social Security: From the Statute of Laborers in 1349 to the Beveridge Report of 1942* (University of Pennsylvania Press, 1943), 72–78; Quigley, "Five Hundred Years," 113–17.

The law of 5th Elizabeth, Chapter 4, 1563, expressed concern for the wages of the poor but empowered the justices of the peace "to limit, rate, and appoint" wages and was really a piece of repressive legislation. The subsequent law of 1st James I, Chapter 6, 1604, was a more liberal attempt at minimum-wage legislation. See discussion in de Schweinitz, *England's Road*, 79.

See also Samuel Mencher, *Poor Law to Poverty Program: Economic Security Policy in Britain and the United States* (University of Pittsburgh Press, 1967), 34–35.

30. Hart, *Bound by Our Constitution*, has a very good history of the efforts for minimum wages in England and the United States.

The New Zealand Industrial Conciliation and Arbitration Act of 1894 gave the Court of Arbitration power to settle industrial disputes by setting binding minimum wages for all workers in certain industries. In 1896, the Australian state of Victoria established a system of wage boards and most all states followed. The British Parliament followed and adopted minimum-wage legislation in 1909 aimed at abolishing "sweating." Gerald Starr, *Minimum Wage Fixing* (Geneva: International Labor Organisation, 1981), 1.

31. Lawrence B. Glickman, *A Living Wage: American Workers and the Making of Consumer Society* (Cornell University Press, 1997), 65–71. The first real push for a governmental right to a living wage was in the efforts of individual states to create minimum wage protections. William P. Quigley, " 'A Fair Day's Pay for a Fair Day's Work': Time to Raise and Index the Minimum Wage," *St. Mary's Law Journal* 27 (1996): 516–19.

32. Glickman, *Living Wage*, 62–77.

33. Ibid., 134–35.

Pope Leo XIII insisted that while employers and workers had to be allowed the freedom to enter into wage agreements,

> yet, there is always underlying such agreements an element of natural justice, and one greater and more ancient than the free consent of contracting parties, namely, that the wage shall not be less than enough to support a worker who is thrifty and upright. If compelled by necessity or moved by fear of a worse evil, a worker accepts a harder condition, which although against his will he must accept because the employer or contractor imposes it, he certainly submits to force, against which justice cries out in protest. . . . If a worker receives a wage sufficiently large to enable him to provide comfortably for himself, his wife, and his children, he will, if prudent, gladly strive to practice thrift.

Rerum Novarum (The Condition of Labor) (1891), paras. 63 and 65, in *Catholic Social Thought*, ed. David J. O'Brien and Thomas A. Shannon (Orbis Books, 2001), 31.

34. Hart, *Bound by Our Constitution*, 14–62. Norlund, *Quest for a Living Wage*, 11–14.

35. Elizabeth Brandeis, "Minimum Wage Legislation," in Don D. Lescohier and Elizabeth Brandeis, *History of Labor in the United States, 1896–1932*, Vol. 3 (Macmillan, 1935), 523.

36. George E. Paulsen, *A Living Wage for the Forgotten Man* (Susquehanna University Press, 1996), 22. Paulsen also notes that in 1912, former president Theodore Roosevelt, as candidate for the Progressive party, endorsed minimum-wage laws, and president-elect Woodrow Wilson condemned employers who objected to paying minimum wages, saying they denied the bread of life to the needy (42).

37. Keith B. Leffler, "Minimum Wages, Welfare, and Wealth Transfer to the Poor," *Journal of Law and Economics* 21 (1978): 345, 364. See also Chapter 9, note 7, above.

38. *Adkins v. Children's Hospital*, 261 U.S. 525 (1923).

39. A five-to-four decision in *Morehead v. New York ex rel. Tipaldo*, 298 U.S. 587 (1936), affirmed *Adkins* and overturned the New York minimum-wage law for women and children as repugnant to the due process clause of the Fourteenth Amendment.

40. *West Coast Hotel Co. v. Parrish*, 300 U.S. 379 (1937).
The story of the organizational and legal strategy involved in this reversal is itself a fascinating story. See Hart, *Bound by Our Constitution*, 87–150.
"State minimum wage legislation was the focal point of the Court's conversion from an opponent into a supporter of social and economic reform." John W. Chambers, "The Big Switch: Justice Roberts and the Minimum Wage Cases," *Labor History* 10 (1969), 44–45.

41. 89 Cong. Rec. 4960 (1937).

42. Norlund, "A Brief History," 715, 719, citing *The Public Papers and Addresses of Franklin D. Roosevelt*, compiled by Samuel I. Rosenman, 1938 volume, *The Continuing Struggle for Liberalism* (Macmillan Company, 1941), 392.

43. Fair Labor Standards Act of 1938, Sec. 6(a), 52 Stat. 1060, 1062. For a summary of the bill's provisions, see Norlund, *Quest for a Living Wage*, 51. Leffler, *Minimum Wages*, 346–47.

44. Quigley, "Fair Day's Pay," 529–36.

45. *Children's Hospital of D.C. v. Adkins*, 284 F. 613, 615 (CA DC 1922).

46. Samuel Herman, "The Administration and Enforcement of the Fair Labor Standards Act," *Law and Contemporary Problems* 5 (1939): 368, footnote 4. For more on the dilution of the living wage goal of the FLSA see Paulsen, *Living Wage*, 82–97.
Of the 11 million workers actually covered by the FLSA at the time of its passage, only about three hundred thousand covered workers earned less than the original $0.25 per hour minimum. Hart, *Bound by Our Constitution*, 152–53. See also Carroll R. Daugherty, "The Economic Coverage of the Fair Labor Standards Act: A Statistical Study," *Law and Contemporary Problems* 5 (1939): 409. Even when the FLSA made mandatory seven years later a forty-hour week at forty cents an hour minimum wage, those workers would still have an income of only one-third of that needed for a true living wage. Paulsen, *Living Wage*, 148.

47. Quigley, "Fair Day's Pay," 531–36.

Marc Linder, "Farm Workers and the Fair Labor Standards Act: Racial Discrimination in the New Deal," *Texas Law Review* 65 (1987): 1335, gives an excellent overview of the role of race in the enactment of the FLSA. See also Quigley, "Fair Day's Pay," 532–35.

Most ironically, the work of chambermaids such as Elsie Parrish, whose case made the FLSA possible, was excluded from coverage. In large part because of these exemptions, one critic noted that "the 'labor' protected by the FLSA was principally the white, male industrial class that needed protection least." Hart, *Bound by Our Constitution*, 152.

48. See earlier discussions in this chapter and in Chapter 11 on support for right to employment and Stephen Kemp Bailey, *Congress Makes a Law: The Story behind the Employment Act of 1946* (Columbia University Press, 1950), 26. *Security, Work and Relief Policies*, December 5, 1941, National Resources Planning Board, Committee on Long Range Work and Relief Policies, 640 pp. See also Alan Brinkley, *The End of Reform: New Deal Liberalism in Recession and War* (Knopf, 1996), 245–50.

49. Bailey, *Congress Makes a Law*, 27, citing *New York Times*, March 11, 1943, 12. See earlier discussion in Chapter 11 on right to employment and a full listing of the proposed rights.

50. 90 Cong. Rec. 57, January 11, 1944.

51. Norlund, *Quest for a Living Wage*, 59–199; Quigley, "Fair Day's Pay," 544–55.

52. S. Rep. No. 6, 101st Cong., 1st Sess. (1989), 12.

53. The EITC was first enacted in 1975 and is currently found at United States Code, Title 26, Section 32. In 1987, the EITC was indexed for inflation. Prior to 1993, the EITC was only available to workers with children. Changes to the EITC in 1993 expanded the EITC in two ways: first, by extending the credit to childless workers between the ages of twenty-five and sixty-five; and, second, by expanding the amount of the credit for families with more than one child.

Under current poverty calculations, the EITC is not to be counted as income or as a resource in the month it was received or the following month for determining the eligibility or amount of benefits for AFDC, Medicaid, SSI, food stamps, or low-income housing programs.

54. See *2000 Green Book*, pp. 808–12, for details about the Earned Income Tax Credit.

55. Rebecca M. Blank, *It Takes a Nation: A New Agenda for Fighting Poverty* (Princeton University Press, 1997), 110–14, 261–62.

56. *2000 Green Book*, 813, Table 13–14.

57. Information on how the Earned Income Tax Credit actually works can be found at the web site of the Internal Revenue Service (<www.irs.gov/individuals/article/0,,id=96406,00.html>).

58. *2000 Green Book*, p. 808.

59. Ibid., p. 811.

60. Ibid., pp. 813–15.

61. Federal Living Wage Responsibility Act, HR 4353, 106 Cong., 2d Sess., May 2, 2000.

62. Chauna Brocht, "The Forgotten Workforce," Briefing Paper No. 101, November 2000, Economic Policy Institute.

While many other federal workers are paid living wages as a result of prevailing wage statutes, the workers who are earning below poverty-level wages constitute 11 percent of the total 1.4 million federal contract workers in the country. The federal government has required contracts to pay "prevailing wages," which are typically much higher than $8.20 an hour, as a result of the Davis-Bacon Act and the Service Contract Act. The Davis-Bacon Act requires government contracts over $2,000 to pay prevailing wages on all construction, alteration, or repair of public buildings or public works. 40 USC, Section 276a. The Service Contract Act requires government contracts for the use of service employees over $2,500 to pay prevailing wages. 41 USC, Section 351.

These workers are mostly female, adult, full-time workers, and disproportionately minorities. Most of the contractors paying these low wages are defense contractors and other large businesses, not small businesses nor non-profits. Brocht, "Forgotten Wages," 1.

63. "Minimum Wage: Santa Cruz Adopts 'Living Wage' Measure of $12 Hourly for City and Contract Employees," BNA Daily Labor Report, October 26, 2000. Santa Cruz joins fifty-five other cities and counties requiring contractors who receive contracts of $10,000 or more to pay a living wage to workers. Campaigns are under way in another seventy-five cities and counties to enact a living wage. Bobbi Murray, "Living Wage Comes of Age," The Nation, July 23, 2001. See also Hirschman, "Paying Up."

64. Michelle Amber, "Low-Wage Workers: AFSCME, Church Group Sponsor Workers' Organization in Baltimore," BNA Daily Labor Report, January 3, 1995.

65. Ibid. See also, "Baltimore Mayor Signs 'Living Wage' Bill," BNA Daily Labor Report, December 14, 1994.

66. John Sweeney, "Building a Labor Movement Strategy for the New Century," Georgetown Journal on Poverty Law & Policy 7 (2000): 163, 165–66. Amber, "Civil Rights."

67. Pollin and Luce, Living Wage, 8. For example, the Association of Community Organizations for Reform Now (ACORN) has worked on numerous local living-wage campaigns with the AFL-CIO and is active in the federal living-wage campaign. Fawn M. Johnson, "Minimum Wage: Nonprofit to Launch National Campaign to Push for Federal Living Wage Legislation," BNA Daily Labor Report, November 29, 2000. See also Amanda Crawford, "Living Wage Campaigns Gain Momentum: Local Debates in Several States," BNA Daily Labor Report, September 26, 1977.

68. Stephen Brull, "What's So Bad about a Living Wage?" Business Week, September 4, 2000. All contracts over $5,000 with the City of Baltimore are required to pay wages of $7.70 per hour. Mike Bowler, "Hopkins Protestors En-

camp for Living Wage," *Baltimore Sun*, March 9, 2000, says that Baltimore's living wage is $7.90 an hour. See also the discussion of Baltimore Ordinance No. 442 (December 13, 1994) in Spectar, "Pay Me Fairly," 83 and 84, footnotes 116–19.

69. In Miami-Dade County, employers bidding on new government contracts of $100,000 or more must pay a living wage of $8.56 plus health benefits. Increases are tied to the consumer price index. William Carlisle, "Minimum Wage: Tucson, Ariz., Adopts 'Living Wage' Ordinance: Applies to City Contractors," *BNA Daily Labor Report*, September 15, 1999.

70. Hirschman, "Paying Up."

71. St. Louis living-wage law sets hourly wages at $8.67 an hour with benefits, or $9.92 without, for city contractors and companies that receive city tax breaks, grant money, or other forms of aid. The hourly rate is set at 130 percent of federal poverty guidelines for a family of three. Betz, "Minimum Wage." See also David Nicklaus, "Living Wage Law," *St. Louis Post Dispatch*, September 6, 2000. Living-wage law applies to city contracts and to companies receiving city tax breaks.

72. Decision of trial court in *Missouri Hotel and Motel Association v. City of St. Louis*, No. 402638, July 18, 2001, 2001 WL882948.

73. Barbara Whitaker, "Living Wage Ordinance Both Delights and Divides," *New York Times*, May 29, 2001.

74. The best source for information opposing the living wage is the Employment Policies Institute, <www.epionline.org>, a comprehensive source for information opposing raising the minimum wage or enacting living-wage ordinances.

75. Jeff Madrick, "Living Wages Are Practical and Don't Let Theory Get in the Way," *New York Times*, July 5, 2001.

According to Chauna Brocht of the Economic Policy Institute, the narrowly drawn living-wage ordinances usually apply to less than 1 percent of a city's total workforce. The Los Angeles ordinance, for example, covers only about seven thousand workers out of a total workforce of 1.8 million. Carolyn Hirschman, "Paying Up."

The Alexandria, Virginia, living-wage ordinance, passed June 17, 2000, was expected to affect about 150 to 200 workers. "Minimum Wage: City in Alexandria Virginia Approves New Living Wage Ordinance for City Contractors," *BNA Daily Labor Report*, June 20, 2000.

But see Don Finerock, "Living Wage Is Approved for Dade," *Miami Herald*, May 12, 1999, which estimated that the Miami living-wage ordinance will raise the salaries of 1,760 full- and part-time employees.

"Minimum Wage: Portland Ordinance Raises Wages, Requires Health Benefits for Contractors' Employees," *BNA Daily Labor Report*, May 6, 1998. Portland's Fair Wage policy required living wages to be paid to companies that contract with the city for the following positions: janitors, security guards, and parking lot attendants. The city estimated that only about one hundred such workers would directly benefit.

The very generous Berkeley ordinance was estimated to apply to only fifty-six workers. Henry K. Lee, "Berkeley Sued by Restaurant: Living Wage Law's Extension Challenged," *San Francisco Chronicle*, October 21, 2000.

76. "Survey of Economists Finds Living Wage Laws Reduce Jobs, Promote Hiring of Skilled Workers," *BNA Daily Labor Report*, August 18, 2000. The results of the survey, "The Living Wage: Survey of Labor Economists," can be viewed at <www.epionline.org/study_epi_part-time_07-2000.html> on the web site for the Employment Policies Institute.

77. Rick Ruggles, "Pay Law Results Mixed: Three Cities Have Experienced Varying Costs from Living Wage Ordinances Similar to One Proposed in Omaha," *Omaha World Herald*, April 17, 2000.

78. Janine DeFao and Pia Sarkar, "Beyond Minimum Wage: Living Wage Costs Easily Absorbed," *San Francisco Chronicle*, June 3, 2001.

Even the *Wall Street Journal* observed that "in recent years, researchers have found little evidence to support that view [that raising minimum wages makes small businesses unprofitable and reduces job opportunities for low skill workers]." Peter Waldman, "Prosperity Is Good for Living Wage Drive," *Wall Street Journal*, December 20, 1999. See also Pollin and Luce, *Living Wage*, 87–135.

Christopher Niedt et al., "The Effects of the Living Wage in Baltimore," Working Paper No. 119, February 1999, Economic Policy Institute.

See Madrick, "Living Wages Are Practical."

79. Rick Wartzman, "How Minimum Wage Lost Its Status as a Tool of Social Progress in the U.S.: Washington Now Considers the Minimum Wage Law a Drag on Employment; Two Shifts for Pat Williams," *Wall Street Journal*, July 19, 2001.

80. While an economic analysis is beyond the scope of this book, there are substantial resources available for those seeking more on this phase of the living-wage discussion. Some of the cost issues will be discussed later in Chapter 13.

81. Pollin and Luce, *Living Wage*, have made the most comprehensive study of the economic impact of living-wage ordinances to date. Those interested in an economic analysis of the various types of living wage ordinances should review their excellent book. Pollin and Luce conclude that there is a significant economic impact in these ordinances but that the wage and benefit increases amount to less than 1 percent of the total spending of the covered businesses (87–135). See also Madrick, "Living Wages Are Practical."

82. See note 76 above.

83. As Professor Galbraith noted in 1998, "Though roundly denounced by conservatives as a source of inflation and a barrier to the creation of new jobs, [the raises in the minimum wage in 1996–1997] proved to be instead an essentially harmless measure that transferred some income from some of the nation's more voracious exploiters of low-wage workers (in particular, the fast-food franchise restaurant industry) to a significant number of their least powerful employees. No adverse effects, of any kind, were observed." James K. Galbraith, *Created Unequal: The Crisis in American Pay* (Free Press, 1998), 242.

84. See discussion in Quigley, "State of the Living Wage Movement," 937–38.

85. Tripp Baltz, "State Laws: Utah Measures on Pay Deductions, Local Minimum Wage Go to Governor," *BNA Daily Labor Report*, March 1, 2001. In Utah, S.B. 138, sponsored by Sen. Howard Stephenson (R) and approved by the House February 26, 2001, bars local governments from setting a minimum wage higher than the state minimum wage. Stephenson told the Bureau of National Affairs that the minimum wage bill is "one of the most family-friendly pieces of legislation we have passed this session." He said the ban on higher municipal minimum wages will make it easier "for young people and people who have just entered this country" to find entry-level work. Opponents of the bill have characterized local minimum wages as a way for cities and towns to enact a "living wage." Stephenson has said the state should work for a fair "entry-level wage." "We should not allow municipalities to arbitrarily set a wage that denies entry to those trying to get a foothold" in the job market, he added. Baltz, "State Laws."

86. Louisiana legislature enacted Louisiana Revised Statute 23:642, which attempted to preempt any local government from enacting a local minimum wage. The validity of the state attempt to prevent local minimum wages will not be determined until after voters have a chance to pass the bill. *Johnson v. Carter*, 767 So. 2d 790 (La. App. 4th Cir. 2000), writ denied October 27, 2000.

87. Oregon passed the law in 2001. Brad Cain, "Smokers and Bullies Targeted by Oregon Laws," *Columbian*, December 30, 2001. The law prohibits cities and counties from requiring businesses to pay more than the state minimum wage of $6.50 an hour, unless they contract with a public agency that requires higher minimum wages.

Arizona's statute is at Arizona Statutes Section 23-362; Colorado's is at Colorado Statutes Section 8-6-101; Missouri's is at Missouri Statute 67.1571.

Michigan considered similar legislation prohibiting local living-wage ordinances. "Senate to Consider Living Wage Requirement," *Detroit News*, February 2, 2001.

Kansas also considered state laws prohibiting living wages. Hirschman, "Paying Up."

Criticisms of the business community included the increased cost to public entities such as the Tucson convention center. Carlisle, "Minimum Wage."

88. For general discussion see William P. Quigley, "Full-Time Workers Should Not Be Poor," *Mississippi Law Journal* 70 (2001): 889, 894–895, 902–905.

For the history of religious support for living wages, see Brandeis, "Minimum Wage Legislation," 513; Harris, "Conceptions of Fairness," 19, 39–46; and Don D. Lescohier and Elizabeth Brandeis, *History of Labor in the United States, 1896–1932*, Vol. 3 (Macmillan, 1935), 63, outlining some of the history of efforts of Protestant churches to help living and just wage efforts.

John A. Ryan, *Economic Justice: Selections from Distributive Justice and a Living Wage*, ed. Harlan R. Beckley (Westminster John Knox Press, 1996), 124.

For specific church advocacy for living wages, see:

Catholic: David L. Gregory, "Catholic Social Teaching on Work," *Labor Law Journal* (March 1998): 912–19. See also David L. Gregory, "Breaking the Exploitation of Labor?: Tensions Regarding the Welfare Workforce," *Fordham Urban Law Journal* 25 (1997): 1, 30–35.

Episcopalian: See discussions of living-wage resolutions at <www.episcopalchurch.org/peace-justice/ENEJ/Living_Wage.htm>.

Jewish: See "Resolution on Living Wage and Low-Income Workers," February 28, 2000, at <www.jewishpublicaffairs.org/resolutions/main.html> on the web site of the Jewish Council of Public Affairs.

Unitarian: The Unitarian Universalist Association, 1997 UUA General Resolution, "Working for a Just Economic Community," called for "A true single minimum wage, applicable to all workers, that provides an adequate standard of living." <www.uua.org/actions/economic-justice/97community.html>.

For contemporary advocacy for living wages see Amber, "Civil Rights," and Katie Hetter, "Labor Has Ally in the Pulpits," *Newsday,* December 12, 2000, describing the sixty local groups of the National Interfaith Coalition for Worker Justice (<www.nicwj.org/pages/issues.LWC.html>), which works to bring concerned religious people and organizations together with progressive labor leaders.

Patricia Ann Lamoureux, "Is a Living Wage a Just Wage?" *America,* February 19, 2001. Lamoureux, a theologian, observes that "A living wage is the minimum of justice, not the full measure of justice."

89. Glickman, *Living Wage,* 134–35.

90. "Quadregesimo Anno" (After Forty Years) (1931), in *Catholic Social Thought,* ed. David J. O'Brien and Thomas A. Shannon (Orbis Books, 2001), para. 71, p. 58.

91. "Statement on Church and Social Order," February 7, 1940, paras. 41–42, *Justice in the Marketplace: Collected Statements of the Vatican and the U.S. Catholic Bishops on Economic Policy, 1891–1984,* ed. David M. Byers (U.S. Catholic Conference, 1985), 435.

92. In 1961, responding to those who said wages should be left to the dictates of the market, Pope John XXIII proclaimed that a living wage was a justice issue too important:

> We therefore consider it our duty to reaffirm that the remuneration of work is not something that can be left to the laws of the marketplace; nor should it be a decision left to the will of the more powerful. "Mater et Magister," para. 71 (1961)

In 1963, he challenged governments to implement the right to work for a living wage:

> The government should make similarly effective efforts to see that those who are able to work can find employment in keeping with their aptitudes, and that each worker receive a wage in keeping with the laws of justice and equity. Peace on Earth, para. 64 (1963)

A worldwide assembly of Catholic bishops in 1965 challenged world governments to ensure that "payment for labor must be such as to furnish a man with the means to cultivate his own material, social, cultural and spiritual life worthily, and that of his dependents." Second Vatican Council, *Gaudium et Spes, Pastoral Constitution on the Church in the Modern World*, para. 67 (December 7, 1965).

In 1981, Pope John Paul II indicated that payment of living wages was a critical criteria for determining the legitimacy of the entire economic system. John Paul II, *On Human Work*, para. 89 (1981). See also further explanation of living wage in paras. 90 and 91.

In 1986, U.S. Catholic Bishops in "Economic Justice For All: Pastoral Letter on Catholic Social Teaching and the U.S. Economy" (U.S. Catholic Conference, 1986), placed economic inequality squarely on the social justice agenda for the American economy:

> The first line of attack against poverty must be to build and sustain a healthy economy that provides employment opportunities at just wages for all adults who are able to work. (para. 196, p. 97)

Again in 1991, John Paul II pointed out that guaranteeing a living wage to the working poor is part of the responsibility of government:

> The richer class has many ways of shielding itself, and stands less in need of help from the state; whereas the mass of the poor have no resources of their own to fall back upon, and must chiefly depend on the assistance of the state. It is for this reason that wage-earners, since they mostly belong to the latter class, should be specially cared for and protected by the government.

Pope John Paul II, "Centesimus Annus," para. 10 (1991).

John Paul II also reaffirmed that "A workman's wages should be sufficient to enable him to support himself, his wife and his children." "Centesimus Annus," para. 8 (1991).

Refusing to pay just wages even if allowed to do so by law is a violation of the seventh commandment, according to the 1992 Catechism of the Catholic Church:

> Even if it does not contradict the provisions of civil law, any form of unjustly taking or keeping the property of others is against the seventh commandment: thus, deliberate retention of goods lent or objects lost; business fraud; paying unjust wages; forcing up prices by taking advantage of the ignorance or hardship of another.

Catechism of the Catholic Church (Doubleday, 1995), para. 2409. See also para. 2434.

93. Paul O'Neill quote from BBC News, January 14, 2002.

94. Chamber of Commerce quote, April 25, 2002, Press Release of U.S. Chamber of Commerce, "U.S. Chamber Challenges 'Living Wage' Law Amicus Brief Filed in New Orleans."

For more on the religious nature of belief in the free market, see Robert H. Nelson, *Economics as Religion: From Samuelson to Chicago and Beyond* (Penn State University Press, 2001).

95. Restaurant quote from Eric Roston, "How Much Is a Living Wage?" *Time,* March 31, 2002.

96. Pollin and Luce, *Living Wage,* 149–62. Robert Pollin's New Orleans, "Economic Analysis of the New Orleans Minimum Wage Proposal," can be found at <www.acorn.org/acorn10/livingwage/neworleans.htm>.

97. Neumark quote from Justin Pritchard, "Living Wage Laws Prove Effective," *Capital Times,* March 14, 2002. See also David Neumark, "How Living Wage Laws Affect Low-Wage Workers and Low-Income Families," Public Policy Institute of California, 2002, <www.ppic.org/publications/PPIC156/index. html>. And see Timothy Bartik, "Thinking about Local Living Wage Requirements," Staff Working Paper No. WP02-76, March 2002, W. E. Upjohn Institute for Employment Research, <www.upjohninst.org/publications/wp/02-76.pdf>. This report suggests that living-wage laws show mixed results, with the more modest raises showing less displacement of workers.

98. Jared Bernstein and Jeff Chapman, "Time to Repair the Wage Floor," Economic Policy Institute Issue Brief No. 180, May 22, 2002, <www.epinet.org/ Issuebriefs/ib180.html>. See also Jared Bernstein and John Schmitt, "The Impact of the Minimum Wage: Policy Lifts Wages, Maintains Floor for Low-Wage Labor Market," Economic Policy Institute Briefing Paper, June 2000, <www. epinet.org/briefingpapers/min_%20wage_bp.html>.

For more on the job-loss argument see the discussions in Sklar, Mykyta, and Wefald, *Raise the Floor,* 66–782, and Card and Krueger, *Myth and Measurement,* 387–90, concluding that increases in minimum wages may actually increase employment rates.

99. Pollin and Luce, *Living Wage,* 134, for quote; Pollin, "New Orleans Study."

100. Roston, "How Much Is a Living Wage?"

101. *West Coast Hotel Co. v. Parrish,* 300 US 379, 399–400 (1937).

CHAPTER 13: HOW MIGHT A CONSTITUTIONAL RIGHT WORK?

1. Mark Tushnet, "Civil Rights and Social Rights: The Future of the Reconstruction Amendments," *Loyola of Los Angeles Law Review* 25 (1992): 1211–19, notes that many of the problems of interpreting and enforcing economic or social rights are the same as those involved in interpreting and enforcing the civil rights of the reconstruction era. See, e.g., p. 1217.

2. These scholars present a ten-point agenda for an entitlement to work and to welfare:

1. Provide public assistance to anyone unable to find a job that is accessible, roughly matches their qualifications, and pays a living wage. 2. Strengthen the unemployment insurance system by raising wage-replacement rates and greatly increasing the proportion of the unemployed who are eligible. Create jobs for the unemployed at wages comparable to those paid for similar private-sector work. 3. Make work

pay by raising the minimum wage to at least $7.50 an hour, equivalent to its peak value in 1968, and index it to average wages. 4. Support and extend "living wage" ordinances to the national level. (Living wage ordinances require firms doing business with governments to pay all their employees at least a decent or living wage.) 5. Guarantee affordable quality child care to all parents regardless of their welfare or income status, who need it in order to be employed or participate in education and training, and prohibit states from requiring welfare recipients to take work assignments in the absence of quality licensed care for their children. 6. Provide opportunities for education and training for all people unable to get jobs due to lack of preparation for work—regardless of their welfare status. 7. Restructure benefits as care allowances to recognize work done in the home caring for the young and the frail of any age. 8. Raise benefit levels to a standard commensurate with health and a decent standard of living. 9. Institute a universal health insurance system—one covering the whole population. 10. Create a national housing program to guarantee decent, affordable housing for all people and to create socially useful jobs for the unemployed.

Gertrude Schaffner Goldberg and Sheila D. Collins, "The Right to Work and to Welfare," National Jobs for All Coalition, Special Report 2, February 2002, <www.njfac.org/sr2.htm>.

Jesse L. Jackson Jr. and Frank E. Watkins, *A More Perfect Union: Advancing New American Rights* (Welcome Rain Publishers, 2001), 252–84. Rep. Jackson proposes the following amendment:

> Proposed Full-Employment Amendment to the U.S. Constitution. Section 1. Every citizen has the right to work, to free choice of employment, to just and favorable conditions of work, and to protection against unemployment. Section 2. Every citizen, without any discrimination, has the right to equal pay for equal work. Section 3. Every citizen who works has the right to just and favorable remuneration ensuring for themselves and their family an existence worthy of human dignity, and supplemented, if necessary, by other means of social protection. Section 4. Every citizen who works has the right to form and join trade unions for the protection of their interests. Section 5. The Congress shall have power to implement this article by legislation. (252)

3. See Adolph Reed, "A New Minimum: $10 an Hour," *Progressive* 61(4) (April 1, 1997): 16; William P. Quigley, "The Right to Work and Earn a Living Wage: A Proposed Constitutional Amendment," *New York City Law Review* 2 (1998): 139; Dick Meister, "A Right to a Job and a Living Wage: Campaigns for a Constitutional Amendment," *Sacramento Bee*, August 5, 1997, B7.

4. Charles L. Black, "Further Reflections on the Constitutional Justice of Livelihood," *Columbia Law Review* 96 (1986): 1101, 1113. Black sees parallels to his vision of a right to a constitutional justice of livelihood in the congressional duty to appropriate money. The duty to appropriate money "cannot be given exact arithmetical shape, but are nonetheless constitutional duties" (1113).

5. Helen Lachs Ginsburg et al., "The Challenge of Full Employment in the Global Economy," 29, National Jobs for All Coalition, (212) 870-3449.

6. See the section "Suggested Web Resources for Further Reading" in this book.

7. See the excellent analysis of this by Gertrude Schaffner Goldberg and Sheila D. Collins, *Washington's New Poor Law: Welfare "Reform" and the Roads Not Taken, 1935 to the Present* (Apex Press, 2001).

8. Edmund S. Phelps, *Rewarding Work: How to Restore Participation and Self-Support to Free Enterprise* (Harvard University Press, 1997), 105–21.

9. Lester C. Thurow, *The Zero-Sum Society: Distribution and the Possibilities for Economic Change* (Basic Books, 1980), 200–210.

10. Katherine S. Newman, *No Shame in My Game: The Working Poor in the Inner City* (Knopf, 1999), 268–98.

11. Rebecca M. Blank, "Enhancing the Opportunities, Skills, and Security of American Workers," in *A Working Nation: Workers, Work, and Government in the New Economy*, ed. David T. Ellwood et al. (Russell Sage Foundation 2000), 105.

12. Lawrence F. Katz, "Wage Subsidies for the Disadvantaged," in *Generating Jobs: How to Increase Demand for Less-Skilled Workers*, ed. Richard B. Freeman and Peter Gottschalk (Russell Sage Foundation, 1998), 21–52.

13. Timothy J. Bartik, *Jobs for the Poor: Can Labor Demand Policies Help?* (Russell Sage Foundation and Upjohn Institute, 2001), 287–302.

14. Charles A. Cerami, "Three New Ways to Create Jobs," *Atlantic Monthly*, March 1994, <www.theatlantic.com/politics/ecbig/eccerami.htm>.

15. "More often than not, the wisdom in the hard-nosed decision to downsize wins Wall Street's approval." W. Michael Cox and Richard Alm, *Myths of Rich and Poor: Why We're Better Off Than We Think* (Basic Books, 1999), 130.

16. Cerami, "Three New Ways."

17. Robert H. Haveman, "Equity with Employment," *Boston Review,* Summer 1997, <http://bostonreview.mit.edu/BR22.3/haveman.html>.

18. L. Randall Wray, *Understanding Modern Money: The Key to Full Employment and Price Stability* (Edward Elgar, 1998), 122–54.

19. Nancy E. Rose, *Put to Work: Relief Programs in the Great Depression* (Monthly Review Press, 1994), 115–22; Nancy E. Rose, *Workfare or Fair Work: Women, Welfare, and Government Work Programs* (Rutgers University Press, 1995), 179–85.

20. Clifford M. Johnson and Alex Goldenberg, "Work to be Done: Designing Publicly-Funded Jobs to Meet Community Needs," Center on Budget and Policy Priorities, September 24, 1999, <www.cbpp.org/9-24-99wtw.htm>.

21. "Stronger Links: New Ways to Connect Low-Skilled Workers to Better Jobs," Annie E. Casey Foundation Jobs Initiative, <www.aecf.org/initiatives/jobsinitiative/strongerlinks.pdf>.

22. See Hans Bos et al., "New Hope for People with Low Incomes: Two Year Results of a Program to Reduce Poverty and Reform Welfare," Manpower Demonstration Research Corporation, <www.mdrc.org/Reports99/NewHope 4-99/NH-ExecSum4-8-99.html>.

23. We already know that one experiment to give people a chance to work themselves out of poverty worked only for a small number of people. A pro-

gram in Milwaukee offered more than six hundred adults the opportunity to work thirty hours a week and earn enough to lift themselves over the poverty threshold. Yet despite this offer, only 27 percent of those invited managed to stay with the program. Employee-employer conflicts arose, abusive relationships intervened, drug and alcohol abuse scrambled the best intentions, and for many workers the opportunity did not work. Psychological problems and a "culture of defeat" were cited as possible reasons for the lack of success. Jason DeParle, "Project to Rescue Needy Stumbles against the Persistence of Poverty," *New York Times*, May 15, 1999.

24. Mary Jo Bane, "Body (Re)Building: Book Review of *Dry Bones Rattling: Community Building to Revitalize American Democracy* by Mark R. Warren," *America*, November 5, 2001. See also Mark R. Warren, *Dry Bones Rattling: Community Building to Revitalize American Democracy* (Princeton University Press, 2001), 162–90. This chapter is a case study on Project Quest, a community-based employment program geared to assist in the transition of unemployed people to living-wage jobs.

25. James Aldridge, "Project Quest Inks Training Pact with Boeing Aerospace," *San Antonio Business Journal*, November 13, 2000, <www.sanantonio. bizjournals.com/sanantonio/stories/2000/11/13/story5.html>. See also the web site of Project Quest at <www.questsa.com>, particularly the link to the 1996 Report to the Ford Foundation by Paul Osterman and Brenda A. Lautsch. Project Hope is also briefly described, but in more depth than here, in Newman, *No Shame*, 294–96.

26. Clifford M. Johnson and Steve Savner, "Federal Funding Sources for Public Job Creation Initiatives," Center on Budget and Policy Priorities and Center on Law and Social Policy, December 1999, <www.cbpp.org/12-21-99wtw.htm>.

27. See Roberta Rehner Iversen, *Moving Up Is a Steep Climb: Parents' Work and Children's Welfare in the Annie E. Casey Foundation's Jobs Initiative* (Annie E. Casey Foundation, April 2002), <www.aecf.org/initiatives/jobsinitiative/ethnography.htm>.

28. See the many reports about welfare-to-work programs collected by the Center on Budget and Policy Priorities web site, <www.cbpp.org>, especially reports such as Clifford M. Johnson and Lana Kim, "Competitive Welfare-to-Work Grantees Utilize Publicly-Funded, Transitional Jobs to Aid Hard-to-Employ Welfare Recipients," September 17, 1999, which describes programs in San Antonio, Los Angeles, Denver, and Roanoke.

29. See Economic Opportunity Community Jobs, <www.econop.org/CJ-OutcomesAssessmentSummary0402.htm>.

30. "Statewide Jail/Prison Project, Welfare-to-Work (Non-Custodial Parent)," August 16, 1999. For a copy contact Gerri Woolf, <gwoolf@esd.wa. gov> or (360) 438-4037.

31. "Thinking Creatively about Welfare to Work Job Creation," July 1998, AF-SCME, <www.afscme.org/pol-leg/wtow02.htm>.

32. John E. Schwarz, *Illusions of Opportunity: The American Dream in Question* (W. W. Norton 1997), 147–52.

33. National survey conducted October 2001 by Lake Snell Perry & Associates for Jobs for the Future. Available by calling Jobs for the Future, (617) 728-4446, or Lake Snell Perry & Associates, (202) 776-9066.

34. *Statistical Abstract of the United States, 2000,* 479, Table 762.

35. Mark C. Weber, "Beyond the ADA: A National Employment Policy for People with Disabilities," *Buffalo Law Review* 46 (1998): 123, 127–28.

36. Ibid., 123 and 128, citing 1994 Louis Harris & Associates survey showing that 72 percent of unemployed persons with disabilities want to work.

37. HR 2812, Minimum Wage Restoration Act, 107th Congress, August 2, 2001. See Chapter 12, note 7.

38. Poll conducted January 2002 by Lake Snell Perry & Associates for the Ms. Foundation for Women. To obtain a copy contact Ms. Foundation for Women, (212) 742-2300.

39. *2000 Green Book,* U.S. House of Representatives Committee on Ways and Means, p. 811.

40. Ibid., pp. 813–15.

41. Annie E. Casey Foundation poll conducted by Peter D. Hart Research Associates, March 2001, <www.aecf.org/specialprojects/taxsurvey/Summary.pdf>.

42. Robert Greenstein, "The Changes the New Tax Law Makes in Refundable Tax Credits for Low-Income Working Families," Center on Budget and Policy Priorities, June 18, 2001, <www.cbpp.org/6-14-01tax.htm>.

43. Schwarz, *Illusions of Opportunity,* 145–56.

44. Robert Cherry and Max B. Sawicky, "Giving Tax Credit Where Credit Is Due: A 'Universal Unified Child Credit' That Expands the EITC and Cuts Taxes for Working Families," Economic Policy Briefing Paper, April 2000, <www.epinet.org/briefingpapers/eitc.html>.

45. Ibid.

46. Robert Pollin and Stephanie Luce, *The Living Wage: Building a Fair Economy* (New Press, 1998).

47. Newman, *No Shame,* 268–98.

48. Isabel Sawhill and Adam Thomas, "A Hand Up for the Bottom Third: Toward a New Agenda for Low-Income Working Families," May 2001, p. 4, <www.brook.edu/views/papers/sawhill/20010522.htm>.

49. Blank, "Enhancing the Opportunities," 105–23.

50. Theda Skocpol, *The Missing Middle: Working Families and the Future of American Social Policy* (W. W. Norton, 2000), 154–60.

51. Haveman, "Equity with Employment."

52. Barry Bluestone and Bennett Harrison, *Growing Prosperity: The Battle for Growth with Equity in the 21st Century* (Houghton Mifflin, 2000), 249–50.

53. Stephen A. Herzenberg, John A. Alic, and Howard Wial, *New Rules for a New Economy: Employment and Opportunity in Postindustrial America* (Cornell University Press, 1998), 167.

54. John Atlee, "Requirements for a 'Job-Full' Recovery," March 14, 2002, <www.iea-macro-economics.org/job-full-recovery.html>.

55. Tome Redburn, "Honoring, and Paying, All Those Who Serve," *New York Times*, October 28, 2001.

56. Lawrence Mishel, Jared Bernstein, and John Schmitt, *The State of Working America, 2000/2001* (ILR Press, 2001), 211. Some say the ratio is even higher: The 2001 ratio of executive pay to the average check of workers rose to 531:1. Geneva Overholser, "CEO's Get Richer," *Washington Post*, August 31, 2001.

57. "A startling surge in corporate tax welfare is expected to drive corporate income taxes over the next two years down to only 1.3 percent of the gross domestic product. That will be the lowest level since the early 1980s—and the second lowest level in at least six decades.

Driven in part by the new corporate tax breaks just enacted in the so-called 'stimulus' bill, the total cost to ordinary American taxpayers of corporate tax welfare will exceed $170 billion annually in each of the next two years. . . .

From 1996 through 2000, just ten large profitable companies enjoyed a total of $50 billion in corporate tax breaks. That brought their combined tax bills down to only 8.9 percent of their $191 billion in U.S. profits over the five years. In just the most recent two years for which data are available, these ten companies got $29 billion in tax welfare, and paid a mere 5.9 percent of their profits in federal income taxes.

[For example,] Microsoft enjoyed more than $12 billion in total tax breaks over the past five years. In fact, Microsoft actually paid no tax at all in 1999, despite $12.3 billion in reported U.S. profits. Microsoft's tax rate for the past two years was only 1.8 percent on $21.9 billion in pretax U.S. profits."

"Surge in Corporate Tax Welfare Drives Corporate Tax Payments Down to Near Record Low," April 17, 2002, Citizens for Tax Justice, available at <www.ctj.org/html/corp0402.htm>.

58. Philip Harvey, "Responding to Rising Unemployment: Can We Afford Jobs for All?" Part 14 of the Uncommon Sense Series, National Jobs for All Coalition, October 2001, <www.njfac.org/us14.html>. See also Philip Harvey, *Securing the Right to Employment: Social Welfare Policy and the Unemployed in the United States* (Princeton University Press, 1989), 50.

59. Sawhill and Thomas, "Hand Up," 4.

60. Schwarz, *Illusions of Opportunity*, 145–58.

61. Phelps, *Rewarding Work*, 116–18.

62. Bartik, *Jobs for the Poor*, 299–302.

63. Jeff Madrick, "Economic Scene: Living Wages Are Practical and Don't Let Theory Get in the Way," *New York Times*, July 5, 2001.

64. William Julius Wilson and Andrew J. Cherlin, "The Real Test of Welfare Reform Still Lies Ahead," *New York Times*, July 13, 2001.

65. Ginsburg et al., "Challenge of Full Employment," 21.

66. Jared Bernstein and Ellen Houston, *Crime and Work: What We Can Learn from the Low-Wage Labor Market* (Economic Policy Institute, 2000), vii–viii.

67. Ibid.

68. Jeff Madrick, "In America, to the Richest Go the Biggest Tax Benefits. So What Else Is New?" *New York Times*, June 7, 2001.

69. James K. Galbraith, *Created Unequal: The Crisis in American Pay* (Free Press, 1998), 232–46.

70. Ibid., 242.

71. Ibid.

72. Wray, *Understanding Modern Money*, 122–54.

73. Thurow, *Zero-Sum Society*, 205.

74. Vivien Hart, *Bound by Our Constitution: Women, Workers, and the Minimum Wage* (Princeton University Press, 1994), 23.

75. President Warren G. Harding, 1921, Report of the President's Conference (Washington, 1921), 27, as quoted in Steven Kemp Bailey, *Congress Makes a Law: The Story behind the Employment Act of 1946* (Columbia University Press, 1950), 6, footnote 7.

76. DeParle, "Project to Rescue Needy."

77. That this will cause problems is clear. There will be cries that there will be "pain" of economic sorts, and creating such rights will make a "mess" of current economic relationships. These are familiar objections, heard in response to all efforts to improve society. As ethicist James Gaffney notes: "The moral aberrations of culture have never been corrected without pain and mess." James Gaffney, "She Who Laughs Last: The Gender-Inclusive Language Debate," *America*, August 26, 1995, 8, 12.

CHAPTER 14: THE WAY TO END POVERTY AS WE KNOW IT

1. Taylor Branch, *Parting the Waters: America in the King Years, 1954–1963* (Touchstone, 1988), 197.

2. Michael Kelly, "77 North Washington Street," *Atlantic Monthly* 287(6) (June 2001): 4.

3. I saw this quote carved into the walls in the public library in New York, the one with the big stone lions out front and best known in our family from the scene in *Ghostbusters*.

Suggested Web Resources
for Further Reading

AFL-CIO, <www.aflcio.org>

American Federation of State, County and Municipal Employees (AFSCME),
  <www.afscme.org>

Annie E. Casey Foundation (AECF), <www.aecf.org>

Association of Community Organizations for Reform Now (ACORN),
  <www.acorn.org> and <www.livingwagecampaign.org>

Center on Budget and Policy Priorities, <www.cbpp.org>

Center on Law and Social Policy (CLASP), <www.clasp.org>

Economic Opportunity Institute (EOI), <www.econop.org>

Economic Policy Institute (EPI), <www.epinet.org>

Employment Policies Institute (EPI), <www.epionline.org>

Joint Center for Poverty Research, <www.jcpr.org>

Labor Party Press, <www.igc.org/lpa/lppress>

Manpower Demonstration Research Corporation, <www.mdrc.org>

Making Wages Work (MWW), <www.makingwageswork.org>

Ms. Foundation for Women "Raise the Floor" Campaign,
  <www.raisethefloor.org>

National Interfaith Coalition for Worker Justice, <www.nicwj.org>

National Jobs for All Coalition (NJFAC), <www.njfac.org>

W. E. Upjohn Institute for Employment Research, <www.upjohninst.org>

Wider Opportunities for Women "Six Strategies for Family Economic
  Self-Sufficiency" Project, <www.sixstrategies.org>

Women's Educational and Industrial Union, <www.weiu.org>

Selected Bibliography

Abramovitz, Mimi. *Regulating the Lives of Women* (South End Press, 1988).

Ackerman, Bruce, and Anne Alstott. *The Stake Holder Society* (Yale University Press, 1999).

Aldridge, James. "Project Quest Inks Training Pact with Boeing Aerospace." *San Antonio Business Journal,* November 13, 2000, <www.sanantonio.bizjournals.com/sanantonio/stories/2000/11/13/story5.html>.

Alpert, Bruce, and Bill Walsh. "Few Low-Skill Jobs." *Times-Picayune,* June 21, 1998.

Alwitt, Linda F., and Thomas D. Donley. *The Low-Income Consumer: Adjusting the Balance of Exchange* (Sage Publications, 1996).

Amar, Akhil Reed. "The Consent of the Governed: Constitutional Amendment Outside of Article V." *Columbia Law Review* 457 (1994): 94.

———. "Philadelphia Revisited: Amending the Constitution Outside Article V." *University of Chicago Law Review* 1043 (1988): 55.

Amber, Michelle. "Civil Rights: Labor, Religious Leaders Announce Plans to Work Together to Promote Worker Rights." *BNA Daily Labor Report,* October 13, 2000.

———. "Low-Wage Workers: AFSCME, Church Group Sponsor Workers' Organization in Baltimore." *BNA Daily Labor Report,* January 3, 1995.

Appelbaum, Eileen, ed. *Balancing Acts: Easing Burdens and Improving the Options for Working Families* (Economic Policy Institute, 2000).

Atlee, John. "Requirements for a 'Job-Full' Recovery." Institute for Economic Analysis, March 14, 2002. <www.iea-macro-economics.org/job-full-recovery.html>

Axinn, June, and Herman Levin. *Social Welfare: A History of the American Response to Need,* 3rd ed. (Longman, 1992).

Backer, Larry Cata. "Medieval Poor Law in Twentieth Century America: Looking Backwards towards a General Theory of Modern American Poor Relief." *Case Western Law Review* 871 (1995): 871.

Bailey, Steven Kemp. *Congress Makes a Law: The Story behind the Employment Act of 1946* (Columbia University Press, 1950).

Bane, Mary Jo. "Body (Re)Building: Book Review of *Dry Bones Rattling: Community Building to Revitalize American Democracy* by Mark R. Warren." *America,* November 5, 2001.

Barber, Benjamin R. *Jihad vs. McWorld: How Globalism and Tribalism Are Reshaping the World* (Ballantine, 1996).

Bartik, Timothy. "Employment as a 'Solution' to Welfare: Changes over the Next Ten Years." *Employment Research,* April 2000, <www.upjohninst.org/publications/newsletter/tjb_400.pdf>.

———. *Jobs for the Poor: Can Labor Demand Policies Help?* (Russell Sage Foundation and W. E Upjohn Institute for Employment Research, 2001).

———. "Thinking about Local Living Wage Requirements." Staff Working Paper No. WP02-76, March 2002, W. E. Upjohn Institute for Employment Research, <www.upjohninst.org/publications/wp/0276wp.html>.

Baxandall, Rosalyn, and Linda Gordon. *America's Working Women: A Documentary History, 1600 to the Present,* rev. ed. (Norton, 1995).

Beckley, Harlan R., ed. *Economic Justice: Selections from Distributive Justice and A Living Wage* (Westminster John Knox Press, 1996).

Berke, Richard L., and Janet Elder. "Bush Loses Favor Despite Tax Cut and Overseas Trip." *New York Times,* June 21, 2002.

Bernstein, Jared, Chauna Brocht, and Maggie Spade-Aguilar. *How Much Is Enough? Basic Family Budgets for Working Families* (Economic Policy Institute, 2000).

Bernstein, Jared, and Jeff Chapman. "Time to Repair the Wage Floor." Economic Policy Institute Issue Brief No. 180, May 22, 2002, <www.epinet.org/Issuebriefs/ib180.html>.

Bernstein, Jared, and Ellen Houston. *Crime and Work: What We Can Learn from the Low-Wage Labor Market* (Economic Policy Institute, 2000).

Bernstein, Jared, Lawrence Mishel, and Chauna Brocht. "Any Way You Cut It: Income Inequality on the Rise Regardless of How It Is Measured." Briefing Paper, Economic Policy Institute, September 2000, <www.epinet.org/briefingpapers/inequality/inequality.html>.

Bernstein, Jared, and John Schmitt. "The Impact of the Minimum Wage: Policy Lifts Wages, Maintains Floor for Low-Wage Labor Market," Economic Policy Institute, June 2000, <www.epinet.org/briefingpapers/min_%20wage_bp.html>.

Bernstein, Nina. "With a Job, Without a Home." *New York Times,* March 4, 1999.

Betz, Kip. "Minimum Wage: St. Louis Voters Approve 'Living Wage' Requirement for City Contract Workers." *BNA Daily Labor Report,* August 11, 2000.

Beveridge, William H. *Full Employment in a Free Society* (Great Britain, 1944).

Black, Charles. "Further Reflections on the Constitutional Justice of Livelihood." *Columbia Law Review* 86 (1986): 1103.

Blank, Rebecca M. "The Employment Strategy: Public Policies to Increase Work and Earnings." Pp. 168–204 in *Confronting Poverty: Prescriptions for Change,* ed. Sheldon H. Danziger, Gary D. Sandifur, and Daniel H. Weinberg (Harvard University Press, 1994).

———. "Enhancing the Opportunities, Skills, and Security of American Workers." Pp. 105–23 in *A Working Nation: Workers, Work, and Government in the New Economy,* David T. Ellwood et al. (Russell Sage Foundation, 2000).

———. *It Takes a Nation: A New Agenda for Fighting Poverty* (Princeton University Press, 1997).

Block, Fred, et al. *The Mean Season: The Attack on the Welfare State* (Pantheon, 1987).

Bluestone, Barry, and Bennett Harrison. *Growing Prosperity: The Battle for Growth with Equity in the 21st Century* (Houghton Mifflin, 2000).

Bork, Robert H. "Commentary: The Impossibility of Finding Welfare Rights in the Constitution." *Washington University Law Quarterly* (Summer 1979): 695.

Bos, Hans, et al. "New Hope for People with Low Incomes: Two Year Results of a Program to Reduce Poverty and Reform Welfare," 2d Report on New Hope Project, Milwaukee, Wisconsin (Manpower Demonstration Research Corporation, April 1999).

Boushey, Heather, et al. *Hardships in America: The Real Story of Working Families* (Economic Policy Institute, 2001).

Branch, Taylor. *Parting the Waters: America in the King Years, 1954–1963* (Touchstone, 1988).

Brandeis, Elizabeth. "Minimum Wage Legislation." Pp. 501–39 in *History of Labor in the United States, 1896–1932*, Vol. 3 (Macmillan, 1935).

Breckinridge, Sophonisba P. *Public Welfare Administration in the United States, Select Documents*, 2d ed. (University of Chicago Press, 1938).

Bremner, Robert H. *Children and Youth in America: A Documentary History, Volume I: 1600–1865* (Harvard University Press, 1970).

———. *From the Depths: The Discovery of Poverty in the United States* (New York University Press, 1964).

Breul, Frank R., and Steven J. Diner, eds. *Compassion and Responsibility: Readings in the History of Social Welfare Policy in the United States* (University of Chicago Press, 1980).

Brinkley, Alan. *The End of Reform: New Deal Liberalism in Recession and War* (Knopf, 1996).

Brocht, Chauna. "The Forgotten Workforce." Briefing Paper No. 101, November 2000. Economic Policy Institute.

Brown, Charles. "A Constitutional Amendment for a Right to Earn a Living." *Guild Practitioner* 56 (1999): 109.

Brown, Josephine Chapin. *Public Relief: 1929–1939* (Henry Holt, 1940).

Brull, Stephen. "What's So Bad about a Living Wage?" *Business Week*, September 4, 2000.

Bumpers, Dale. "How the Sunshine Harmed Congress." *New York Times*, January 3, 1999, 9.

Cain, Brad. "Smokers and Bullies Targeted by Oregon Laws." *Columbian*, December 30, 2001.

Canova, Timothy A. "Monologue or Dialogue in Management Decisions: A Comparison of Mandatory Bargaining Duties in the United States and Sweden." *Comparative Labor Law Journal* 12 (1991): 257.

Card, David, and Alan B. Krueger. *Myth and Measurement: The New Economics of the Minimum Wage* (Princeton University Press, 1995).

Casebeer, Kenneth M. "Holder of the Pen: An Interview with Leon Keyserling on Drafting the Wagner Act." *University of Miami Law Review* 42 (1987): 285.

228   Selected Bibliography

Castillo, Monica D. "Persons Outside the Labor Force Who Want a Job." *Monthly Labor Review* 121(7) (July 1998): 34.

Cerami, Charles A. "Three New Ways to Create Jobs." *Atlantic Monthly* (March 1994), <www.theatlantic.com/politics/ecbig/eccerami.htm>.

Cherry, Robert, and Max B. Sawicky. "Giving Tax Credit Where Credit Is Due: A 'Universal Unified Child Credit' That Expands the EITC and Cuts Taxes for Working Families." Briefing Paper No. 91, April 2000, Economic Policy Institute, <www.epinet.org/briefingpapers/eitc.html>.

Chisman, Forrest. "An Effective Employment Policy: The Missing Middle." P. 251 in *Rethinking Employment Policy*, ed. D. Lee Bawden and Felicity Skidmore (Urban Institute Press, 1989).

"Christian Faith and Economic Life, United Church of Christ," in *On Moral Business: Classical and Contemporary Resources for Ethics in Economic Life*, ed. Max L. Stackhouse et al. (William B. Eerdmans, 1995).

Citro, Constance, and Robert Michael, eds. *Measuring Poverty: A New Approach* (National Academy Press, 1995).

Coffin, William Sloane. *A Passion for the Possible* (Knox, 1997).

Cohen, David. "Labor Market Policy in Sweden and the United States: The Cooperative State vs. Enduring Notions of Capitalism." *Comparative Labor Law Journal* 15 (1993): 55.

Collins, Sheila D., Helen Lachs Ginsburg, and Gertrude Schaffner Goldberg. *Jobs for All: A Plan for the Revitalization of America* (Apex, 1994).

Commons, John R. *The Distribution of Wealth* (Macmillan, 1893; reprinted 1905).

Cooper, Kenneth J. "House Approves Amendment on Flag Desecration." *Washington Post*, June 29, 1995, A7.

Cox, W. Michael, and Richard Alm. *Myths of Rich and Poor: Why We're Better Off Than We Think* (Basic Books, 1999).

Danziger, Sheldon, et al. "Does It Pay to Move from Welfare to Work?" Joint Center for Poverty Research, Policy Brief 4(4) (2002).

Danziger, Sheldon, and Peter Gottschalk. *America Unequal* (Harvard University Press, 1995).

Danziger, Sheldon H., Gary D. Sandefur, and Daniel H. Weinberg, eds. *Confronting Poverty: Prescriptions for Change* (Harvard University Press, 1994).

DeFao, Janine, and Pia Sarkar. "Beyond Minimum Wage: Living Wage Costs Easily Absorbed." *San Francisco Chronicle*, June 3, 2001.

DeParle, Jason. "Project to Rescue Needy Stumbles against the Persistence of Poverty." *New York Times*, May 15, 1999.

de Schweinitz, Karl. *England's Road to Social Security: From the Statute of Laborers in 1349 to the Beveridge Report of 1942* (University of Pennsylvania Press, 1943).

Dionne, E. J. "Poll Finds Reagan Support Down but Democrats Still Lacking Fire." *New York Times*, December 1, 1987, A1.

Dow, David R. "When Words Mean What We Believe They Say." *Iowa Law Review* 76 (1990): 41.

Eaton, Leslie. "Changing to Meet the Job Market." *New York Times*, October 20, 1999.

"Economic Justice for All: Pastoral Letter on Catholic Social Teaching and the U.S. Economy." Publication No. 101-6 (U.S. Catholic Conference, 1986).

"Economic Report of the President to Congress, 1998." *Transmittal to the Congress, February 1998* (U.S. Government Printing Office, 1998).

Edelman, Peter B. "The Next Century of Our Constitution: Rethinking Our Duty to the Poor." *Hastings Law Journal* 39 (1987): 1.

———. "The Worst Thing Bill Clinton Has Done." *Atlantic Monthly* 279(3) (March 1997): 43.

Ehrenreich, Barbara. *Nickel and Dimed: On (Not) Getting By in America* (Metropolitan Books, 2001).

Elder, Justin. "Article V, Justifiability, and the Equal Rights Amendment." *Oklahoma Law Review* 31 (1978): 63.

Ellwood, David T., et al. *A Working Nation: Workers, Work, and Government in the New Economy* (Russell Sage Foundation, 2000).

Elster, Jon. "Is There (or Should There Be) a Right to Work?" Pp. 53–78 in *Democracy and the Welfare State,* ed. Amy Gutmann (Princeton University Press, 1988).

Ely, James W., Jr. "Poor Laws of the Post-Revolutionary South, 1776–1800." *Tulsa Law Journal* 21 (1985): 1.

———. " 'There Are Few Subjects in Political Economy of Greater Difficulty': The Poor Laws of the Antebellum South." *American Bar Association Research Journal* 849 (1985).

Ely, John Hart. *Democracy and Distrust: A Theory of Judicial Review* (Harvard University Press, 1980).

Farrell, Christopher, and Michael Mandel. "The Cold War's Grim Aftermath." *Business Week,* February 24, 1992.

Feder, Leah Hannah. *Unemployment Relief in Periods of Depression: A Study of Measures Adopted in Certain American Cities, 1857 through 1922* (Russell Sage Foundation, 1936).

Fisher, Gordon M. "From Hunter to Orshansky: An Overview of (Unofficial) Poverty Lines in the United States from 1904 to 1965—Summary," <www.census.gov/hhes/poverty/povmeas/papers/hstorsp4.html>.

Foot, Michael, and Isaac Kramnick, eds., *The Thomas Paine Reader* (Penguin Books, 1987).

Forbath, William E. "Why Is This Rights Talk Different from All Other Rights Talk? Demoting the Court and Reimagining the Constitution." *Stanford Law Review* 46 (1994): 1771.

Freeman, Richard B., and Peter Gottschalk, eds. *Generating Jobs: How to Increase Demand for Less-Skilled Workers* (Russell Sage Foundation, 1998).

Friedman, Milton. *Capitalism and Freedom* (University of Chicago Press, 1962).

Gaffney, James. "She Who Laughs Last: The Gender-Inclusive Language Debate." *America,* August 26, 1995, 8.

Galbraith, James K. *Created Unequal: The Crisis in American Pay* (Free Press, 1998).

Gans, Herbert J., *The War against the Poor: The Underclass and Antipoverty Policy* (Basic Books, 1995).

Gardener, Jennifer, and Diane Herz. "Working and Poor in 1990." *Monthly Labor Review* 115(12) (December 1992): 20.

Garner, Thesia I., et al. "Experimental Poverty Measurement for the 1990s." *Monthly Labor Review* 121(3) (March 1998): 39.

Gil, David G. "Full Employment: The 'Supreme Law of the Land.' " May 1995, see summary on web site of National Jobs for All Coalition, <www.njfac.org/us6.htm>.

Ginsburg, Helen. "Full Employment as a Policy Issue." P. 15 in *Employment and Labor-Relations Policy,* ed. Charles Bulmer and John L. Carmichael Jr. (Lexington Books, 1980).

Ginsburg, Helen Lachs, et al. "The Challenge of Full Employment in the Global Economy." National Jobs for All Coalition.

Ginsburg, Ruth Bater. "Ratification of the Equal Rights Amendment: A Question of Time." *Texas Law Review* 57 (1979): 919.

Glickman, Lawrence B. *A Living Wage: American Workers and the Making of Consumer Society* (Cornell University Press, 1997).

Goldberg, Gertrude Schaffner, and Sheila D. Collins. "The Right to Work and to Welfare." National Jobs for All Coalition, Special Report 2, February 2002, <www.njfac.org/sr2.htm>.

―――. *Washington's New Poor Law: Welfare "Reform" and the Roads Not Taken, 1935 to the Present* (Apex Press, 2001).

Greenhouse, Steven. "Low-Wage Jobs Leading Gains in Employment." *New York Times,* October 1, 2000.

―――. "A Rising Tide, but Some Boats Rise Higher Than Others." *New York Times,* September 3, 2000.

Greenstein, Robert. "The Changes the Next Tax Law Makes in Refundable Tax Credits for Low-Income Working Families." Center on Budget and Policy Priorities, June 18, 2001, <www.cbpp.org/6-14-01tax.htm>.

Gregory, David. "Breaking the Exploitation of Labor." *Fordham Law Journal* 25 (1997): 1.

―――. "Catholic Labor Theory and the Transformation of Work." *Washington and Lee Law Review* 119 (1988): 124.

―――. "Catholic Social Teaching on Work." *Labor Law Journal* (1998): 912.

Gremillion, Joseph, ed. *The Gospel of Peace and Justice: Catholic Social Teaching Since Pope John* (Orbis, 1976).

Guinier, Lani, and Gerald Torres. *The Miner's Canary: Enlisting Race, Resisting Power, Transforming Democracy* (Harvard University Press, 2002).

Gutfeld, Rose. "The Real Cost of Living: 'Self-Sufficiency' May Be the Next Frontier for U.S. Welfare Reform." Ford Foundation Report, Winter 2001, <www.fordfound.org/publications/ff_report/view_ff_report_detail.cfm?report_index=261>.

Handler, Joel F. *The Poverty of Welfare Reform* (Yale University Press, 1995).

Handler, Joel F., and Yeheskel Hasenfeld. *We the Poor People: Work, Poverty, and Welfare* (Yale University Press, 1997).

Handler, Joel F., and Lucie White, eds. *Hard Labor: Women and Work in the Post-Welfare Era* (M. E. Sharpe, 1999).

Harrington, Michael. *The Other America: Poverty in the United States* (Collier Books, 1993).

Harris, Seth. "Conceptions of Fairness and the Fair Labor Standards Act." *Hofstra Labor & Employment Law Journal* 18 (2000): 19.

Hart, Vivien. *Bound by Our Constitution: Women, Workers, and the Minimum Wage* (Princeton University Press, 1994).

Harvey, Philip. "Employment as a Human Right." Pp. 351–74 in *Sociology and the Public Agenda,* ed. William Julius Wilson (Sage Publications, 1993).

———. "Fashioning a Work-Based Strategy for Welfare Reform Based on International Human Rights Doctrine." *Journal of Public Health Policy* 16 (1995): 269.

———. "Responding to Rising Unemployment: Can We Afford Jobs for All?" Part 14 of the Uncommon Sense Series, National Jobs for All Coalition, October 2001, <www.njfac.org/us14.html>.

———. *Securing the Right to Employment* (Princeton University Press, 1989).

Haveman, Robert H. "Equity with Employment." *Boston Review* (Summer 1997), <www.bostonreview.mit.edu/BR22.3/haveman.html>.

Herzenberg, Stephen A., John A. Alic, and Howard Wial. *New Rules for a New Economy: Employment and Opportunity in Postindustrial America* (Cornell University Press, 1998).

Hetter, Katie. "Labor Has Ally in the Pulpits." *Newsday,* December 12, 2000.

Hirschman, Carolyn. "Paying Up." *HR Magazine* 45(7) (July 1, 2000).

Hudson, Wade. *Economic Security for All: How to End Poverty in the United States* (Economic Security Project, 1996). Available online at <www.inlet.org/esp/>.

Hurt, Charles. "Living Wage Foes Make Plans." *Detroit News,* November 5, 1998.

Iceland, John. "Poverty among Working Families: Findings from Experimental Poverty Measures, 1998." Special Studies, Current Population Reports No. P23–203, September 2000. U.S. Census Bureau, Economics and Statistics Administration.

Iversen, Roberta Rehner. *Moving Up Is a Steep Climb: Parents' Work and Children's Welfare in the Annie E. Casey Foundation's Jobs Initiative* (Annie E. Casey Foundation, April 2002). Available online at <www.aecf.org/initiatives/jobsinitiative/ethnography.htm>.

Ivins, Molly. "Old Issue of Pay Inequity for Women Just Won't Go Away." *Buffalo News,* May 8, 1999.

Jackson, Jesse L., Jr., and Frank E. Watkins, *A More Perfect Union: Advancing New American Rights* (Welcome Rain Publishers, 2001).

John Paul II, "Respect for Human Rights: The Secret of True Peace." January 1, 1999, <www.vatican.va/holy_father/john_paul_ii/messages/peace/documents/hf_jp-ii_mes_14121998_xxxii-world-day-for-peace_en.html>.

Johnson, Clifford M., and Alex Goldenberg. "Work to Be Done: Designing Publicly-Funded Jobs to Meet Community Needs." Center on Budget and Policy Priorities, September 24, 1999. Available online at <www.cbpp.org/9-24-99wtw.htm>.

Johnson, Clifford M., and Lana Kim. "Competitive Welfare-to-Work Grantees Utilize Publicly-Funded, Transitional Jobs to Aid Hard-to-Employ Welfare Recipients." Center on Budget and Policy Priorities, September 17, 1999. Available online at <www.cbpp.org/9-17-99wtw.htm>.

Johnson, Clifford M., and Steve Savner. "Federal Funding Sources for Public Job Creation Initiatives." Center on Budget and Policy Priorities and Center on Law and Social Policy, December 1999. Available online at <www.cbpp.org/12-21-99wtw.htm>.

Jones, Jacqueline. *American Work: Four Centuries of Black and White Labor* (W. W. Norton, 1998).

———. *The Dispossessed: America's Underclass from the Civil War to the Present* (Basic Books, 1992).

———. *Labor of Love, Labor of Sorrow: Black Women, Work, and the Family from Slavery to the Present* (Vintage Books, 1985).

Karst, Kenneth L. *Belonging to America: Equal Citizenship and the Constitution* (Yale University Press, 1989).

———. "Foreword: Equal Citizenship under the Fourteenth Amendment." *Harvard Law Review* 91 (1977): 1.

Kasarda, John D. "Jobs, Migration, and Emerging Mismatches." Pp. 148–98 in *Urban Change and Poverty*, ed. Michael McGeary and Laurence E. Lynn Jr. (National Academy Press, 1988).

Katz, Lawrence F. "Wage Subsidies for the Disadvantaged." Pp. 21–52 in *Generating Jobs: How to Increase Demand for Less-Skilled Workers*, ed. Richard B. Freeman and Peter Gottschalk (Russell Sage Foundation, 1998).

Katz, Michael B. *The Price of Citizenship: Redefining the American Welfare State* (Henry Holt, 2001).

———. *In the Shadow of the Poorhouse: A Social History of Welfare in America* (Basic Books, 1986).

———. *The Undeserving Poor: From the War on Poverty to the War on Welfare* (Pantheon, 1989).

Kaus, Mickey. *The End of Equality* (Basic Books, 1992).

Keister, Lisa A. *Wealth in America: Trends in Wealth Inequality* (Cambridge University Press, 2000).

Kelvin, Peter, and Joanna E. Jarrett. *Unemployment: Its Social Psychological Effects* (Cambridge University Press, 1985).

Keyserling, Leon H. "The New Deal and Its Current Significance." *Washington Law Review* 59 (1984): 795.

Kim, Marlene. "Women Paid Low Wages: Who They Are and Where They Work." *Monthly Labor Review* 123(9) (September 2000): 26.

King, Martin Luther, Jr., *Where Do We Go From Here: Chaos or Community?* (Beacon Press, 1967).

Klebaner, Benjamin Joseph. "Poverty and Its Relief in American Thought, 1815–61." *Social Service Review* 382 (1964): 38.

———. *Public Poor Relief in America, 1790 to 1860* (Ayer Co. Publishing, 1976).

Klein, Bruce W., and Philip L. Rones. "A Profile of the Working Poor." *Monthly Labor Review* 112(10) (October 1989): 3–13.

Kleinfield, N. R. "The Company as Family No More." *New York Times,* March 4, 1996.

Krueger, Alan B. "How Computers Have Changed the Wage Structure: Evidence from Microdata, 1984–1989." *Quarterly Journal of Economics* 108(1) (February 1993): 33–60.

Krupa, Michelle. "In Search of a Home: Crisis of the Working Poor." *Beacon News,* September 6, 1999.

Kunkle, Frederick, and Craig Thomas. "Alexandria Officials Aim to Defend Living Wage." *Washington Post,* February 1, 2001.

Lamoureux, Patricia Ann. "Is a Living Wage a Just Wage?" *America,* February 19, 2001.

Lee, Henry K. "Berkeley Sued by Restaurant: Living Wage Law's Extension Challenged." *San Francisco Chronicle,* October 21, 2000.

Lescohier, Don. "Working Conditions." P. 63 in *History of Labor in the United States, 1896–1932,* Vol. 3 (Macmillan, 1935).

Lescohier, Don D., and Elizeth Brandeis. *History of Labor in the United States, 1896–1932,* Vol. 3 (Macmillan, 1935).

Levitan, Sar A., Frank Gallo, and Isaac Shapiro. *Working but Poor: America's Contradiction,* rev. ed. (Johns Hopkins University Press, 1993).

Levy, Frank. *The New Dollars and Dreams: American Incomes and Economic Change* (Russell Sage Foundation, 1998).

Lichtenstein, Nelson. *State of the Union: A Century of American Labor* (Princeton University Press, 2002).

Linder, Marc. "Farm Workers and the Fair Labor Standards Act: Racial Discrimination in the New Deal." *Texas Law Review* 65 (1987): 1335.

Loury, Glenn C. "Tenuous Trickle-Down." *New York Times,* May 29, 1999.

Madrick, Jeff. "Living Wages Are Practical and Don't Let Theory Get in the Way." *New York Times,* July 5, 2001.

Marvel, Mary K. "The Social and Political Consequences of Manpower Training Programs: The Case of CETA." P. 41 in *Employment and Labor-Relations Policy,* ed. Charles Bulmer and John L. Carmichael Jr. (Lexington Books, 1980).

"Mater et Magister, On Christianity and Social Progress." May 15, 1961, in David J. O'Brien and Thomas A. Shannon, *Catholic Social Thought* (Orbis Books, 2001).

Matheny, Ken, and Marion Crain. "Making Labor's Rhetoric Reality." *Green Bag* 5 (2001): 17.

McCaffrey, Shannon. "Minimum Wage Can't Pay Rent." *Wisconsin State Journal,* September 21, 2000.

Meister, Dick. "A Right to a Job and a Living Wage: Campaigns for a Constitutional Amendment." *Sacramento Bee,* August 5, 1997, B7.

Mena, Jennifer. "Poor Renters Find Shelter on Floors." *Orange County Register,* May 17, 1999.

Mencher, Samuel. *Poor Law to Poverty Program: Economic Security Policy in Britain and the United States* (University of Pittsburgh Press, 1967).

Michelman, Frank I. "The Supreme Court, 1968 Term—Foreword: On Protecting the Poor through the Fourteenth Amendment." *Harvard Law Review* 83 (1969): 7.

Milbank, Dana. "Working Poor Fear Welfare Cutbacks Aimed at the Idle Will Inevitably Strike Them, Too." *Wall Street Journal,* August 9, 1995, A10.

Miller, Arthur. "Toward Recognition of a Constitutional Right to a Job." Pp. 319–26 in *Politics, Democracy and the Supreme Court: Essays on the Frontier of Constitutional Theory* (Greenwood Publishing, 1985).

Mink, Gwendolyn. "TANF Reauthorization: An Opportunity to Invest in America's Future." Issue Brief No. 13, ADA Economic Policy Committee, December 10, 2001, <www.adaction.org/TANF.htm>.

———. *Welfare's End* (Cornell University Press, 1998).

Mishel, Lawrence, Jared Bernstein, and John Schmitt. *The State of Working America, 1996–97* (M. E. Sharpe, 1997).

———. *The State of Working America, 1998–99* (Cornell University Press, 1998).

———. *The State of Working America, 2000/2001* (Cornell University Press, 2001).

Morris, Richard B. *Government and Labor in Early America* (Columbia University Press, 1946).

Murray, Bobbi. "Living Wage Comes of Age." *The Nation,* July 23, 2001.

Nelson, Robert H. *Economics as Religion: From Samuelson to Chicago and Beyond* (Penn State University Press, 2001).

Neuman, Gerald L. "The Lost Century of American Immigration Law (1776–1875)." *Columbia Law Review* 93 (1993): 1833, 1846–59.

Neumark, David. "How Living Wage Laws Affect Low-Wage Workers and Low-Income Families." Public Policy Institute of California, 2002, <www.ppic.org/publications/PPIC156/index.html>.

Newman, Katherine S. *Declining Fortunes: The Withering of the American Dream* (Basic Books, 1993).

———. *Falling from Grace: Downward Mobility in the Age of Affluence* (University of California Press, 1988).

———. *No Shame in My Game: The Working Poor in the Inner City* (Knopf, 1999).

Nicklaus, David. "Living Wage Law." *St. Louis Post Dispatch,* September 6, 2000.

Niedt, Christopher, et al. "The Effects of the Living Wage in Baltimore." Working Paper No. 119, February 1999, Economic Policy Institute.

Nieves, Evelyn. "California Counties Pay Jobless to Move Away." *New York Times,* June 18, 2001.

Niskanen, William A. "Creating Good Jobs and Good Wages." Pp. 92–104 in *A Working Nation: Workers, Work, and Government in the New Economy,* David T. Ellwood et al. (Russell Sage Foundation, 2000).

Norlund, Willis J. "A Brief History of the Fair Labor Standards Act." *Labor Law Journal* 39 (1988): 715.

———. *The Quest for a Living Wage: The History of the Federal Minimum Wage Program* (Greenwood Press, 1997).

Novak, Michael. "What Wealth Gap?" *Wall Street Journal*, July 11, 1995, A14.

Offner, Paul, and Harry Holzer. "Left Behind in the Labor Market: Recent Employment Trends among Young Black Men." Brookings Institution Center on Urban and Metropolitan Policy, April 2002, <www.brookings.edu/dybdocroot/urban/publications/offnerexsum.htm>.

Olasky, Marvin. *The Tragedy of American Compassion* (Regnery Publishing, 1992).

Orloff, Ann Shola. *The Politics of Pensions: A Comparative Analysis of Britain, Canada, and the United States 1880–1940* (University of Wisconsin Press, 1993).

Overholser, Geneva. "CEO's Get Richer." *Washington Post*, August 31, 2001.

Passell, Peter. "Benefits Dwindle along with Wages for the Unskilled." *New York Times*, June 14, 1998, A1.

Patterson, James T. *America's Struggle against Poverty, 1900–1994* (Harvard University Press, 1994).

Paulsen, George E. *A Living Wage for the Forgotten Man: The Quest for Fair Labor Standards, 1933–1941* (Susquehanna University Press, 1996).

Paulsen, Michael Stokes. "A General Theory of Article V: The Constitutional Lessons of the Twenty-Seventh Amendment." *Yale Law Journal* 677 (1993): 103.

Pear, Robert. "Infant Mortality Rate Drops But Racial Disparity Grows." *New York Times*, July 10, 1995, p. A8.

Phelps, Edmund S. *Rewarding Work: How to Restore Participation and Self-Support to Free Enterprise* (Harvard University Press, 1997).

Piven, Frances Fox, and Richard A. Cloward. *The New Class War: Reagan's Attack on the Welfare State and Its Consequences* (Pantheon, 1985).

———. *Regulating the Poor: The Functions of Public Welfare* (Vintage Books, 1971).

Pollin, Robert. "Economic Analysis of the New Orleans Minimum Wage Proposal," <www.acorn.org/acorn10/livingwage/neworleans.htm>.

Pollin, Robert, and Stephanie Luce. *The Living Wage: Building a Fair Economy* (New Press, 1998).

Porter, Kathryn H., and Allen Dupree. "Poverty Trends for Families Headed by Working Single Mothers, 1993 to 1999," Table 3, Center on Budget and Policy Priorities, August 2001, <www.cbpp.org/8-16-01wel.pdf>.

Pritchard, Justin. "Living Wage Laws Prove Effective." *Capital Times*, March 14, 2002.

———. "Study Supports Living Wage Laws." *Columbian*, March 14, 2002.

"A Profile of the Working Poor, 1999." U.S. Department of Labor, Bureau of Labor Statistics, Report No. 947, February 2001, p. 1. <http://stats.bls.gov/CPS/CPSWP99.pdf>.

"Quadregesimo Anno" (After Forty Years) (1931), in *Catholic Social Thought*, ed. David J. O'Brien and Thomas A. Shannon (Orbis Books, 2001).

Quigley, Fran. "24 Hours of Welfare Reform." *NUVO Weekly,* January 13, 2000.

Quigley, William P. "Backwards into the Future: How Welfare Changes in the Millennium Resemble Poor Law of the Middle Ages." *Stanford Law and Policy Review* 9 (1998): 101–13.

———. "The Earliest Years of Federal Social Welfare Legislation: Federal Poor Relief Prior to the Civil War." *University of Detroit Mercy Law Review* 79 (2001): 157.

———. " 'A Fair Day's Pay for a Fair Day's Work': Time to Raise and Index the Minimum Wage." *St. Mary's Law Journal* 27 (1996): 513.

———. "Five Hundred Years of English Poor Laws, 1349–1834: Regulating the Working and Nonworking Poor." *Akron Law Review* 30 (1996): 73–128.

———. "Full-Time Workers Should Not Be Poor." *Mississippi Law Journal* 70 (2001): 889.

———. "Primer on Minimum Wage and Overtime Issues under the Fair Labor Standards Act for Low-Wage Workers and Their Advocates." *Clearinghouse Review* 29 (February 1996): 925.

———. "The Quicksands of the Poor Law: Poor Relief Legislation from 1790 to 1820." *Northern Illinois University Law Review* 18 (1997): 1.

———. "Reluctant Charity: Poor Laws in the Original Thirteen States." *University of Richmond Law Review* 31 (1997): 111–78.

———. "The Right to Work and Earn a Living Wage: A Proposed Amendment to the U. S. Constitution." *Blueprint for Social Justice* 50 (May 1997).

———. "The Right to Work and Earn a Living Wage: A Proposed Constitutional Amendment." *New York City Law Review* 2 (1998): 139.

———. "Rumblings of Reform: Northern Poor Relief Legislation in Antebellum America, 1820–1860." *Capital University Law Review* 26 (1997): 739.

———. "The State of the Living Wage Movement." *University of Mississippi Law Journal* 70 (2001): 889.

———. "Work or Starve: Regulation of the Poor in Colonial America." *University of San Francisco Law Review* 31 (1996): 35.

Ranalli, Ralph. "Bill Offers New Gauge for Poverty: Backers Insist U.S. Benchmark Doesn't Reflect Mass Realities." *Boston Globe,* May 8, 2001.

Rasell, Edith, Jared Bernstein, and Heather Boushey. "Step Up, Not Out: The Case for Raising the Federal Minimum Wage for Workers in Every State." Economic Policy Institute, Issue Brief No. 149, February 7, 2001, p. 2.

Redburn, Tome. "Honoring, and Paying, All Those Who Serve." *New York Times,* October 28, 2001.

Reed, Adolph, Jr. "A Right to a Job—By Constitutional Amendment." *People's Tribune,* June 1998, <www.lrna.org/league/PT/PT.1998.06/PT.1998.06.3.html>.

———. "A New Minimum: $10 an Hour." *Progressive* 61(4) (April 1, 1997): 16.

Reich, Robert B. *The Work of Nations: Preparing Ourselves for 21st Century Capitalism* (Addison-Wesley, 1992).

Reingold, Jennifer. "Executive Pay." *Business Week,* April 21, 1997.

Riesenfeld, Stefan A. "The Formative Era of American Public Assistance Law." *California Law Review* 43 (1955): 175.

Rifkin, Jeremy. *The End of Work: The Decline of the Global Labor Force and the Dawn of the Post-Market Era* (G. P. Putnam, 1995).

Roberts, J. M. *The Penguin History of the World* (Penguin USA, 1992).

Rodes, Robert E. *Law and Liberation* (University of Notre Dame Press, 1986).

Roeder, Linda. "Minimum Wage: Survey Shows Support for Living Wage, Economists Say at Washington Summit." *BNA Daily Labor Report*, Thursday, May 25, 2000.

Rose, Nancy E. *Put to Work: Relief Programs in the Great Depression* (Monthly Review Press, 1994).

———. *Workfare or Fair Work: Women, Welfare, and Government Work Programs* (Rutgers University Press, 1995).

Roston, Eric. "How Much Is a Living Wage?" *Time,* March 31, 2002.

Rothman, David J. *The Discovery of the Asylum: Social Order and Disorder in the New Republic* (Little, Brown and Co., 1971).

Ruggles, Patricia. *Drawing the Line: Alternative Poverty Measures and Their Implications for Public Policy* (Urban Institute Press, 1990).

Ryan, John A. *Economic Justice: Selections from Distributive Justice and a Living Wage,* ed. Harlan R. Beckley (Westminster John Knox, 1996).

Samuelson, Robert J. *The Good Life and Its Discontents: The American Dream in the Age of Entitlement, 1945–1995* (Times Books, 1995).

Saunders, Lisa. "Relative Earnings of Black Men to White Men by Region, Industry." *Monthly Labor Review* 118(4) (April 1995): 68.

Sawhill, Isabel, and Adam Thomas. "A Hand Up for the Bottom Third: Toward a New Agenda for Low-Income Working Families," May 2001, <www.brook.edu/views/papers/sawhill/20010522.htm>.

Schantz, Harvey L., and Richard H. Schmidt. "Politics and Policy: The Humphrey-Hawkins Story." Pp. 25–34 in *Employment and Labor-Relations Policy,* ed. Charles Bulmer and John L. Carmichael Jr. (Lexington Books, 1980).

Schiller, Bradley R. *Economics of Poverty and Discrimination,* 7th ed. (Prentice Hall, 1998).

Schneider, David M. *The History of Public Welfare in New York State, 1609–1866* (University of Chicago Press, 1938).

Schwartz, Bonnie Fox. *The Civil Works Administration, 1933–1934: The Business of Emergency Employment in the New Deal* (Princeton University Press, 1984).

Schwarz, John E. "The Hidden Side of the Clinton Economy." *Atlantic Monthly,* 282(4) (October 1998): 8.

———. *Illusions of Opportunity: The American Dream in Question* (W. W. Norton, 1997).

Schwarz, John E., and Thomas J. Volgy. *The Forgotten Americans: Thirty Million Working Poor in the Land of Opportunity* (W. W. Norton, 1993).

Shapiro, Fred R. *Oxford Dictionary of American Legal Quotations* (Oxford University Press, 1993).

Shapiro, Robert Y., et al. "The Polls—A Report: Employment and Social Welfare." *Public Opinion Quarterly* (51) (1987): 268.

Siegel, Richard Lewis. *Employment and Human Rights* (University of Pennsylvania Press, 1994).

Sklar, Holly, Laryssa Mykyta, and Susan Wefald. *Raise the Floor: Wages and Policies That Work for All of Us* (South End Press, 2001).

Skocpol, Theda. " 'Brother Can You Spare A Job?': Work and Welfare in the United States." Pp. 228–49 in *Social Policy in the United States: Future Possibilities in Historical Perspective* (Princeton University Press, 1995).

————. *The Missing Middle: Working Families and the Future of American Social Policy* (W. W. Norton, 2000).

————. *Protecting Soldiers and Mothers: The Political Origins of Social Policy in the United States* (Belknap Harvard Press, 1992).

————. *Social Policy in the United States: Future Possibilities in Historical Perspective* (Princeton University Press, 1995).

Solow, Robert M. *Work and Welfare* (Princeton University Press, 1998).

Smith, Adam. *The Wealth of Nations* (1776; Modern Library Edition, 1937).

Spectar, J. M. "Pay Me Fairly, Kathie Lee! The WTO, The Right to a Living Wage, and a Proposed Protocol." *New York Law School Journal of International & Corporate Law* 20 (2000): 61.

Starr, Gerald. *Minimum Wage Fixing* (International Labor Organisation, Geneva, 1981).

"Statement on Church and Social Order." February 7, 1940, in *Justice in the Marketplace: Collected Statements of the Vatican and the U.S. Catholic Bishops on Economic Policy, 1891–1984*, ed. David M. Byers (U.S. Catholic Conference, 1985).

Statistical Abstract of the United States, 1995, 115th ed. (U.S. Census Bureau, 1995).

Statistical Abstract of the United States, 1997, 117th ed. (U.S. Census Bureau, 1997).

Statistical Abstract of the United States, 2000, 120th ed. (U.S. Census Bureau, 2000).

Statistical Abstract of the United States, 2001, 121st ed. (U.S. Census Bureau, 2001).

Steinfeld, Robert J. *The Invention of Unfree labor: The Employment Relationship in English and American Culture, 1350–1870* (University of North Carolina Press, 1991).

"Stronger Links: New Ways to Connect Low-Skilled Workers to Better Jobs." Annie E. Casey Foundation Jobs Initiative, <www.aecf.org/initiatives/jobsinitiative/strongerlinks.pdf>.

Sullivan, Kathleen M. "What's Wrong with Constitutional Amendments?" Pp. 64–65 in *New Federalists Papers: Essays in Defense of the Constitution*, Alan Brinkley, Nelson Polsby, and Kathleen M. Sullivan (W. W. Norton, 1997).

Sweeney, John. "Building a Labor Movement Strategy for the New Century." *Georgetown Journal on Poverty Law and Policy* 7 (2000): 163.

Swift, Pat. "A Way to Figure What the Pay Gap Will Cost You." *Buffalo News*, September 12, 1998.

Thurow, Lester C. "The Boom That Wasn't." *New York Times*, January 18, 1999, A19.

————. *The Zero-Sum Society: Distribution and the Possibilities for Economic Change* (Basic Books, 1980).

Tobin, James. "Poverty in Relation to Macroeconomic Trends, Cycles, and Policies." Pp. 147, 162 in *Confronting Poverty: Prescriptions for Change,* ed. Sheldon H. Danziger, Gary D. Sandefur, and Daniel H. Weinberg (Harvard University Press, 1994).

Trattner, Walter I. *From Poor Law to Welfare State: A History of Social Welfare in America,* 6th ed. (Free Press, 1999).

Tribe, Laurence H. *American Constitutional Law* (Foundation Press, 1978).

————. "Unraveling National League of Cities: The New Federalism and Affirmative Rights to Essential Governmental Services." *Harvard Law Review* 90 (1977): 1065.

Tushnet, Mark. "Civil Rights and Social Rights: The Future of the Reconstruction Amendments." *Loyola of Los Angeles Law Review* 25 (1992): 1211–19.

2000 Green Book. Background Material and Data on Programs within the Jurisdiction of the Committee on Ways and Means. U.S. House of Representatives, Committee on Ways and Means (U.S. Government Printing Office, 2000).

Uchitelle, Louis. "Devising New Math to Define Poverty." *New York Times,* October 18, 1999.

————. "The Quiet Help of Family Members." *New York Times,* October 24, 1999.

Uchitelle, Louis, and N. R. Kleinfield. "On the Battlefields of Business, Millions of Casualties." *New York Times,* March 3, 1996.

van der Vyver, Johan D. "Book Review: Human Rights in the Twenty-First Century: A Global Challenge." *Emory International Law Review* 787 (1993): 799.

"Villars Statement on Relief and Development," in *On Moral Business: Classical and Contemporary Resources for Ethics in Economic Life,* ed. Max L. Stackhouse et al. (William B. Eerdmans, 1995).

Waldman, Amy. "Long Line in the Bronx, But for Jobs, Not the Yankees." *New York Times,* October 20, 1999.

Waldman, Peter. "Prosperity Is Good for Living Wage Drive." *Wall Street Journal,* December 20, 1999.

Waltman, Jerald. *The Politics of the Minimum Wage* (University of Illinois Press, 2000).

Warren, Mark R. *Dry Bones Rattling: Community Building to Revitalize American Democracy* (Princeton University Press, 2001), 162–90.

Wartzman, Rick. "How Minimum Wage Lost Its Status as a Tool of Social Progress in the U.S.: Washington Now Considers the Minimum Wage Law a Drag on Employment; Two Shifts for Pat Williams." *Wall Street Journal,* July 19, 2001.

Webb, Sidney, and Beatrice Webb. *English Local Government—English Poor Law Policy,* Vol. 10 (Frank Cass and Co., 1910; reprinted 1963).

Weir, Margaret. *Politics and Jobs: The Boundaries of Employment Policy in the United States* (Princeton University Press, 1992).

Weisbrot, Mark. "From Welfare to Poverty." *Sunday Journal* (Suburban D.C.), December 21, 1997, p. 8.

Wilson, William Julius. *The Truly Disadvantaged: The Inner City, the Underclass, and Public Policy* (University of Chicago Press, 1987).

————. *When Work Disappears: The World of the New Urban Poor* (Knopf, 1996).

Wilson, William Julius, and Andrew J. Cherlin. "The Real Test of Welfare Reform Still Lies Ahead." *New York Times,* July 13, 2001.

Winter, Ralf K., Jr. "Poverty, Economic Equality, and the Equal Protection Clause." P. 41 in *Supreme Court Review 1972,* ed. Philip B. Kurland (University of Chicago Press, 1973).

Wolff, Edward N. *Top Heavy: A Study of the Increasing Inequality of Wealth in America* (New Press, 1995).

Woolf, Gerri. "Statewide Jail/Prison Project, Welfare-to-Work (Non-custodial Parent)." Washington State Jobs Program.

"Working Hard, Earning Less: The Story of Job Growth in America." National Priorities Project 1999. Available through the National Priorities Project, (413) 584–9566, or Jobs with Justice, (202) 434–1106.

"Working Women Count: A Report to the Nation." U.S. Department of Labor, Women's Bureau, 1994.

Wray, L. Randall. *Understanding Modern Money: The Key to Full Employment and Price Stability* (Edward Elgar, 1998).

Wronka, Joseph. *Human Rights and Social Policy in the 21st Century* (University Press of America, 1992).

Index